Sickert and the Ripper Crimes

For the memory of my Mother
and of Florence

Sickert and the Ripper Crimes

An investigation into the relationship between the Whitechapel murders of 1888 and the English tonal painter Walter Richard Sickert

Mandrake

PO Box 250

Oxford

OX1 1AP (UK)

Sickert and The Ripper Crimes
(c) Mandrake of Oxford Ltd and Jean Overton Fuller

By the same author
Madeleine: A Biography of Noor Inayat Khan, GC
The Starr Affair
Double Webs
Horoscope for a Double Agent
Shelley, a Biography
Swinburne, A Biography
Noor-un-Nisa Inayat Khan (Madeleine)
The German Penetration of S O E
Sir Francis Bacon, A Biography
The Comte de Saint-Germain, Last Scion of the House of Rákóczy
Blavatsky and Her Teachers
Déricourt, The Chequered Spy
The Magical Dilemma of Victor Neuburg (Mandrake 1990)

Forthcoming
In Camera: Ivor Cook and the Court Lees Affair (Mandrake 1991)

Fuller, Jean Overton
Sickert and the Ripper Crimes
November 1990
1. London. Murderers: Jack the Ripper
2. Title
364.1523092
ISBN 1-65882-815-6

Contents

Acknowledgements

My first acknowledgement must be to my friend Dr Margaret Little, for I had so long kept to myself this strange story that, but for her letters from Glasgow repeatedly urging me to write it, I probably should have continued to hold my peace.

It is with particular pleasure I acknowledge the generosity of Dr David E Coombe of Christ's College, Cambridge, the owner of Sickert's portrait of Florence, not merely for giving his permission to reproduce the picture, which has never been reproduced before, but for motoring from Cambridge to bring me a set of high quality photographs of it, from which reproduction could be made.

Mrs Patricia S Karet, Secretary of University College School and Mr Frank Miles, Archivist of King's College School, looked out for me details of Sickert's days there.

Dr Stanley Sadie put me in touch with Dr James Harding, who gave me the dates of Saint-Saëns' last movements and so enabled me to fine down the date of the portrait of Sickert by Florence.

Mr William Wardle, Curator of Scotland Yard's Black Museum answered my particular queries, and the Public Record Office sent me photostats of the case papers of the murders.

I am particularly grateful to Peter R Burroughs, Acting Unit General Manager of Guy's Hospital, for granting me permission to see Guy's Admission Register for years otherwise still covered by the Hundred Years Rule, and to Miss J Coburn, Head Archivist of the City of London Record Office and Library for laying them before me.

Miss Margaret J Swarbrick, Chief Archivist, Westminster, found information for me concerning Victoria Street and Mr Richard A Bowden, Archivist, Marylebone Library, found information for me concerning Cleveland Street.

Emma Chambers, Print Room Supervisor at the Ashmolean, Oxford, did her best to read for me the writing in Sickert's hand in the corner of their squared up sketch for their version of *Ennui*, and Dr Vernon Harrison gave me an informal opinion on the same.

Miss R Featherstone of the Courtauld Institute took considerable pains for me.

My friend, Timothy d'Arch Smith, gave me some of his own insights into the period. As always, he has read my proofs.

Jean Overton Fuller

List of Illustrations

Chronology

1860, 30 May	Sickert born
1862, 2 August	Florence born
1881-2	Sickert at Slade School of Art .
1883-4	Sickert studying under Whistler
1884	Florence finishes at Royal College of Art
1885 February	Florence at Whistler's Ten o'clock lecture in Piccadilly
1885 April	Annie Elizabeth Crook, confectionery assistant from 6 Cleveland Street gives birth at Marylebone Workhouse to Alice Margaret
1885 summer	Florence in Paris and Dieppe, studying under Gervex, painted by Blanche
1885, 10 June	Sickert married to Ellen Cobden
1885 December	Sickert and Florence meet at RBA
1886-7	Florence comes to know Sickert's Cleveland Street neighbours, Annie Crook, the little Alice Margaret, and Mary Kelly, and becomes aware of existence of house of prostitution a couple of doors down the road
1887 (c)	Mary Kelly gives up her job as governess to Alice Margaret to become a prostitute, disappears from the neighbourhood but sends Sickert blackmailing letters from the East End. Forms liaison with Joseph Barnett
1888, August	*Jekyll & Hyde* opens at Lyceum
31 August	Mary Anne Nichols murdered
8 September	Annie Chapman murdered
30 September	Elizabeth Stride and Catherine Eddowes murdered
9 November	Mary Kelly murdered

Note: on the value of money

I am informed by the Bank of England that £1 in 1888 would have the equivalent purchasing power of £35.38 today (January 1888 to January 1989). Approximate equivalents for the sums of money mentioned in this story can therefore be worked out, bearing in mind that 1s = 5p and 6d = 2 1/2 p.

8

Chapter 1

The Artist Florence Pash

'She says he knew who Jack the Ripper was!' It was my mother who said this to me, on 12 April, 1948. I had just returned from some months in Paris, where I had been studying painting at the Académie Julien. Mother, who had come to stay in my flat, at 4 Guilford Place, while I was away, had polished everything up, bright and shining for my return, and let me settle to the dinner she had ready, for I was tired after my crossing from Dieppe to Newhaven. I had things to tell her about Paris and she had something further to tell me about a project of which I had first heard when I came home for Christmas. Mother was an artist, accustomed to exhibit at, and for some years a Committee Member of, the Chelsea Arts, and she had become friends with another artist, a Mrs Humphrey Holland, née Florence Pash, older than herself. Florence had known Sickert and had letters from him, and it had been agreed between them that these should be typed out, and, with an introduction and linking passages by my mother, offered to a publisher. They proved to be, unfortunately, rather slight, and it was a pity Florence would not allow her to put in the one thing that was really startling: 'She says he knew who Jack the Ripper was!'

I was very much surprised he should know anything about Jack the Ripper, and asked, 'Who?'

That, he had been afraid to say in a plain manner.

'How did he know?' I asked.

'He saw the bodies.' Later, he painted them. The quiet tonal studies we knew were not the only kind of thing he did. There was another series, unknown to us, never exhibited, which Florence felt could never be exhibited, because they were too horrible. She could not bear to look at them. Paintings of bleeding, mutilated corpses, which he had done from his memory. He was haunted by it, all through his life, and it invaded everything that he did.

'How did he come to see them?' I asked. Were they all laid out in a mortuary, and why was an artist invited to look?

Mother shook her head. She did not think it had been like that he had seen them.

'Did he just come on them in the street?'

Mother supposed so. She kept referring to 'bodies' in the plural.

'I don't understand this,' I said. 'It could happen just once that he was, by accident, the first person to see a body on the street, mutilated and bleeding. He could not be the first person to see all of them, accidentally. All of them makes him the Ripper.'

'Yes!' said my mother, wide-eyed.

From that moment, I think we both thought he was the Ripper. Yet we tried to allow for the possibility of there having been a misunderstanding; that perhaps only one of the bodies was all he had claimed to have seen, and that one was enough to affect him. He could, in that case, be innocent.

I asked. 'Did he see a man hurrying away, and recognize him?'

Florence had not said he saw a man hurrying away.

'Then how did he know who he was?'

Florence had not explained.

'Did he go to the police?'

'No. He was afraid to.'

I asked myself aloud, 'If I found a body, what would I do? I would walk straight on past it - not appearing to notice - and make straight for the nearest police station.'

Yes, said my mother, 'but a man might be afraid in case the police thought the murderer was him.'

I still thought the greater safety would lie in going to them. It would look so bad if it came out later that he had passed by the body and not reported it.

But, said mother, he could be afraid the murderer would kill him.

'He could be in danger from the murderer only until he reached the police station,' I insisted. Once there, he could ask police protection. To have kept it to himself seemed terrible.

It weighed on him, Florence had assured her. Although he had been afraid to tell outright, he wanted it known after his death, and so he had painted clues in to his pictures. They were distributed through several of them, which had to be taken together. They formed a 'riddle'. The 'supreme clue' was a gull, which he had placed on Queen Victoria's shoulder (see photograph). Did I know of any mythological or emblematical meaning of a seagull?

'No'.

Florence had asked her not to tell anybody what she had told her about this, but she had felt it was too big to keep from me, and she hoped I might be able to help with the clue. 'I thought there might be something about it in one of your books.'

I was sorry to disappoint her but I knew there was nothing in them about seagulls.

Suppose one said, 'the Ripper is a seagull,' or 'the Ripper is a gull', what would that mean?

There was, I suggested, the old meaning of 'gull', as 'dupe', but if one said, 'The Ripper is a dupe', where would that get one?

That it was on Queen Victoria's shoulder was not accidental, but of significance, Mother said. 'I thought you and I, Jean, could try to solve the Ripper mystery, together, with this clue'.

This was a bracing challenge.

The next morning I walked down to Foyle's bookshop. I asked them if they had a book 'on the crimes of Jack the Ripper?' No, they had not. What I wanted to see was the circumstances in which the bodies of the victims had been found, and whether it was possible for Sickert to have stumbled over them in the street and walked on, or whether they had all been laid out in one mortuary in which he could have seen them all. What was the interval between the crimes, how many were they and who were the women? Without these elementary particulars, it did not seem possible to make a start at checking up on this strange story.

I very distinctly remember my thoughts as I walked back up Charing Cross Road that morning. Sickert was not my favourite painter. I had my eye 'in' for the brilliant colours of the Post Impressionists and Impressionists in the Jeu de Paume and Orangérie, and remembered those of Sickert as dingy. Indeed, I could only remember *Ennui*, in the Tate. My favourite paintings were Van Gogh's *Cornfield with Cypresses*, Franz Marc's *Red Horses* and Paul Nash's *Wood on the Downs*, amongst the moderns; earlier, Dürer's *Large Piece of Turf* and Botticelli's *Nascita di Venere (Birth of Venus)*. I had even had in mind to write a monograph on the girl, Simonetta Vespucci, whom he painted as Venus and who was perhaps, like himself, a Neo-Platonist.

However, if Sickert was the Ripper, that was a change of plane, yet perhaps something that I ought to take up.

So, on getting back, I asked my mother some questions about him. For what, in particular, was his work admired?

He was, she said, a 'tonal painter'. He noted all the different gradations between dark and light - the depth of one shadow, relative to another. She agreed to his being rather dingy, but his subjects were largely scenes of low life in Camden Town. He was the father of what was known as the Camden Town School, all of whom showed somewhat subdued colouration. Unlike the Impressionists, Sickert used a lot of tertiary colour, mixtures of greys, browns and ochres. Yet, there were rich reds in his music hall pictures. 'He went on the stage first, like you.' He also did a lot of pictures of Dieppe.

That he spent so much time in Dieppe, Florence had said, was because it got him out of the streets in which the murders had been committed. Anywhere in London, he still felt too near to the scenes of the crimes. Only a bus journey could take him back there and he didn't really feel safe. In Dieppe, he could almost feel like a different person, a person who had not walked in the dark streets.

Yet even there, he was visited. Somebody - I think she said the Chief Commissioner of the Police of London - or Lord Salisbury, walked into his studio in Dieppe, took a brief look round, gave him £500 and went out with a picture of boats under his arm.

It was a small indifferent picture. Sickert was not yet well known as an artist, and that picture could not possibly have been worth £500, which was an enormous sum in those days.

'It was a bribe! He took it unblushingly.'

'A bribe to do what?' I asked.

'Not to reveal what he knew about the murders. The Government, the Prime Minister, Lord Salisbury, and the Commissioner of the Police of London were all very anxious for it not to come out.'

'You don't think Florence is a little dotty do you?'

Mother confessed that she had asked herself that question, because the tale did seem so extraordinary. Yet Florence did not sound like a person making things up, though she told the story in bits, disconnectedly, in a way that made it difficult to understand what exactly she was trying to say had happened. The whole thing was in some way connected with the Royal Family. That was why Lord Salisbury, who was Prime Minister, wanted it hushed up. There was a little girl born illegitimate, to some male member of Queen Victoria's family. Salisbury did not want it to come out that there was this child, because the father was a member of the Royal Family. 'She says, in direct line of succession to the throne!' Mother raised her eyebrows, as though she found this a bit much to take.

'What has this to do with Jack the Ripper?'

'I don't know. She says it's the background to the crimes she is giving me.' Unless this background was understood, the crimes would not be understood. There was nothing for it but to wait in patience until Florence, in her own time, drew the connection. She was giving out the data, and there had to be some connecting thread, on which the beads could be strung in the right order.

We did what we could with what seemed to be the pieces of a broken necklace.

The putative father had not been named by Florence. Obviously she knew, but was holding it back, not because she wished to hold anything in reserve but because she felt it too indiscreet and dangerous. Mother read a good deal of historical biography and was fairly well up on Queen Victoria's family. In direct line of succession to the throne were only the Prince of Wales who later became Edward VII, and the two grandsons, the one who became George V and that elder brother of his, the Duke of Clarence, who predeceased him. There was a scandal about him, but it was of a different order, and suggested an orientation towards boys. Mother's suspicions centred upon Edward VII. There were a number of scandals connecting his name with women: actresses or other men's wives.

This set me wondering whether we should have had a Queen Florence, if such things went by the blood. I worked out that Florence, in her late eighties, would have been born within the lifetime of Edward VII.

Florence had told Mother that she, herself, had been in danger of her life. She had lived through very frightening years. She had been afraid she could be killed, like those other poor women. She had been in such a state of terror, she did not think she had ever got over it or ever would. Even after all these years, when Sickert was dead (he had died on 22 January 1942). The habit of being afraid to speak of it persisted. Indeed, said Mother, she had looked very 'trembly' as she did so. That was why it was impossible to press her upon any point.

She had not witnessed the murders, which took place in the East End. But an attempt had been made on her own life, in broad daylight, near Charing Cross. Coming from St Martin's Lane...

'On Trafalgar Square, then, in front of St Martin's-in-The-Fields.'

'Not in front of the church. Where it broadens out at the junction with the Strand, near Charing Cross.' They were making for the station. She had been taking a little girl out for a walk and meant to take her back to her place for tea. They were stepping off the curb when a coach came straight at them. Florence had jumped back on to the pavement and tried to lift the child back on to it but the coach mounted the pavement and the child was hit by a wheel, and had to be taken to hospital. Florence felt dreadful having to go back, alone, and tell Sickert the child he had confided to her care had been injured and was in hospital. He had been very nice about it and told her not to blame herself. He said he was sure it was a case of attempted murder!

Florence had been very specific about the location because, while she had not seen the murders in Whitehchapel, this was the one thing to which she had been a witness, and the details were etched in her mind as though it had happened yesterday.

I was almost disappointed. I had been expecting to hear Florence had been chased by a man with a knife. This sounded merely like an accident. The coachman could have lost control of his horse. How did she know it was attempted murder?

Probably she accepted what Sickert told her about it because it was part of the whole situation. She had always been told an illegitimate child for the heir to the throne could be a target, and this seemed to prove it. It enforced her conviction she must never speak of it, to anyone. Even now, 'She says she could even be bringing *me* into danger by telling *me*, which I find hard to believe.'

Mother was not sure I was right in assuming Florence was the illegitimate child. From the way she had told it, Mother thought the target was the child she had by the hand.

I know now that I should have given more weight to this. What wrong-footed me was an apparent mystery about Florence's own origins. Mother had thought it would be nice to begin her book by saying something about Florence, and asked her for some biographical details. Would she tell her something about her parents and early surroundings? Florence said she would rather not. I thought that if Florence was the illegitimate daughter of Edward VII, she would not want to identify her mother. I insufficiently regarded the reason Florence did give for her reticence. Her beginnings had not been happy. Her parents had been against her going to France. Indeed, it was unusual in those days for girls to go anywhere unchaperoned. But Florence knew it would not be easy for her to make a career as an artist, and although she had been to the Royal College of Art, felt that, to stand a chance, she needed the extra qualification of having studied in Paris. Her parents contributed nothing to her expenses over there. She managed to find work tinting portrait photographs for a studio in Paris - strengthening the eyelashes and adding touches of colour. Work not to be spoken of in serious artists' circles, but it paid Henri Gervex's fees, as well as her living expenses. To speak truth, she had even after her return to England done such tinting, for the Court photographers, Bassano, in Dover Street, but that was a secret, because if critics knew it they might think it influenced her style. Having gone to France cost her her relations with her family. She had made her own life entirely.

So, she would rather be introduced without childhood or early years. She thought Mother could perfectly well start just by saying that in 1885 she returned from Paris where she had been studying under Henri Gervex, and met Sickert.

Mother regretted not being allowed to introduce anything about the early struggle Florence had had, for she admired her independence.

Florence had given Mother a good deal of information about the irregular Sickert household. There was an illegitimate son, Joseph, 'Who is *always* called Sickert' - I particularly remember the emphasis which mother placed upon the *always*. Florence had not kept in with Joseph since he grew up, but she knew his mother very well. She had not been married to Sickert but Joseph was his child. I gathered she meant, his mother told her so. Florence made the point that, if Mother wanted to write to Joseph she should address him as Sickert. He was still living. There had been a lot of women in Walter Sickert's life. His attitude to marriage was very casual. For his first marriage (to Ellen Cooden) he was very nearly late. Instead of having ordered a carriage, he stood waiting by the kerb-side for a bus. It was a long time in coming. Another man, also waiting at the stop, grumbled, 'If it doesn't come I shall be late for the office.'

'And I shall be late for my wedding,' Sickert said.

'Your wedding!' exclaimed the other. It was the other who, to avert such a calamity, hailed a hansom cab.

Amongst the papers lent to Mother was a telegram dated 3 July 1911, reading SORRY MARRIAGE OFF. Florence explained that he had on that date arranged to be married to a student at his newly opened school, Rowlandson House. When he arrived at the Registry Office, in Hampstead, he found another man there. She had let both men make appointments to be married to her at the same time. The Registrar said to the girl, 'you can't marry two men!' He advised them to go for a walk on Hampstead Heath, and it was decided she should marry the other one. This Sickert told Florence and Albert Humphrey when he came to see them that evening. He did not appear much upset, and on 29 July married another student at Rowlandson House. He wrote to Florence and her husband apologizing for not having asked them to the wedding, as he had not known he was going to marry 'rather suddenly'. He would, however, like them to come to the first house-warming, to meet Christine.

Florence said there was a girl engaged for a time to act as nanny; an Irish girl, named Mary Kelly.

The irony of this story is that I did not know who Mary Kelly was. Neither, from the way she told it, did Mother. Florence, living all the time in the atmosphere of the Ripper Crimes, may have assumed everyone in the world knew who Mary Kelly was, and that the significance of this name, as she dropped it, would be instantly appreciated. That name had no resonance, either for Mother or for me. Yet something in the way Florence had spoken of this must have impressed Mother with its being in some way relevent, and it was as something Florence told as significant she told it to me. I only wish that I had written down every jot that was told me about Mary Kelly. All I can remember is that she was in some way difficult. Strong willed, with ideas of her own. She was dissatisfied. She did not think Sickert treated her with sufficient respect and consideration. She was ambitious for better things, and not really cut out to be a nanny. Indeed, she could have made a career as an artists' model, if only anyone had thought of it. She was quite good looking. Good hair, dark, bushy. One of the Art Schools might have been persuaded to take her on, on a regular basis. But nobody looked into the future. Florence was not expecting things to blow up in the way they did.

Mary Kelly eventually flounced off, leaving Sickert holding the baby, almost literally. After she had gone, she started blackmailing.

'Blackmailing!' I was astonished. 'What had Sickert done that he could be blackmailed for?'

Mother thought the nanny could have seen something of his affair with some woman, and threatened to tell his wife, unless he produced some money. Not that he had any to produce. He was very poor.

It did not sound like a blackmailer's passport to fortune.

The practical effect, as seen by Florence, was that, the nanny having ceased to come, Sickert had to look after the child himself. The chief impression made upon Florence was the spectacle of his having to bath and change a little girl. It was not so much that she worried him while he was painting but that he had to go out, to meet dealers, to whom he was trying to sell his paintings, and he was a man who liked to go out in the evenings. Sickert was always asking Florence to come over to take charge of the child so that he could go out. It was not particularly convenient for Florence, either. It meant she had to cross London, and there was no convenient underground or bus service. It took her away from her own work and she found it tiring. She went over when he sounded really desperate for someone to come and be with the little girl while he went out.

I wondered why his wife did not do it, but Mother had referred to Christine as delicate. Hence I wrongly assumed that the child in question was Sickert and Christine's.

I was introduced to Florence, during the time that I was hearing all this. It was at an art exhibition, in which both she and Mother had something hanging. She was a tall woman, but because of her age, stooping. She was very thin, and must once have been willowy. Her hair was quite white. Her speech and manner were those of good breeding. However, she did not look at all like Edward VII or Queen Victoria. I scrutinised her very carefully from that point of view. Naturally, I betrayed no knowledge of the strange story I was not supposed to have been told. Her pictures in the exhibition were both pastels. One was a portrait of a little girl, the other a picture of children playing in a garden. She had caught their fleeting attitudes well.

Although the strangeness of the story Mother had been relaying had made me wonder whether she was unstable, she appeared a self-collected, orderly sort of person.

I should state plainly that Florence never told Mother Sickert was the Ripper. I asked Mother whether she thought Florence believed it was he who had committed the Ripper crimes She hesitated a little, but said, low, 'yes'.

But, I said, if she had believed he was the Ripper would she have kept silent, or dared to remain friends with him?

Mother, who had read a good deal of Freud and Jung, thought he could have had a Madonna/whore complex, in which case only prostitutes might be in danger from him. Also, if it was a long time ago, Florence might have felt he had got over it.

Florence really was a puzzle to Mother. Mother thought of herself as being open minded, but from the way in which she said one day, 'Florence was at one time familiar with a *dreadful* neighbourhood,' I realized she had sustained a slight shock. Florence had said there had been a house of prostitution only a couple of doors down the street.

'Where was this?' I asked. I had been expecting the answer to be Paris, where so many of the Impressionists had lived in what was practically a red light district, on the Buttes de Montmartre.

'Some low district of London', was the unexpected reply.

London! 'What part of London?'

Florence had not named the street. She had referred to it as being near a Square, but had not named the Square, either. Some run down, low district.

'Why was Florence living in a low district?'

She did not say living in. She referred to a studio in. A studio where she used to visit an artist. Probably Sickert. Going in or out of the studio, to visit him, she could see the prostitutes with their clients going in and out, a couple of houses down. There was no mystery about what they were doing. If it was a purpose built studio, it would have large windows, facing north. Too cold to want to live in. An artist might feel it was not for him to move out because prostitutes had moved into the neighbourhood. But if Florence went into a shop to buy anything, she could find herself standing in the queue with one of the women from *that* house.

On another occasion, Mother - obviously a bit shaken - said that Florence had spoken of a house in the street at which boys were available to men. 'Only a couple of doors down.'

Mother said Florence appeared to have 'attained to total unshockability'. If she were to be told that somebody she knew was in the habit of going out at night and murdering prostitutes, she would hardly start. She had seen it all.

If she believed someone had been Jack the Ripper, she would just say in her mild way, 'He had his problems.'

Florence had had a friend who had been a governess but became a prostitute.

This seemed to me an unlikely transition, and I queried it. A governess would be a woman of some education. The descent was too precipitous.

Not a trained governess, said Mother. Her previous employment had been as a shop assistant. She was not a happy girl. She had come to London from Wales. She had a job in an infirmary in Cardiff, washing floors. She came to London, hoping to get something better. London had not offered the kind of opportunity she sought. She had found nothing better than that job in that shoddy shop. What did not help was that she tended to compare her situation, much to her own disadvantage, with that of Florence. Florence appeared to her as the independent mistress of her own hours. 'If only she knew how hard I worked!' Florence had interjected.

Florence was unusual. In those days, there were very few women who were not dependent on a man. For a girl without any particular gift, or training to qualify her for anything, the only employments available were in truth rather miserable.

When it was suggested she look after the child, it was thought that at least it would get her out of standing on her feet all day in that tawdry shop, and that working for an artist would be agreeable and interesting. It was a bohemian, irregular family, for the child's mother was not the artist's wife, but to come in and take care of the little girl brought their friend into the kind of artistic and intellectual environment she apparently craved.

Unfortunately, her wages, which were never promised to be great, were not regularly paid. 'Really, they were not the sort of people who should ever have employed a governess.' They had not the means. She was pleased with the job at first, But then, there were the days on which she was not paid. Waiting until he had sold a picture, to have the money, was not good enough. She had no reserves, and could not wait. Gratitude turned to recriminations. She had been better off in the shop. 'And she became a prostitute.'

For a time she was seen about, obviously soliciting. Then she was seen no more. That was all Florence knew. It was only much later that she learned that her poor friend must have drifted downwards, to the East End.

'How did she learn it?'

'From the papers. She had been murdered. It was only from reading the papers, which gave quite a lot of details about the crime and reported the inquest, that Florence realized how miserably her one-time friend must have been living, for some considerable time. It affected her.

Florence had met Sickert in December 1885, at a private view of the RBA (Royal Society of British Artists) in Suffold Street. Her picture, *The Disputed Point,* was her first to be hung at the RBA. She found herself in conversation with Henry Tonks, Theodore Roussell and Sidney Starr, but she noticed, standing near to the fireplace, a man rather taller than the average, a man with blue or blue-grey eyes, and curly fair hair, which he had a trick of pushing back with his hand to flatten it. He was in animated conversation with other people, but presently left them in order to join her group. He was Walter Richard Sickert.

He, too, was exhibiting that year for the first time at the RBA. He was at that time twenty-five, and she was twenty-three. As he was very fond of music halls, they went sometimes together, and sketched together. Among the artistes they drew were Dan Leno, R.G. Knowles, Marie Lloyd, Vesta Tilley, Little Tich and Albert Chevalier. They drew in pencil, in small note-books, four or five inches long, but later Sickert used to take packets of postcards, as he found them easier to handle. Afterwards, she would sometimes help him with the squaring up. (Sickert believed in making lightning drawings, but then transferred them to canvas by the slowest imaginable means. That is - rejecting the Impressionists' revolution in taking their easels into into the open air - he divided his sketches into small numbered squares, similarly squared the canvas on which he wished to transfer them, but in squares that multiplied the size, so that the transferred design came up larger.

One of his favourite music halls was the Old Bedford, in Camden High Street.

They often ate together at a small restaurant close to Warren Street

Florence Pash

underground station.

It was for Florence a time of meeting people. She met Whistler, whose pupil Sickert had been until his recent meeting with Degas. Florence had attended Whistler's famous Ten o'Clock lecture at Princes, in Piccadilly in February, 1885, just before she left for France - and though she was at the back, his diction was so clear she heard every word. During her summer in France she spent, for the first time, a few days in Dieppe, where so many of the Impressionists gathered to paint by the sea, and after a champagne lunch Jacques-Emile Blanche asked her to pose for him, which she did there and then, standing in front of a bathing hut in the pink hat and dress she happened to be wearing, and the picture was later exhibited by him in London and reproduced in his memoirs. He gave it to her and she still had it. F.J. O'Sullivan also, painted her.

1890 was the year in which she and Sickert first sat for one another. Her pastel of him was later hung at the Royal Academy (though not hung until 1924, her first picture hung there having been *Fairy Tales*, which had been already exhibited at the Paris Salon in 1888).

In the opening months of 1890, Sickert made four paintings of her. She did not, of course, commission these. He did them for his own pleasure and so kept them, and she did not know where they were now.

The earliest of his letters to 'Dear Miss Pash,' from 12 Pembroke Gardens, Kensington, asked her to be 'so very charitable' as to sit for him on Sunday morning. She always enjoyed sitting for Sickert, as during the rests she could inspect the progress of the portrait and see the technique. 'I always learned something,' she said.

The first three portraits were done in her own studio-flat, in Sloane Street, where she was already taking pupils. The fourth, which she liked the best, was done in his mother's home, in Edwardes Square, West Kensington, where he posed her, wearing a black dress and black hat, on a black sofa. It was really in his brother Bernard Sickert's studio but he was away and Walter was using it. It was at the end of May 1890. Between sessions, he took her upstairs to introduce to his mother. Mrs Sickert (Nellie) was above average height, and looked very like her son. His attitude to her was reverential. She showed Florence drawings and paintings by his father, Oswald Adalbert Sickert, which were very good. As they talked about Walter's childhood, he told her he had stood in for the young Nelson in the picture by George William Joy, *Thirty Years before Trafalgar, Young Nelson with his Grandmother*. This was later reproduced in *The Boy Through The Ages*, by D.M. Stuart.

Mrs Sickert also showed Florence a letter Walter had written to her when he was ten. Florence saw with surprise that it was in German. Walter's father had been a Dane, born in Altona, but with the German annexation of Schleswig-Holstein in 1866, he found himself a German national. He joined the staff of the *Fliegende Blätter*, as a regular draughtsman, in the year before Walter was

19

born, which was why Walter, their first child, was born, on 30 May 1860, in Munich. Oswald did not want his children to grow up German. That was why, in 1868, he had come to his wife's country and taken British nationality.

Florence lent Mother Walter's ten year old letter in his mother's translation. It was written from the seaside, where he and the younger children had been flying a kite and digging in the sand. Papa had bought a spade for each of them. They saw a man drown. 'It was terrible.' They had been for a long walk and crossed the railway line twice.

Florence believed this had been written from Lowestoft, though she advised Mother not to state that for a fact as the Sickerts also spent holidays at Morthoe and in St. Ives. I am sure it was Lowestoft, for there was no railway line to either Morthoe or St. Ives.

Sickert did a fifth painting of Florence a few years later in his studio in Robert Street, near Cumberland Square and Regent's Park.

When Florence had assembled a sufficient number of pupils, she moved to a larger studio-flat, at 36 Victoria Street, in Members Mansions, now demolished, the site being occupied by New Scotland Yard. According to the street directory, with which I have recently checked, she was there in 1896, but from the tone of the manuscript Florence seemed to think she had been here much earlier than that. She invited Sickert to give some of the classes, for which he expressed himself extremely grateful. She must have replied that there was no need for him to feel so, as his name might draw pupils. So he wrote again, 'I remain grateful...So I am grateful. I chose to be grateful. I feel grateful. I'll see you hanged but I'll be grateful.'

Several letters concern the preliminary arrangements. He would come on a Monday. He would come on Thursdays. He would perhaps come on both Thursdays and Mondays. He would not say on which days he could come; the pupils would thus have to come every day, so as not to miss the chance of being there when he came. She had accommodation for thirty easels, and designed a circular advertising her Art School for Ladies, offering 'the opportunity of studying from the living model, still life, flowers, drapery etc., on the system pursued at Parisian studios.'

It should be explained that in those days the sexes were still generally segregated for the teaching of art. It was thought that if both sexes were set to draw from the nude model side by side, they would feel embarrassed. (Sickert would later open an Art School for gentlemen). She took beginners in the morning, from 10-2, daily. There were also evening classes for more advanced students, and it was at these that Sickert would come in.

The financial basis of the arrangement does not appear clearly, but there is one in which he asks if she would let him retain for a few days a cheque that he ought to hand over, as he was penniless. This was the first letter written after the classes had started, and Mother had added to the typescript, in her handwriting 'August 1893', which Florence had told her from the context. As it started, 'what a good beginning!' it was probably written directly after the first class which he had taken, which would have been some time during the first week. It looks to me, therefore, as though the classes started in 1893, despite the street directory.

Though not tidy, Sickert was obsessive about cleanliness, in the studio and of his person, and everything that touched it. Once, at his mother's, he accidentally put on someone else's hat. On discovering his mistake, he was so horrified he immediately went upstairs and washed his hair. Nevertheless, the one thing that he never washed was his palette; he just scraped it down when it became too mountainous. But psychiatrists have something to say about obsessive washing. In Dieppe he would hang the whole of his bed-linen and even his mattress out of his window every morning.

He found it more interesting to paint slightly misshapen models than standard beauties. His favourite was a very fat model who had a squint and deformed feet. However, he was full of compassion for a pretty one he found crying. When he enquired the cause of her tears, she said the dentist had told her she would have to have all her teeth out. 'Why that's no great matter', he exclaimed, thinking she could have false ones. She said she had not the money to buy false ones. It would mean that she would no longer be employed as an artist's model and no man would want to marry her, either, so it was the end of her prospects altogether and she did not know how she would live. Sickert came to tell Florence, and the two of them paid for artificial teeth and a few weeks later she put her head round the door, smiling broadly to show them the beautiful dentures and told them she was engaged to be married.

When Florence appealed to him on behalf of a C.E. Holloway, a former pupil of Whistler who was in dire straits, he was, however unable to help. Although he was now writing for various papers, they delayed paying him, and consequently, 'I live on my landlady's credit.' (Whistler stepped into the breach and went and sat with Holloway in hospital every day until his death, while an exhibition of his works was still running).

A near neighbour of Florence at 92 Victoria Street was George Moore, the Irish novelist. They would invite one another for tea, and it was at his place she met Yeats and Lady Gregory.

Early in 1898 Florence told her friends she was going to be married. Sickert, leaving Florence's class, encountered Moore in the street, not looking well. Explaining his condition, Moore said, 'I had a glass of milk last night and it feels as if it had turned to Camembert cheese, and Miss Pash is going to be married.' It was Sickert who told Florence this. Moore was always a bit sweet on Florence, but, a bachelor by ingrained habit, had never proposed.

Albert Alexander Humphrey was a six-foot Canadian, straightforward, open-hearted, 'would do anyone a good turn'. He had been born in Quebec, and was a survivor of Sherman's 1864 march through Georgia in the American Civil War. He was a kind of financial diplomatist, interested in Argentinian affairs. He had come to England in 1897 to sell a mine, but met Florence and liked it so well here that he stayed for the rest of his life.

Just after her marriage, on 2 July, Sickert wrote to her (from Robert Street), a letter that was a model for such occasions: 'You have always been one of my best and most valued friends...I am a believer in love and marriage and still more in the conjunction of both...All I know about your husband is that his marriage shows him to have taste and wisdom.' As a wedding present, he gave her and her husband one of his paintings, *The Acting Manager*.

Albert Humphrey did not know much about art or artists, but he made Florence's friends welcome. She had given up her art school as soon as she married, but in the top floor flat of 122 Victoria Street, where he joined her, they gave a dinner party every Sunday evening. They were seldom less than twelve or fifteen round the table, the regulars being Sickert, Moore, Max Beerbohm with his sister Aggie (Agnes) and Charles Conder, who specialized in painting on silk and on fans. His pretty, wistful pictures were as different from Sickert's as could be imagined, but Sickert taught him to etch and he taught Sickert to paint on chicken skins and Florence to paint on silk. Florence's creativity went perhaps more into her painting than her cooking, for she gave them every Sunday the same menu, roast beef with sweet corn followed by jelly and trifle. Nevertheless, they always came, and after the meal all went up into the big studio which Florence had had built onto the roof in the days of her school, and danced.

One year, Florence went to the Chelsea Arts Ball in a silk dress made by Aggie (who was a professional dressmaker) and hand-painted by Conder. She still had it, folded away in a drawer from which it had lately been taken out for loan to an exhibition. When Moore was writing *Evelyn Innes* he asked her what his heroine should wear to some function. She had the evening before been to a dance at which the hostess wore mauve silk embroidered with lilies, so described that garment to him and the description went into the book. Albert Alexander Humphrey had a sister, Mrs Green, who had a daughter, christened Stella Maris, now Mrs Bedford but young to be a widow. She came to stay with them and was with Florence when Charles Conder called, and after Stella had gone out he said to Florence, 'I'm going to marry that girl!' He did. (She wished that Rothenstein, in his biography of Conder, had not written so much about his drinking. He did drink, but out of consideration for Stella he made efforts to conquer the habit, twice going voluntarily into a home for treatment, though on coming out he relapsed). He made of Florence the lithographic portrait now in the British Museum.

Speaking about the Ripper crimes again, Florence had said to Mother, 'I'm telling you things I have never told anybody!' She had not told her son, and did not intend to. She had not told her husband. Albert thought of her as having lived a bohemian life amongst artists, which was true as far as it went, but he thought of it as having been a gay and carefree life. He did not know she had lived for years of her life in terror. She kept back from him anything that was sordid or frightening. He knew of her friendship with Sickert, but not of the brothel in the street where Sickert had the studio or of Mary Kelly. She did not tell him anything that could possibly connect with the Ripper crimes. He had no idea she had been in a position such that she had feared to be the next victim. In that sense, he never really knew her.

Sickert, after his move to Dieppe, where he stayed for about six years, asked her to assure his creditors he would return one day, and gave her detailed instructions as to what to do with all the pictures and other possessions he had left at Robert Street. Amongst the paintings he lists 'Yourself by Whistler'. There must surely have been a painting of Florence by Whistler that has disappeared or gone unidentified. Sickert wanted her to have first refusal on his easel, and his throne as a present. When she used the key he had given her to let herself in, she found none of the pictures (save one small head) or palettes he had spoken of, Wheatley's having come and removed all for store, but she accepted the easel and throne. The latter was far too big for her studio at Victoria Street, so she had it cut down.

He wrote to Florence a good deal from Dieppe. Largely it was about painting. He was painting Dieppe scenes, trying to make some money. He had evolved painting techniques, which, generously, he told her, while asking her not to pass them on to other painters. Yet there were personal touches: 'Nice to see a handwriting that suggests pleasure and nothing but pleasure year in year out...I am very much cut off from fun by two things - work and the absence of the one luxury in life, which is a sympathetic English woman who is at home in a studio and would now and then spend an hour with me...Write, write, write.'

(If this sounds lonely, he was not physically so. The letter was written from the Villa Villain, in which he had set up house with a Dieppe fishwife, Madam Villain, who had a stall on the quay. During the years he lived with her he dressed as a fisherman, and one of her children was believed to be his. Nevertheless, he may genuinely have missed a sympathetic English woman who could enter into his life as an artist).

In another letter, written from the Rue Aguardo, he compared Florence with another woman. The latter had always haggled and bargained her way through life, yet had not got much. On the contrary, 'You have spent always, everything, work, love, money, fatigue, health, and look how full and rich your existence is...The thing is to give, give, give. You always get back more than you can give.'

He sounded in this letter so nice, it seemed mean to think he could be the

Ripper.

He came back to England in 1905. In 1911 there was his broken engagement after the debacle at the Registry Office on 3 July, and second marriage only just over a fortnight later, on 29 July, to Christine Angus.

Sickert returned to Dieppe with his second wife, Christine, and it was there that Christine died, in October, 1920.

Florence's husband was about fifteen years her senior, and his health now began to go. She had a long period of looking after him until he died, on 24 September 1917, in her presence, at 122 Victoria Street, aged seventy, of a carcimona of the stomach. It was she who, on the next day, provided the details for the death certificate (on which his occupation is given as 'formerly a press agent.' Her consolation was their son, Cecil. The Earl of Argyll, as a friend of her late husband, wanted to send Cecil to the frightfully good public school where he himself had been educated. This was a terrific offer, but she did not wish her son separated from herself during terms, and sent him to a nearby day-school, instead.

It was not long afterwards that Florence received a commission to make a portrait of the composer, Camille Saint-Saëns, now nearing the end of his long life. Taking Cecil with her, she crossed the channel and whilst in Dieppe took the occasion to see Sickert and condole with him in his bereavement. She found him very depressed. If he had married Christine on the rebound, yet he had become much attached to her. He sat for Florence to make a second portrait of him, another pastel (now in the Islington Public Library), and she felt that this depression showed in the picture.

Later, she married a Major C.T. Holland. For a while they lived in Broadhurst Gardens, Kensington. Then they went to live abroad in France and Italy for three or four years. Soon after their return, she found herself widowed for the second time.

It was then that she went to share a home with her sister, Miss Annie Pash. They divided 4 Briardale Gardens, Hampstead, into two flats.

On 16 May, 1932, George Moore wrote to her, asking if she knew anyone in her neighbourhood who would let him have a room to sleep in. He would arrive in the evening and leave early in the morning to work in his own flat in Ebury Street, and so be no trouble. He was obviously hoping that she would respond by suggesting he move in with them, and she had a dreadful feeling it could be the prelude to his asking her to marry him. He was over eighty, and she did not feel she could take the strain of looking after him, so she made some other suggestions as to where he could stay, which he did not take up. At the end of the year, she received a cable from her son, Cecil, asking her to come out to India to join him, as he was concerned about the health of his wife. She had been going to take tea with George Moore at Ebury Street, and felt rather mean in sending him a card to excuse herself as she was on her way to the ship.

She remained in India for six years, and when she came back, he was amongst the old friends who had died.

After a total absence of more than ten years, she found it difficult to pick up the threads again. The London art world no longer knew her. The persons had changed. Sickert was in Bathampton. He, too, within months, was dead.

That was probably why she liked the company of my mother, also a widow, who liked to hear about the past. (They had also in common that they had both lived several years in India; my father had been a British Officer in the old Indian army).

They had been businesslike, and had a contract drawn up between Florence Humphrey Holland and Violet Overton Fuller concerning the book to be entitled *Letters to Florence, from Sickert, Conder and Moore*, and placed it in the hands of Curtis Brown, who sent it round, but it failed to find a publisher. Home & Van Thal, Dennis Dobson and Phoenix all found it charming but too slight, and really they agreed. Mother lamented that Florence made her take out anything that had 'the least bit of spice.' Florence had helped Stella Maris nurse Conder during his last illness, and noticed it was her practice to smoke a cigarette while reading in bed. This seemed to Florence a dangerous habit, since if she dropped off to sleep while it was still lighted, it would fall from her hand on to the bedclothes or floor, and when, not long after Conder's death, Florence learned Stella had been burned to death in her flat in Ebury Street, the bed having caught fire, she had not the least doubt that was what had happened. She would not, however, permit that to go into the book in case anyone should criticize Stella for having had that habit. Mother had, regretfully, to replace the specific detail with a vague reference to 'an accident'. (It is so long ago now I hope the truth about that fire in April 1912, cannot hurt anybody).

Mother returned Sickert's letters and the photographs of pictures intended for use as illustrations, to Florence. They remained friends, however. I was invited with Mother to tea with Florence at 4a Briardale Gardens - and cautioned by Mother beforehand not to mention the Ripper, as Cecil and his wife would be there and they did not know anything about it, and Florence did not know she had told me.

The only time I really talked with Florence was at an exhibition when unintentionally I cut across her. I said I found painting relaxing. She bridled, and said it required intellectual vigour. One had to make decisions. Yes, I knew one could have to decide, for instance, whether something in the background should be eliminated or brought into the picture and featured. The last thing I had meant to do was disparage painting as an art requiring acumen. But it belonged to a different plane from work at the typewriter. Just at that moment, an unexpected invitation to tea with Professor Daniel Jones, Principal of the Phonetics Department at University College, had ended with his suggesting to me that, as I already had an Honours Degree in English, I should under his supervision undertake an intensive study of phonetics. This occasioned me some brain fatigue and I was, from May 1949 onwards, involved with the research into the fate of Noor Inayat Khan that went into my book *Madeleine* and plunged me into rather sinister mysteries concerning SOE and the world of wartime secret agents, and, yes, I did find painting relaxing. I could not find a way of putting it that did not sound to her slighting.

In January she sent Mother a cutting from the *Hampstead and Highgate Express* that must have appeared about the 20th, in which she was referred to as 'an old lady of 87.' It was entitled ' An Old Lady Remembers.' All the things she had remembered for the benefit of the interviewer were happy ones, dinners at Victoria Street, and a champagne lunch. Six months later, on the occasion of the opening of the Pastel Society's annual exhibition, the *Evening Standard* had a piece about her, entitled 'Artist at 87.' Again, Sickert was mentioned, but not the Ripper.

She had the grief of her son's death. Her eyesight failed so that she could no longer draw, for fear of submitting work with mistakes she could not see. She nevertheless did me the honour of coming to the Festival Exhibition of the Women's International Art Club, 1951, to see the two pictures I had hanging.

She was silent for some time. Then Mother had a letter from her lawyer, saying she had died on 25 June 1951, and had left her an artist's mirror and two easels.

These bequests were more than Mother had room for in her flat. She sold the artist's mirror and one of the easels, and kept the one that Florence had bought from Sickert, more than fifty years ago.

When Mother died, on 12 September 1967, - a still wet painting on it - I brought it, with the rest of her things, from her place to mine. However I sold it to Rowney's. This was not merely because it was enormous, and, as I had no need for one that size took up a disproportionate space in my flat. It was because I could not quite put from my mind the thought that this had been the easel of the Ripper and carried the atmosphere of his crimes.

Chapter 2

Stephen Knight's 'Final Solution'

More than a decade later, a Glasgow friend, Dr Margaret Little, sent me the paperback edition of *Jack the Ripper, The Final Solution* by Stephen Knight (Panther, 1977). I had missed the original edition, as also an associated television programme, so it was quite new to me, and it was by chance Margaret had sent it. She was a psychiatrist, who had first written to me after reading my *Swinburne*.

My eyes travelled down the table of contents and picked out the chapter heading, 'Sir William Gull.' Gull! The clue that Florence had given Mother! We had never thought of it as being the name of a person. And Sickert was mentioned all through.

Knight's informant was Joseph Sickert, the artist's son. When he was fourteen, his father had told him a terrible story. In the early 1880s, he had a studio at 15, Cleveland Street. At 22 Cleveland Street was a tobacconists's where there were two assistants, Annie Elizabeth Crook and Mary Jane Kelly. The latter was Irish. Annie who lodged at number six, used sometimes to visit Sickert. So did the Duke of Clarence, the Heir Presumptive. He got her with child. The child was named Alice Margaret.

This, and not Florence herself, must be the illegitimate daughter of a relation of Queen Victoria in direct line of succession to the throne, of whom Florence had talked to Mother.

Knight had obtained a birth certificate, which he reproduced in facsimile. It gave these details:

When and where born: Eighteenth April 1885 Marylebone Workhouse
Name: Alice Margaret
Sex: Girl
Name and surname of father:
Name, surname and maiden surname of Mother:
Annie Elizabeth Crook, Confectionery assistant from Cleveland Street
Occupation of Father:
Signature, description and residence of informant:
X the mark of Annie Elizabeth Crook Mother
6 Cleveland Street Fitzroy Square.

There, certainly, was an Alice Margaret born to an Annie Elizabeth Crook and the father's name left blank. Annie was illiterate, having had to make her mark. She had had her child in the workhouse but gave her residence as 6 Cleveland Street. She defined herself as a confectionery assistant from Cleveland Street. Joseph Sickert had described the shop where she worked as a tobacconist's; not a significant discrepancy, as it may have been both.

Knight sought to further buttress the information obtained by enquiring the rate-payer of 6 Cleveland Street, from 1888, and found that the rated occupier of the basement of No 6 was Elizabeth Cook. He therefore assumed Annie Elizabeth Crook and Elizabeth Cook to be the same person. Subsequent research by others has shown this not to be so. They had different dates of death, in different places.

I made my own enquiries and found that neither Annie Elizabeth Crook, Mary Jane Kelly or Walter Richard Sickert were rated occupiers of any address in Cleveland Street. This did not mean they were not there; only the owner or principal tenant pays rates. Sub-tenants, for the rating authorities, do not exist. The letting of furnished rooms used to be very much commoner than it is now. I can remember streets in which almost every house had a ROOMS TO LET card in the window.

So far as Annie is concerned, she gave her address on the birth certificate of her child as 6 Cleveland Street.

I also asked the archivist of the Marylebone Library, City of Westminster, who was the rated occupier of 22 Cleveland Street. I received the following reply:

The St Marylebone rate books for 1884 and 1885 both show Charlotte Horton at 22 Cleveland Street. The St Marylebone Directory of 1884 lists James Currier, Confectioner, and Miss Horton at this address.

It seems to me as though, in a premises at 22 Cleveland Street of which the rated occupier was Charlotte Horton, James Currier and she opened a confectioner's with a tobacconist's side to it, in which Annie Elizabeth Crook and Mary Jane Kelly were employed as assistants.

Sickert's association with the area is supported by Florence's reminiscence that they often ate in a restaurant near Warren Street underground station. That was not specially convenient for her; living in Sloane Street, one of Chelsea's many restaurants would have suited her better. Neither was Warren Street specially near to any place of entertainment or culture where they would continually go. But if he had his studio in Cleveland Street, that was only a few minutes' walk. Probably, she got out at Warren Street Station when she went to see him.

I have found further support for his connection with the area at that time in the catalogue of his works in Wendy Baron's *Sickert.* (1) In this she lists 'Sheet with Four Restaurant Studies 1884'. It comprises, she says, four pencil drawings, one of which is inscribed, 'Restaurant Benoit Charlotte Street, Fitzroy Square, Oct 6 Déjeunér', and one of which is inscribed, 'Moreau's Sunday 9 pm, Oct 5...' the whole sheet being inscribed, obviously retrospectively, '1881 or thereabouts/82?/83?/84?' Dr Baron checked that it was in 1884 that October 5 fell on a Sunday, and therefore ascribed the whole set of restaurant drawings to that year. Now, that is the year that we want, the year in which Annie's union with Clarence must have taken place. Charlotte Street, which is full of restaurants, is very near to Warren Street and to Cleveland Street, so it does look as though Sickert was at that time constantly in that area. It had, of course, a long association with artists. The Rossetti family grew up at 50 Charlotte Street,(2) and their father, Gabriel Rossetti, for a while shared a studio with Holman Hunt at 7 Cleveland Street, while Millais, at 83 Gower Street, was not far away. The Rossettis had, by now, migrated to the opulence of Cheyne Walk, Chelsea. One could say Chelsea was for well-off artists, Fitzrovia for artists not well off; yet it is not for nothing the two main manufactures of artists' materials, Winsor and Newton's and Rowney's have their retail outlets where they do, in the area earlier trodden by the Pre-Raphaelites and now by Sickert.

What did not satisfy me was the account of how the Heir Presumptive came to meet Annie, at Sickert's. Knight wrote that Sickert's 'father and grandfather having been artists to the Royal Court of Denmark,' the Princess of Wales (the future Queen Alexandra), being from the Danish Royal Family, found it natural to write to Sickert and ask him to take her son 'under his artistic wing'(3). I thought that if Oswald Adalbert had been a painter to the Danish Royal Family, Mrs Sickert, when she showed Florence his paintings and drawings, would have mentioned it, and Florence would have told Mother. Moreover, what Sickert himself wrote of his ancestry was:(4)

My grandfather, Johann Jurgen Sickert, was born in 1803, in Flensburg. He was at the same time a painter of easel pictures and head of a firm of decorators, who were employed in the Royal Palaces by Christian VIII of Denmark. He lived and carried on his business in Altona..Oswald Adalbert Sickert...was born in Altona in 1828. The astonishing portrait of himself at the age of sixteen, certainly justified the gracious interest that was taken in him by HM Christian VIII of Denmark, who conferred on him a travelling purse to Copenhagen...He studied in Paris under Courture...

Whilst one could see here the genesis of the idea, it did not read to me as though either his grandfather or father had been a court painter. Altona, the old capital of Schleswig-Holstein, was too far from Copenhagen for anybody who might be summoned to paint a member of the Royal Family. It was not stated that Oswald availed himself of the purse to go to Copenhagen. He went, instead, to Paris to study. There was no indication that either father or grandfather ever met any member of the Danish Royal Family, and, as Sickert was not yet known, I did not think the Princess of Wales would ever have heard of him, let alone written to him.

It is not essential to the story that she should have introduced them. Clarence - HRH Prince Albert Victor Christian Edward, grandson of Queen Victoria and Heir Presumptive to the throne, known to his intimates as Eddie and to the vulgar as 'Collar and Cuffs', was created Duke of Clarence and Avondale only on his grandmother's birthday, 24 May 1890, but for simplicity's sake I shall call him Clarence throughout - Clarence, whether or not he visited Sickert, visited Cleveland Street.

On 4 July 1889, within the headquarters of the General Post Office at St Martin's Le Grand, a Post Office Police Constable asked a fifteen year old Post Office messenger boy, Charles Swinscow, to account for a large sum of money he was carrying. Swinscow said it had been paid to him by a Mr Charles Hammond 'for going to bed with gentlemen' at his house, at 19 Cleveland Street. The Post Office Police informed the Metropolitan Police immediately. Swinscow gave away a lot of names, and as the first arrests were made, a lot more names were shaken loose. Hammond, however, had plainly been tipped off, for, when the police arrived at 19 Cleveland Street they did not find him. He had gone briefly to a brother at Gravesend, whence he had taken ship to France. The police wanted an application to be made for his extradition, but Lord Salisbury did not make the application.

The whole matter had a political aspect, explored by Lewis Chester, David Leitch and Colin Simpson in their book *The Cleveland Street Affair*. Hammond's junior assistant and chief procurer, Henry Newlove, complained it was unfair people such as he should be arrested when patrons of the establishment included the Earl of Euston and Lord Arthur Somerset, the equerry to the Prince of Wales. This was indeed the view taken by the radical side in the House of Commons. Henry du Pre Labouchere (of Huguenot descent), the radical MP for Northampton, delved into what seemed to have been moves behind the scenes, and attacked the Government, both in the House and in *Truth* of which he was editor. In the issue of 14 November, he wrote: 'It would really be too monstrous if crimes which, when committed by poor, ignorant men, lead to sentences of penal servitude, were to be done with impunity by those whom the Tory Government delights to honour. The names are known.'

The editor of the *North London Press,* Ernest Parke, who felt in the same way, was so rash as, in its issue of 10 November, to name Euston and Somerset. These two, Parke alleged, had been allowed to flee the country, 'because their prosecution would disclose the fact that a far more distinguished and more highly placed personage than themselves was inculpated in their disgusting crimes.' He meant, of course, Clarence.

Somerset had, indeed, slipped out of the country, but Euston not. He was still in London, and instituted proceedings for criminal libel.

Euston said in evidence he was accosted by a tout who gave him a card reading, 'C Hammond. Poses Plastiques. 19 Cleveland Street.'

I do not know what this phrase - plastic poses - may convey to others. To me, it conjures up memories of what used to be on display at the Windmill, Piccadilly, when a change in the law allowed women to appear on the stage naked, on condition of their remaining immobile. Chester, Leitch and Simpson think it then meant strip-tease. Whatever precisely it meant at that time, Euston thought it meant that women would be found there, and so he went. When he discovered the true character of the house, he left at once.

The jury believed him. Parke, the puritan radical, was sentenced to twelve months, which was longer than had been meted out to any of Hammond's associates. Truly, it seemed the crime was not so much the committing as the disclosing. The judge's summing up was entirely hostile to him, as being merely a muck-raker.

The continental and American press, unrestrained by our libel laws, did not hesitate to suggest the real beneficiary of the cover-up was Clarence.

I have discussed this matter with my friend Timothy d'Arch Smith, who researched it for his book *Love in Earnest*(5). Whereas the Cleveland Street affair is generally taken as the proof Clarence was homosexual, he thinks that not proven. 'Poses plastiques. What would a man think that meant? He would think it meant women.' Unless women as well as boys were available, such a card would be an uneconomic way of advertising, for it would bring in men who wanted women and who would go away if they found none. 'There must have been both. Probably, when you got inside, there was a dividing of the ways. Euston must have got shown the wrong way by mistake.'

But later, when we were again discussing the subject, he suggested there need not have been 'resident prostitutes', and that 19 Cleveland Street was more of what the French call 'une maison de passe' - 'where you went with your own partner, and asked for a room'. From his reading of *My Secret Life:* (an anonymous Victorian autobiography) and other sources, he gathered most of the brothels in London at that time were like that. 'It might be that at 19 Cleveland Street, if you came with a boy instead of a woman, no objection was made.' Indeed, in one of Somerset's letters, I notice a line which could support that. Yet, from what Florence said, it is evident that there were at least some resident women prostitutes.

That Salisbury was the cover up gives us a side-light on his character, but it is the argument of Chester, Leitch and Simpson that (unknown even to Labouchere) the real pressure for the cover up came not from Salisbury but from the Prince of Wales. There is a letter of his which shows he wanted Somerset to escape, but, they think, not because he cared about his equerry but because he feared that the interrogation of Somerset in court would disclose the involvement of Clarence (Somerset's own letters show he was thinking about this, too). The Prince and Princess of Wales knew more about their son than did Queen Victoria. She was very fond of him.

Clarence, however, was far from wholly homosexual. He did have affairs with women, and fell in love with the politically inconvenient Princess Hélène d'Orleans, daughter of the pretender to the French throne, and a Catholic - though she was willing to give up her religion if their marriage were permitted. (It was her father who stopped it.) His eventual engagement, to Princess Mary of Teck was not arranged for him. He proposed to her off his own bat, and wrote to inform the Queen after she had accepted him.

But the question for us is whether Clarence knew Cleveland Street early enough to have met Annie Crook there and got her with a child born in 1885. One of Hammond's associates, John Saul, of 150 Old Compton Street, 'of no occupation,' told the police he had known Hammond from 1 May, 1879. 'We both earned our livelihood as Sodomites.' Hammond, he said, moved around, seldom for long at one address, though usually within the Soho area. Saul, who had been away for a while, returned to find Hammond at Cleveland Street just before Christmas, 1885. He thought he had recently moved in. Hammond had with him a wife, a French prostitute, Madame Caroline, who lived with him there.

Hammond was not the rated occupier of 19 Cleveland Street, hence the date of his moving in cannot be checked from rate books. If he was anywhere in that area during 1884, Clarence, visiting him, could easily have run into Annie. But there is something else. Michael Harrison, in his book *Clarence,* asserts that Clarence was, in any case, a member of the Hundred Guineas Club, which was a club for transvestites, wherein all were known by women's Christian names, Clarence's being Victoria. This club, says Harrison, was 'off Great Portland Street.' That could refer to Cleveland Street, but Saul said in evidence that, dissatisfied by the meanness with which Hammond shared the takings, he moved to the place in Nassau Street. Now, the Middlesex Hospital is flanked by Cleveland Street on the one side and Nassau Street on the other, Nassau Street being the nearer to Great Portland Street. If it was not on his way to or from Hammond's place in Cleveland Street, it could have been on his way to or from the place in Nassau Street, which was probably the Hundred Guineas Club, that Clarence met Annie Crook.

We do not need the Princess of Wales to have asked Sickert to introduce him to girls. If Sickert ever met the Heir Presumptive, it is more likely to have been Annie Crook who performed the introduction.

Clarence was out of England from 18 June to 18 August, 1884, but this does not matter, as it leaves eight clear months. Except for the silly bit about Princess Alexandra, the story so far contains nothing impossible to believe. It is what follows that defies credulity.

1886 and 1887, says Joseph Sickert, were peaceful. When Clarence was away, Sickert took Annie and the baby, and sometimes Mary Kelly as well, to Dieppe. (Does this mean in simple friendship, or that he became the lover of Annie or Mary or both?)

But then, says Joseph, one dreadful day in 1888, returning from Maple Street, he saw two cabs turn from Tottenham Court Road into Cleveland Street. Men descended from them, and he saw Annie dragged from number 6 and Clarence dragged from his own studio, and the two bundled into the two cabs and driven off in different directions.

Myself, I would think that what Sickert saw was the raid on the brothel at number 19 in the following year.

But to continue with Knight: Mary Kelly had some time before been persuaded by Sickert to give up her employment at the tobacconist's, move in with Annie and become, as his employee, a nanny to Alice. When the raid was mounted, Mary escaped taking the child with her, though, in some way not clear to Joseph, the child came back to Sickert. He placed her at different times with different people, but she became in an overall though unofficial sense his ward.

This was because Annie was unable to look after her. For a hundred and fifty-six days, according to Joseph, she had been kept in Guy's hospital, to which Sir William Gull, Physician in Ordinary to Queen Victoria was attached. Gull was a brain specialist, and Sickert believed he had performed some operation on Annie's brain, to make her incapable of remembering her relationship with Clarence. But I do not believe he would have mutilated the brain of a patient. If we deny the kidnap, we have still to explain the disappearance of Annie from Cleveland Street. Perhaps she was genuinely taken ill, and taken to hospital. When she reappeared, she seemed to Sickert not her normal self. Subsequent research has shown that in 1913 she was admitted to St Pancras Workhouse suffering from epilepsy, her occupation being given then as 'casual hand [at] Crosse and Blackwells.' When she died, in 1920, at Fulham Workhouse, it was in the lunacy ward. I incline to think she suffered from a natural infirmity, which Sickert did not at first notice.

I attempted to check the story about Annie Elizabeth Crook's having been in Guy's hospital. This was not an easy matter. Guy's told me their records were now in the City of London Record Office and Library. I applied there, and was told that they had the records, but could not spare time to search them for me. Neither could they permit me to search them, because of the 'hundred year rule.' The years I wanted, 1887-8, were bound into a file that contained the records of later years, and consequently could not be shown before the end of 1992 - unless I obtained special permission from the person in authority at Guy's hospital. So I wrote to Guy's again, and this time received written permission to inspect their admissions and discharges register, 1887-1888.

According to Joseph Sickert, Annie had been taken in early in 1888 and discharged during the period of the Ripper crimes, having been inside one hundred and fifty-six days. I went right through the register from 1 June 1887 to the end of December, 1888. I had a moment's excitement when I found an Annie Eliza Crook, admitted on 30 July, but she was only ten, and discharged after a few days, her doctor having been Perry, not Gull. But Gull's name does not appear against any of the patients.

This was negative evidence which undermined a great part of the Knight book, at least in so far as regarded the thesis of Gull's having had Annie hospitalised.

Yet where had I read something about Gull's having had lunatics at Guy's? I short-circuited my researches by writing to Dr Margaret Little, because I thought that, as a practising psychiatrist attached to a hospital, she would know what to look up. She sent me, by return, a great packet full of photostats of papers, including many pages from *A Biographical History of Guy's Hospital* by Samuel Wilks MD, ILD FRS and G T Bettany, MA, BSC (Ward, Lock, Rowen & Co, 1892) with all references to Gull marked in red. In her accompanying letter, of 17 November 1989, she summarized and commented upon the matter to be gleaned:

Sir William's biography itself is on p 261-274 and doesn't contain any surprises. It does confirm (p 263) that he was put in charge of the 'lunatic ward' at Guy's though this seems to have been early in his career (1840s), and that subsequently (p 265) he did some research on spinal diseases. There is also quite a bit (p 264) about his role as clinician, lecturer and professor at the Guy's hospital Medical School.

Page 96...tells us that the Guy's 'lunatics' (at least in theory) were all females.

There is certainly no reference to Sir William's having taken private or 'special' patients at Guy's, and I really think this would have been rather unlikely...the role of hospital Treasurers would be paramount, and one imagines that (at least in the absence of corruption) it would be quite difficult for patients to be admitted without going through the books. I have copied Wilks and Bettany's account (pp 141-148) of the absolute powers of nineteenth century Guy's treasurers, who hired and fired doctors...

On the other hand W & B do say (p 145) that one of the early treasurers, who unfortunately died in 1856 was very much under Gull's influence, and also that hospital Governors had power to overrule the Treasurer. Gull became a governor of Guy's in 1887 (p 148)

So there one has all that seems to be available. The 'lunatic' wards belonged to a period long anterior to that which concerns us. In the period we want, Gull was a Governor, but that a Governor should be able to put pressure on a Treasurer and staff to keep a patient for 156 days secretly, does seem to me unlikely.

In the story my mother received from Florence, there was nothing about anybody's having been put in Guy's or in a 'lunatic ward'. As this part of the story appeared not to have come from the imagination of Walter Sickert, it must be of later generation.

But to return to Knight's story, in which the focus of interest now becomes Mary Kelly(6):

In late July or August 1888...A shoddy and unsophisticated attempt at blackmail was initiated. The old painter never revealed who had been the victim of the demand, but it was for a paltry - in other circumstances he might have said laughable - sum. It emanated from the East End.

That is, from Mary Kelly. Note that if Mary Kelly could write, she was better educated than Annie, who could only make her mark.

Knight all along assumes two things, that there had been a secret marriage between Annie and Clarence, and that she was Catholic. As regards the latter point, the record of her death gives her religion as Church of England, though of course that may be because her religion was unknown to the entrant. Joseph grew up to understand his grandmother was a Catholic. As to the secret marriage, witnessed by Mary Kelly, I do not believe in it. No proof is offered. Even if had taken place, Clarence would at the time have been under twenty-five, so that it could have been set aside, as not having had the Sovereign's permission. There was, therefore, surely no danger of England's being faced with the prospect of a Catholic sovereign, Queen Alice Margaret. It is, however, on that assumption the rest of Knight's story - as he had it from Joseph - is based.

The thesis is, Lord Salisbury, as Prime Minister, was so concerned about the impending crisis for the monarchy that he intimated to Sir William Gull, as a fellow Freemason, that it was necessary to get rid of Mary Kelly, and also of certain other prostitutes in the East End to whom she had communicated the secrets which conferred the power to blackmail. Gull, accompanied by the Assistant Commissioner of the Metropolitan Police, Sir Robert Anderson, would therefore go out in a hansom, driven by John Charles Netley, Clarence's coachman, to range the streets on either side of the Commercial Road, Whitechapel - that is, the Spitalfields-Whitechapel area - in search of the women. When one was sighted, Netley would stop the coach, Anderson would get out and lure the woman in, Gull would give her poisoned black grapes, to weaken her struggles, and then cut her throat and perform the famous mutilations, after which her body would be deposited on the street - except, of course in the final case, of Mary Kelly, who was murdered within her own room.

Not one word of this do I believe.

There were, however, two stories that were obviously versions of those I had heard so long ago from my mother, as she had heard them from Florence.

Sickert went to Dieppe because his knowledge of what had happened made him feel unsafe when in England. But one day in Dieppe, Lord Salisbury had walked into his studio and paid him £500 for a painting he hardly looked at. No mention had been made of Cleveland Street or the Whitechapel murders, but he would have had to be a dullard not to have seen that the exorbitant fee was hush-money.(7)

The other concerned the illegitimate child Alice. There had, Knight understood from Joseph, been two attempts on her life. The first was in 1888, when she had been knocked down by Netley's coach in Fleet Street or the Strand.

The second occurred in February, 1892.(8)

On this occasion Netley charged along Drury Lane in his carriage just as Alice Margaret was crossing the road with an elderly relative who was helping to bring her up. The child was not so badly hurt on this occasion because she was spun out of the way of the wheels when the corner of the carriage struck her. She was taken to hospital unconscious but released after a day, having been treated for concussion. The elderly woman who had been with her later described the driver of the coach to Sickert. He knew at once it was Netley.

Later, Sickert took Alice to Dieppe, and settled her with some people, so that most of the rest of her childhood was spent there.

When she grew up she married a man called Gorman. In 1925, Joseph was born to her; but his father was Sickert.

Knight, as he listened to the strange story which he retold, became puzzled as to how Sickert could have known so much about the organization of the murders as he had professed to Joseph. Knight put it to Joseph that his father could not have known what took place within the coach unless he had been within it himself- and that Gull's companion had not been Anderson, but Sickert!

Joseph Sickert was naturally very much distressed. He had always supposed it was in some innocent manner his father had come by his terrible knowledge, though he had not asked him. Perhaps when only fourteen one does not cross-question one's father. Now, Knight was making him accessory to the fact.

Nevertheless, he wrote an afterword to the book, saying he took no pleasure in being the grandson of the Duke of Clarence, and that although his first reaction to Knight's implication of his father in the crimes had been one of anger:(9)

later I had to admit that my father must have known more than he told me. It was a fact that I had half-realised all along. And possibly one of the reasons I allowed my story to be investigated in the first place, was that I hoped new facts might be uncovered that would somehow dispel my worst private fears about my father. In the event, the investigation has had the opposite effect and my fears have been confirmed.

I should like to say that my concern all along has been for my mother and my grandmother...

So, he gave his blessing to the book. Yet it must have continued to gnaw at him. He must have felt he had been disloyal to his father in allowing the book to go out, despite that he had appeared on television to give it his support. In 1978, that is two years after the paperback reprint, *The Sunday Times* of 18 June carried an article by David May entitled, 'Jack the Ripper 'solution was a hoax, man confesses.' To clear his father's name, Joseph had sacrificed his own - and Knight's for there were not lacking other writers to insinuate that Knight published Joseph's story knowing Joseph to be making it up as he went along. But it was only in 1973 that Joseph met Knight.

What Joseph did not know when he made the recantation was that Florence had told a great part of the story to my mother in 1948.

Florence had now become an important person, and though she had told Mother she did not want to talk about her background and early years, I felt I should have the particulars of it, and made application for a certificate of her birth, which should be found in the registers for 1862 or 1863.

The certificate showed the birth to have taken place in the registration district of Hackney's sub-district, West Hackney, in the county of Middlesex. The particulars it bore read:

When and where born: Second August, 1862, 10 Kingsland
Name: Florence
Sex: Girl
Name and surname of father: Daniel John Pash
Name, surname and maiden name of Mother:
Martha Pash, formerly Bassett
Occupation of father: Shoemaker
Signature, description and residence of informant:
Daniel John Pash, father, 10 Kingsland.

Some of these details surprised me. She had seemed to me distinctly upper middle class. Where did she get that dignity of speech and bearing? In these days of mass production when clothing comes out of factories, shoemakers, like dressmakers, have practically ceased to exist. Daniel John Pash will have been a man who made shoes by hand for people in his locality. How did his daughter come to be, at nineteen, sitting for a portrait to Jacques-Emile Blanche and studying painting in Paris?

I also wrote to Charing Cross hospital, now removed to Fulham Palace Road, and asked if their records for February 1892, showed a child, Alice Margaret Crook, aged six, to have been brought in having been run over in Trafalgar Square and if the name of the person who brought her in was recorded as Florence Pash. Sadly, I received a reply from their Mrs L Powell, Medical Records Officer, saying that although they did have some records of the old hospital, 'they do not go back as far as the year you require.'

Footnotes:
1 *Sickert*, Wendy Baron (Phaidon, 1973) p 298
2 *The Pre-Raphaelite Dream*, William Gaunt (reprint and Cape, 1943), p 35; *Christina Rossetti*, Lona Mosk Packer (Cambridge, 1963) p 13; *A Victorian Romantic, Dante Gabriel Rossetti*, Oswald Doughty, (Oxford, 1960) pp 65, 87
3 *Jack the Ripper, the Final Solution*, Stephen Knight (Panther, 1977), p 24
4 *A Free House, or The Artist as Craftsman, being the Writings of Walter Richard Sickert*, ed. Osbert Sitwell (Macmillan, 1947), p.1
5 *Love In Earnest*, Timothy d'Arch Smith (Routledge, 1970) pp 28-29
6 Knight, p 35
7 Knight, p 39
8 Knight, p 213-14
9 Knight, p 264

Chapter 3
An attempt to probe the story

There are obvious parallels between what I heard from my mother and what I read in Knight; as there are obvious differences. The closest parallel concerns the incident in which the child was hit by a coach, which mounted the pavement.

Florence was not a relative of Alice Margaret Crook. Neither was she, then, elderly. In February, 1892, I was glad to have the happening dated - she would have been just twenty-nine, at the height of her artistic career. Knight plainly had no idea the child's escort was a person so glamorous. I still think the occurrence was an accident. What is interesting is that Sickert was talking to Florence as early as 1892 of murder and attempted murder, to silence those who could speak of the royal bastardy.

From the transcript of his original statement to the BBC, Joseph himself had said, in telling of this incident, 'a woman friend was taking her for a walk.'

As regards the alleged bribe incident in Dieppe, Salisbury did spend a summer in Dieppe. A version of the story was also told to Sir Osbert Sitwell:(1)

> Lord Salisbury had felt sorry for the artist and had determined to help him. And so, on being shown a picture of the river at Dieppe, he had generously said: 'I will buy that river scene for five hundred pounds if you will paint in a boat, containing my family and myself.'

Here there is no mention of a bribe. On the other hand, this version does not ring true to me either. A painting is a whole. One cannot just add one thing without changing everything. Sickert would surely have preferred to make a completely fresh painting. And the point of the story as told by Florence was that Salisbury had walked off with the picture under his arm without having really looked at it. These accounts do, however, support one another upon the point that Sickert kept talking about some episode that occurred, in which an unusually high price was paid for one of his paintings. He made it sinister or comic to suit his listener. It may be Salisbury did pay a high price for a picture, perhaps out of generosity, and just possibly with the *arrière pensée* that the sweetener might keep Sickert quiet about the royal bastardy, if Salisbury knew about that.

There were things that dawned on me only gradually as I read and re-read Knight - and as I read, for the first time, all the books on the life and work of Sickert that I could obtain. When Mother had told me Florence had said that a nanny's departure had left Sickert having to bath and change a little baby girl. I had supposed the child to be that of himself and one of his wives. Now I realized that although he had been married three times, all three of these marriages had been childless. So whose little baby daughter was this, that he had been left to tend? It must have been Alice Margaret. The vanished nanny must have been Mary Kelly - Florence had said she was Irish and had attempted blackmail - and Florence must have been in contact with Sickert and his irregular 'family' in Cleveland Street during the period leading up to and throughout the murders. Now, I understood why Florence had been very frightened indeed. She had stepped into the shoes of Mary Kelly. In case anybody does not know what happened to Mary Kelly, she had been found on the morning of Sunday, 9 November 1888 on the bed in her room, her breasts cut off in slices and laid side by side on her bedside table, her nose and ears cut off and laid beside her breasts on the table, her throat and neck so deeply cut her head was nearly severed, her left arm so nearly severed it was attached to her body by skin only, her heart and kidneys taken out and laid beside the breasts, ears and nose on the table, her liver taken out and laid upon her right thigh, her abdomen ripped and her intestines thrown about, her right thigh defleshed to the bone and her shins partly flayed.

Florence had been told by Sickert this atrocity had been performed upon Mary Kelly because she had known about the child of Clarence and Annie, and had talked. Florence had felt she could not refuse to continue to help with looking after the child, but although she was careful not to talk, how could it be known she was not talking? She must have been terribly afraid she could end the same way as Mary Kelly. Florence was a very brave woman. If I had the awarding of medals I would give her one.

But how had Mary Kelly descended from Cleveland Street to Whitechapel? Sickert could not have afforded to pay her much, and if it is correct, as said by Knight, that he persuaded her to give up her job as shop assistant to act as nanny, she may have had little to live on, and pressed for more. If he said he could not afford more, she could have retorted that was ridiculous. The child was that of the Heir Presumptive. Clarence should be made to pay maintenance. If he refused to pay, Sickert should write to the Princess of Wales, or better, the Queen. Victoria would not like a thing like this to come out!

In *Love in Earnest,* by Timothy d'Arch Smith, soldiers from the Household Cavalry were said to be amongst the users of rooms at 19 Cleveland Street.(2) It is not in the book, but the author told me that, according to one of his informant's, homosexual contacts were sometimes made via a tobacconist's: 'The thing was, you asked for a box of matches and paid for it with a ten shilling note. You were then given an assignation.' That was not in Cleveland Street, but it was not far from it, in Camden Town, in Albany Street. That suggested that the tobacconist's in Albany Street was run in connection with Hammond's and so probably was the tobacconist's in Cleveland Street itself. Although Annie had described the shop as a confectioner's we both thought it was probably the sort of small shop in which you could buy a packet of cigarettes, a newspaper, a bar of chocolate or other sweetmeats.

On the same page, Crowley was said to have boasted the possession of letters from Clarence to a 'Boy' Morgan. This was not enlarged upon in the book, but, consulting his ancient notes for me, Timothy d'Arch Smith found 'a relation of Annie Elizabeth Morgan of 22 Cleveland St'!

Twenty-two was the number of the confectioner-tobacconist at which Annie Crook and Mary Kelly worked. That gives a place where Clarence could have met Annie. He could have gone in for 'Boy' Morgan, who lived there, and noticed those two girls serving behind the counter. Annie Elizabeth were the two Christian names of Annie Elizabeth Crook!

Was this just a coincidence or had someone mistaken Annie for a sister of Morgan?

Did Annie and Mary hand out boxes of matches for ten shilling notes? I do not think either of those girls can have been unknowing. Mary Kelly would have known not only of the child Clarence had had by Annie but of the association of Clarence with 'Boy' Morgan. Certainly she had a lot she could tell, which would interest people very much. It would have been prudent to be nice to her, and make sure that she did not want.

Sickert probably had not the means to do that. His wife had money. The first Mrs Sickert, Ellen, née Cobden, is a person who does not appear in Knight's narrative, and was not I think mentioned by Florence as a person she had met. Yet he had married her in 1885, and their honeymoon had included a summer's stay in Dieppe. She was not too much at ease in Dieppe or with his artistic and unconventional friends and was offended by his infidelities. It was only in 1899 she obtained a divorce from him, but I have the impression they were probably considerably parted in spirit long before that. They lived in Hampstead and I doubt if he ever brought her to Cleveland Street, or told her anything about his friendship with Annie Crook and Mary Kelly. Hence, he was not in a position to ask her to pay a salary to Mary to act as nanny to the child of Annie, and if he had only his own resources to draw upon, they were slender. Selling the occasional picture and helping Florence teach her pupils in Sloane Street would not have paid wages to a nanny sufficient for her to live on. If it is true he had persuaded Mary to give up her job at the tobacconist's to become a full-time nanny, he may have acted irresponsibly, relying on money to pay her which did not come in so regularly as to enable him to pay her with a regularity on which she could rely. It was a case of good intentions...

So, blackmail could come to be in the air, without at first being actively threatened. Sickert not being inclined to trouble the throne, and the situation not improving, it is evident Mary got fed up with washing and changing Alice for a pittance, and decided to become a prostitute. The girls she saw going in and out of Hammond's were probably richly dressed. Perhaps she hoped she might meet there a high placed paramour. After all, Madame du Barry was said to have started in such a house, and ended a King's mistress.

It did not work out like that. But how had she descended in so short a time from prostitution in Cleveland Street, which drew a high class clientele, to prostitution in Whitechapel, and in so short a space of time? Her last companion was a fishporter of Billingsgate, Joseph Barnett. He told the police and Coroner's court what he could of her background. He had gathered from her she was born in Limerick some twenty-five years before, had been the daughter of a John Kelly, who had moved with his family to Wales, where he found employment in an iron works in Carmarthen or Carnarvon, married a collier, Davis or Davies, who had been killed in an explosion, and come from Cardiff to London:

> In London she was in a gay house in the West End of the town. A gentleman there asked her to go to France. She went to France but she told me she did not like the part. She did not stay there long. She lived there about a fortnight.

This accords not too badly with the facts already designated. Cleveland Street was not exactly the West End but it was a long way West of Whitechapel and had a West End clientele. It is surprising she should not have liked Dieppe. Even if her tastes were urban rather than rural, there was a casino and the resort was very fashionable at that time. There would have been lively, rich people, and plenty to do. Sickert is always thought of as having been very attractive, but could she have disliked his holiday companionship? In any case, it seems very strange to have come back from Dieppe, not to Cleveland Street, or but briefly to Cleveland Street, only to sink to Whitechapel.

Searching for clues, I re-read the transcript of Joseph Sickert's statement to the BBC. It contains many things we can now see as probably or certainly incorrect, but it is the nearest we shall get to the voice in which Sickert talked to his son:

> My name is Joseph Sickert. My father was the painter Walter Sickert. When I was a small boy I can remember my mother telling me over and over again I had to be careful not to say or do anything which would give the police or authorities any reason to question me or any excuse for them to take me away. She said that my grandmother had suffered terribly at the hands of the authorities. And a servant had died in a terrible way. And that I had to be very careful. I just thought it was another story that adults tell. A sort of 'if you don't behave the bogey man will get you.'
> Then when I was older, in my teens, I asked my father about the story. Eventually he told me a story that I didn't really believe. He didn't mention any names, but he told it as a sort of fairy story.
> 'Once upon a time there was a Prince, a girl the Prince loved and a baby girl, and her nurse and an artist. The Prince's mother asked the artist to show the prince the world of art. In that world the prince met a Catholic girl and fell in love with her. They had a child - a girl. Then a little later they got married.
> But the Prime Minister heard about the wedding and was very worried because the Prince was a Royal Prince and the bride was a poor girl and a Catholic. The bride was taken away and confined to hospital. And she died without ever seeing her prince or her child again.
> The child was looked after by a servant who disappeared taking the child with her. But she told a friend of hers about the child she was caring for and who its father was.

Important people got to hear of it. And the royal doctor was asked to find the woman and silence her. With some other people's help he did find her and she was killed. To cover up the search for her the doctor killed the other women so that no one would ask why this one woman was killed. The child was looked after, though, by the artist and eventually they fell in love. They had a child, a boy.

That was how my father told me the story first of all. I kept on nagging him and asking questions about it and eventually I broke down his reserve. He said, 'Your grandfather was the Duke of Clarence.' I laughed and he said, 'It's no laughing matter. It's a bit of a mess because you're all bloody Catholics'. And then he told me the whole story.

When Prince Edward went there during his vacation from Cambridge he was passed off as Sickert's younger brother. He also met one of the shop girls who used to model for Sickert. A girl called Ann Elizabeth Crook who worked in a tobacconist's shop. She was very beautiful. In fact she looked like Eddy's mother. Eddy fell in love with her. She became pregnant. They also went through a ceremony of marriage at St Saviour's private chapel in 1888.

The two lovers, Clarence and Ann Elizabeth, were parted after a police raid on a party in Cleveland Street. Ann Elizabeth was in Guy's Hospital for 156 days before being put in a smaller hospital at 367 Fulham Road. She was supposed to be mentally ill. She was kept in the Fulham Road hospital until her death in 1921.

The servant girl also disappeared for a time. Her name was Mary Kelly.

The little girl, Alice Margaret, was then looked after by old Walter Sickert with the help of various local friends. One day when she was about seven years old in 1892 a woman friend was taking her for a walk in Drury Lane. A carriage ran the child down. The driver of the carriage was recognized as John Netley, a man who had been used as an outside coachman by Clarence on his visits to Sickert. A man who would know the story of the lovers and their child - and their Irish servant girl, Mary Kelly.

The child, Alice Margaret, was fortunate. After a spell in Charing Cross Hospital, she recovered from her injuries. Mary Kelly was not so lucky. She was, of course, a Catholic girl, and she was known to the nuns of the convent in nearby Harewood Place. She went first of all to their sister convent in the East End. What then happened was that various people high in government and the royal household became very worried indeed about the possibility of news getting out that the heir presumptive to the throne of England had married, had had a child, and that the child had been born of a Catholic mother. You have to remember it was a time when the possibility of revolution was thought to be a very real one - and the problems and violence surrounding Ireland were at their height.

It was decided that Mary Jane Kelly would have to be silenced. The operation was undertaken by the driver, John Netley, who was a coachman who had regularly driven Clarence although he wasn't on the official Palace staff, and the Royal physician, Sir William Gull.

To conceal the dangerous motive behind Mary Kelly's death - and the enquiries they were making for her, she was killed as the last of five women in a way that made it look like the random work of a madman. The child, however, survived. She was protected by Walter Sickert - and had two sons by him. The first one was Charles, who disappeared at the age of two about 1911 - I am the other son.

This story, I felt, was told in good faith and the inaccuracies are of a kind that can occur very naturally in re-telling a story one has heard from other lips. One thing, however, leaped out at me now, that had not been mentioned by Knight, probably because he thought it silly. That was the reference to Mary Kelly's connection with nuns and a nearby convent. Her only known connections were with prostitutes and a nearby brothel. Sickert had been trying to soften the story for the innocent ears of his young son, choosing his words so as to take out of it what was sordid and replace with terms gently romantic. Yet in making this choice, he had perhaps been aware that in the slang of Elizabethan literature, 'nun' was often used to mean whore, and 'convent' brothel. When Hamlet said to Ophelia, 'Get thee to a nunnery,' there is a doubt as to which sense he meant, lost upon a modern audience. Sickert had played in *Hamlet*, and it might have been common knowledge amongst the actors. Did Hammond have a second house of prostitution, in the East End? This is a question which has not been researched. Suppose that Mary Kelly had got across Hammond, he might have told her she would have to go to his other house, and she might not have had the 'industrial muscle' to resist.

That is how she could have found herself transferred to the East End. If she found her exploitation in the 'sister convent' too degrading to be endured, that could explain how we come to find her, so short a time later, trying to earn her living as a freelance prostitute, based in a wretched room in Miller's Court. She would not have been able to get back to the West End because she would not have had the money saved to pay a West End rental. She was behind with the rent even at Miller's Court. It was a man, John Bower, sent by the landlord, John McCarthy, who called that Sunday morning to try to collect, who, obtaining no answer at the door, looked through the hole in the long-broken window, and saw the horror within. He went back to tell the landlord, and they both went together to the Commercial Road Police Station.

It must have been in her dire straits that she had written to Sickert, asking for money to help her recover and, perhaps abusively, blaming him for her having taken the downward path.

There is no evidence of her having written letters to the palace or to anybody but Sickert. I do not see how Gull would have known of them unless told by Sickert.

I do not believe in the three in a coach rumbling through Whitechapel to pick up and kill.

Whoever the Ripper was, he went alone, on foot.

Was it Sickert? We ought not to forget his love of theatricals. As a child, he put on his own production of *The Three Witches* in a disused quarry near Newquay, impounding his younger brother and sisters as witches, so that he could be Macbeth.(3) Could his theatrical streak have lead him to court suspicion of crimes of which he was innocent? A contrary consideration is that in August 1888, during the weeks leading up to the first of the Ripper murders, *Dr Jekyll and Mr Hyde,* was running at the Lyceum, where Sickert had worshipped Ellen Terry and appeared in Irving's productions. If he had been during that time in a state of crisis, havering on the brink, could that have sent him over it?

What of his childhood? Emmons wrote that Sickert told him he was expelled from University College School for selling doughnuts - but then took the story back.(4) Sutton referred the story to King's College School, but though it unlikely.(5) I wrote to both schools. At University College he had spent, oddly, one year, 1870-1. From King's College he had certainly not been expelled. In 1877 he was awarded the Vice-Master's prize for German. He left after the summer term of 1878, aged eighteen, having sat London Matriculation, in which he gained First Class Honours. Afterwards he was invited back to give a recitation at a prize giving. He performed Clarence's Dream from *Richard III* (It is in Act I, Scene iv).

As to his career on the professional stage, he first walked on in Irving's production at the Lyceum. His first speaking part was in a theatre in Holborn. It was on the cue 'that man Jasper creeping among the laurels' that he had to enter. A friend warned him. 'Take care, Walter, lest it affect your real character'.(6) In *Henry V*, he played five small parts, including the French soldier captured by Pistol. He played the ghost in Irving's *Hamlet* and then, in Isobel Bateman's company at Sadler's Wells, Demetrius in *A Midsummer Night's Dream*.(7)

It was in 1881 that Sickert forsook his first career as an actor for the Slade School of Art which he left for Whistler's studio.

What remained of his earlier enthusiasm for the stage was mainly a love of dressing up, make-up and playing a part. Whatever he did, he dressed for it, threw himself into it, as though it were a stage role. If he cooked, he had to dress as a chef.

Marjorie Lilly writes:(8)

..During a prolonged cooking craze the walls were covered with expensive gadgets and pots and pans with Sickert himself appropriately arrayed in cook's cap and apron. In this rig he looked about eight feet high and a friend of mine, a shy little elderly person who knocked on his door...was so overpowered by the vast white apparition who opened it that she was bereft of words.

In Dieppe, when he took for a while a house with an empty stables attached he bought himself riding-breeches, though this was as near to a horse as he ever got.

He would sometimes be the artist, open shirt and slippers; sometimes the man about town, in morning suit and topper. Once, when 'already famous, he called at Bourlet's, the artists' agents, looking so like a tramp they were throwing him out before they recognized him, and returned a few days later with silk hat, patent leather shoes and cane.'(9)

Perhaps he sought a harmony between the conflicting personas within himself by living them in alternation - to some extent a monkey, watching, copying, and assuming the exterior attitudes and appurtenances of the part as a prelude to putting himself into it to play it in earnest. People observed in him a marked histrionic tendency. His biographer, Dr Robert Emmons, writes that, while he and his first wife were living in Broadhurst Gardens, Hampstead:(10)

He used to go nightly to music halls and walk home from Hoxton, Shoreditch, Camden

Probing the Story

Town or Islington, across Primrose Hill and so on to Hampstead. He wore a loud check coat, long to the ankles, and carried a little bag for his drawings. One night in Copenhagen Street a party of young girls fled from him in terror, yelling 'Jack the Ripper, Jack the Ripper!'

Emmons recognizes that the only source for this story can have been Sickert himself. Now, was this just an example of his fun in dressing a part, and getting an audience for his tale? I do not believe in the bag. A black bag was one of the legendary appurtenances of the Ripper. But Florence told Mother than when they went to music halls they drew in pencil, in tiny notebooks, later on cards. Surely, the convenience of these was that they could be carried in the pocket. Was he just playing at having been taken for the Ripper? Or, if he had really been the Ripper and nobody knew, did he want, as it were the 'credit' for it? After all, he had been clever in outwitting the police.

He told Sir Osbert and Sacheverell Sitwell that he had lodged in a room that had been lodged in by Jack the Ripper. This, the landlady had told him. It had been a poor veterinary student, whose behaviour had invited her suspicion. Eventually his mother had come and taken him to Bournemouth, after which the murders ceased.(11) The Sitwells, however, tell us he was also interested in the case of the Tichborne claimant, and tended to believe the claimant. This, however, was a case which must have interested many people.

Knight attributes to Donald McCormick a story that Sickert told the 'lodger' story to Sir Melville Macnaughton, one of the CID men interested in the case, but with the difference that the lodger was not a veterinary student but Montague Druitt, schoolmaster and barrister, who had been fetched to Bournemouth by his mother and was later found drowned in the Thames.(12) I cannot find the story in McCormick's book, but Macnaughton had, in any case, thought of Druitt, earlier, because of his being found dead, just after the murders ceased. Sickert also told one of the 'lodger' variants to Sir Max Beerbohm.

This one knows from Lord David Cecil's biography of Beerbohm wherein he collects, on one page, private impressions of four artists, Steer, Sickert, Tonks and Augustus John, which Beerbohm had committed to a notebook not intended for publication. Sickert got:(13)

Sickert: His charm - for all women - Duchess or model - kind, shrewd, then domineering...two sides - like Shaw. Cruel mouth - kind eyes. Hair beautiful - peg tops. Extreme of refinement - love of squalor. Lodged in Jack the Ripper house.

If the stories told to Beerbohm, the Sitwells and Emmons stood alone, one could almost take them as humour, or attempts to claim attention. Yet Sickert had no need to draw attention to himself in such a way. A tall, good looking man, with a rising reputation as an artist, and generally sparkling in conversation, he tended to be the centre of attention in almost any group, without having to pretend to know something of Jack the Ripper. It was as though he had a compulsion to make it believed he knew about the crimes, without putting his neck in the noose. If what he said to the Sitwells could be taken lightly, it was certainly not in the way of making humorous conversation that he talked to Florence, to Alice Margaret, and ultimately to his own son, Joseph, in such as way as nearly to scare the wits out of them, very adversely affecting their whole lives.

Marjorie Lillie wrote (14) that a red handkerchief was extraordinarily important to Sickert. While painting his series on the Camden Town murder of 1907, he always wore it round his neck, or hung it on a peg or door-knob where he could see it while he was working. After the publication of her book, Knight interviewed her and she told him a little more. After his stroke, he would *be* the Ripper, turning the light low and walking up and down. As he had in his youth been on the stage, she supposed he did this in the way that an actor feels himself into the part before going on to the stage, to feel himself into the mood for painting the murder pictures. Yet. she also thought that perhaps he knew the truth about the Ripper murders.(15)

A man with whom Catherine Eddowes was seen just before she was found murdered, always supposed to be her murderer, was described in the *Police Gazette* as wearing a red handkerchief:

> At 1.35 am, 30 September, with Catherine Eddowes, in Church passage leading to Mitre Square, where she was found murdered at 1.45 am, same date, a man aged 30, height 5 feet 7 or 8 inches, complexion fair, moustache fair, medium build; dress; pepper and salt colour, loose jacket, grey cloth cap with peak of same material, reddish neckerchief tied in a knot; appearance of a sailor. Information concerning this man to be forwarded to Inspector MacWilliam, 26 Old Jewery, London EC

That description could be of Sickert, who was at that time twenty-eight.

There was also a description in the *Police Gazette* of the man seen with Elizabeth Stride, the earlier victim of that night:

> At 12.35 am, 30 September, with Elizabeth Stride, found murdered on the same date in Berners Street at 1 am, a man, aged 28, height 5 feet 8 inches, complexion dark, small dark moustache; dress, black, diagonal coat, hard felt hat, collar and tie; respectable appearance, carried a parcel wrapped up in a newspaper.

Although 28, being the exact age of Sickert, is tempting, one must be cautious here, because it is not necessarily this man who killed Elizabeth Stride and later Catherine Eddowes.

The black bag entered legend that night with the statement of Albert Backert at the Three Tuns, in Aldgate, that Saturday night, who was spoken to by a man:

> He wanted to know what sort of loose women used the public bar of the Three Tuns and where they were in the habit of going afterwards. It seemed rather odd to me...he was shabby, but a genteel sort of fellow, with black clothes, a black felt hat and carried a black bag.

I am not sure how much weight it would be right to give a letter by an ex-policeman P C Robert Clifford Spicer, published in the *Daily Express* over forty years afterwards.(16) He said that at past 2am on the night of the murder of Stride and Eddowes, he turned from Brick Lane into Henage Court, where he saw a man sitting on a dustbin with a prostitute. The prostitute was one known as Rosy. The constable's lantern showed up that the man had blood on his cuffs, and was carrying a black bag. He took him to Commercial Street police station on suspicion. There, the man declared that he was a respectable doctor, from Brixton, and Rosy, following, said that he had not in any way attempted to molest her, so they let him go - without making him open his bag. The man wore a high hat, a black suit with silk facings and a gold watch and chain. He was about five feet eight inches, 'weighed around twelve stone, had a fair moustache, high forehead and rosy cheeks.'

As it was a letter, not an article, Spicer will not have been paid for it, and the description, as regards height and fair moustache, tallies with that of the man wanted in connection with Catherine Eddowes' murder, though that one was not noticed to be carrying a bag, and was wearing a cap not a high hat.

There was also a man seen with Mary Kelly on the night of the murder. I will quote the statement of the witness, George Hutchinson, later. Here, what imports is just that the man was seen to offer her a red handkerchief.

This may or may not be coincidental. The important red handkerchief is the one knotted round the neck of the man wanted in connection with the murder of Catherine Eddowes. That is enough to establish a significance probably unknown to Marjorie Lilly when she noticed a red handkerchief as being an apparent necessity to Sickert to put him into the mood for painting pictures of murder.

To Marjorie Lilly he appeared a person who soaked up atmospheres and personalities:(17)

He has his Burns days, his Byron days..when his own good nature had involved him with a bore, whose visits in spite of marked hints appeared interminable, he would murmur, 'What would Byron have said to this infliction? He would not have permitted it for a moment.'
His sense of theatre was as keen as that of his idols, Hogarth, Degas and Dickens...

I am sure of it. But this kind of harmless fun seems to me, like his interest in unsolved mysteries such as that of the Tichborne claimant, not in the same dimension with that steady, permanent obsession with the Ripper that dominated his life. If it was only to entertain that he talked of the Ripper.

His preoccupation with the Ripper was not always overt. Marjorie Lilly tells a story of which I do not think she suspects the significance.

When Sickert became a neighbour of hers in Fitzroy Street in 1917, she and the girl with whom she shared a studio were often visitors to his. (18)

One foggy January morning in 1918, Sickert said suddenly: 'let's go to Petticoat Lane'....He had seemed so happy and so busy, resurrecting a battered old Gladstone bag, to which he was greatly attached, from the basement in order to paint on it his new address..

Mrs Sickert - Christine - had sent the girls a note asking them to try to keep him indoors, as he had a bad throat and exposure to the fog would make it worse. They were unable to prevent him from going out, so, feeling ineffectual and guilty, they went with him. They went to Warren Street Underground Station. He gave the impression he had never used the Underground before, but said he wanted to go to Aldgate, and was directed. At Aldgate they all three got out.

Whether they ever reached 'Petticoat Lane' (ie Middlesex Street), she never knew. The district was unfamiliar to her. The fog was now so thick they could not see the names of the streets, and had no idea where they were. Sickert seemed to know and 'every now and then darted down a side street' after something that caught his interest. He was claiming to see paintable subjects. All the girls knew was that they had to stick with him, and they 'plunged after him through the murk.'

What I do not think they knew is that Aldgate is the station for the Ripper district, and that they were very near to Miller's Court, where Mary Kelly was killed and mutilated. They made no connection in their minds between this fog-hugged excursion and the resurrection of the bag, which could have been the one the Ripper carried.

That was an association with the Ripper existing only in his mind, and not made overt for the 'entertainment' of the girls.

One must remember that all the people who have written their reminiscences of him knew only from much later than Florence. Excepting for a momentary encounter on a bus in 1911, Marjorie Lilly knew him only from November 1917, when he took a studio at 15 Fitzroy Street.

The Sitwell brothers knew him only from April 1918, when, sharing a flat in Swan Walk, Chelsea, they saw a tall, grey haired man standing in the road near the Physic Garden, and recognized him. Thus Marjorie Lilly and the Sitwells knew him only from when he was fifty-seven to eight; and Emmons, his eventual biographer, came to him as a pupil only in 1927, when Sickert was sixty-seven. But Florence knew him from 1885, when he was twenty-five. She knew him right through the Ripper period. Florence has an authority with which the friends of his mellowing years, and later Ripperologists, cannot compete. Florence knew Mary Kelly.

1 Sitwell, p xlii
2 d'Arch Smith, p 28-9
3 *The Life and Opinions of Walter Richard Sickert*, Robert Emmons (Faber, 1941), p 24
4 Emmons, p 20
5 *Walter Sickert, a Biography*, Denys Sutton (Michael Joseph, 1976), p 24
6 Emmons, p 28
7 Emmons, pp 28-9
8 *Sickert, The Painter and His Circle*, Marjorie Lilly (Noyes, 1973), p 19
9 *Sickert*, Lillian Browse (Hart-Davis, 1961), p 14
10 Emmons, pp 48-9
11 Sitwell, p xxxix

12 Knight, p 254
13 *Max, A Biography*, David Cecil (Constable, 1964), p 24
14 Lilly, p 15
15 Knight. p 254
16 'I caught Jack the Ripper', Robert Spicer, in the *Daily Express,* 16 March 1931
17 Lilly, p 27
18 Lilly, pp 19-20

Chapter 4
The first Mrs Sickert's Novel

The first Mrs Sickert is hardly characterized, in books about her husband. Marjorie Lilly would have liked to find something to say about her, but found that even the people she interviewed who had met Ellen seemed to have nothing to tell her about her personality.

Yet she was not really a negative person. She may not have expressed herself much in company, but after the divorce she wrote a novel, in which one may hear her speak with her own voice. The plot of *Wistons* is, of course, fictitious, but psychologically one feels that Esther is Ellen (both begin with E) and that Robin is Walter Richard Sickert.

When they meet, she is of a romantic outlook, wishing it might be given her to play Mary Godwin to some Shelley. Then, he walks into her life, and she describes him:(1)

Robin was tall and strongly slim, he had yellow hair and dark blue eyes well cut and placed; his lips were beautifully shaped, the line of his jaw from ear to chin could not have been better drawn, there were no blurred outlines and there was no clumsiness in him.

This is surely a description of Sickert. To disguise the identity a little, she makes him not an artist but a novelist and poet. She is convinced of his genius. She tells her sister, (2) 'he is more wonderful and beautiful than it's possible to imagine.'

There are touches in the characterization that Florence might recognize:

He was cheerfully interested in all that personally concerned him; his morning toilet completely absorbed him; he enjoyed washing his hands, brushing his hair...

He is, in fact, somewhat self-absorbed, as she begins to realize after they are married. Meals had to be punctual, on the chance of his punctuality.

For a week Robin talked to Esther about himself and his work. But:

Once or twice Esther began to tell Robin of her own occupations. The first time he did not listen; the second time, with a sweet anxious expression on his face and in a soft, appealing voice, he told her that his whole mind was so absorbed in his work that he feared to think of anything outside it.

One begins to see the picture: spoiled, and selfish to the bone. This is perhaps commonplace. One could say as much of Professor Higgins in Shaw's *Pygmalion*. Unlike Shaw's creation, he is not, however, helpfully advised by his mother. Robin's relations with his mother are strangely negative. To begin with:(6)

He thought it quite ridiculous to write to his mother and tell her of his engagement.

Indeed, though he is pressed into informing her, she does not come to the wedding. Did Sickert's mother come to his wedding? We do not know. From Florence's account of his waiting for the bus, it does not sound as though his mother were behind the scenes, making sure he did everything properly. Florence received a favourable impression of Sickert's mother, and of the relations between mother and son, but Robin says: (7)

My dear Mother and I understand each other perfectly. she is all gush without a scrap of affection for anyone; and I'm all common sense and satisfied with her as she is.

Yet it is a bitter remark, not the remark of a man content. Had there been, at some time, a withdrawal of affection, upon her side - perhaps as younger children arrived - resulting in a withdrawal on his? This is very unusual, for mothers tend to dote on sons, especially upon first born sons, who are good looking. Yet, though we must remember this is a work of fiction, it seems an unlikely detail for Ellen to have invented, in what is so plainly her own exposition of the breakdown of the marriage.

Even on the journey back from the honeymoon, she had begun to have the feeling she did not really share in his inner life:

Esther looked back as they crossed the long bridge. Robin was absorbed in his papers. She spoke to him once or twice, but he shook a finger at her as a sign that he was not to be disturbed, and she was aware of a hot feeling of resentment that flared up suddenly within her. She remembered how continually he wanted to be away from her in Venice; how often she had wanted him to be with her, on the piazza at night when it was brilliant with light...She had longed for him to look up with her at the dark ceiling overhead...How often she had wanted him to be with her in the gondola...

Why wasn't he? We are told Mrs Sickert did not seem much to enjoy the part of their honeymoon that was spent in Dieppe. Perhaps for this sort of reason?

Soon, Robin is reading a book at meals. Esther exclaims: (9)

I believe he is the most selfish creature alive!

Yet always the feeling hers was the privilege of being married to a genius caused her to rein back her resentment and strive to be understanding.(10)

'What am I,' she asked herself, 'compared to him.'

When she wavers, one of his men-friends assures her: (11)

Robin is phenomenal. I believe that his genius is absolutely original, epoch-making. Let me add that he is marvellously fortunate to have a wife who understands him and who is willing to give up her own wishes for his.'

She replies (12)

'I will try, indeed I will try. It is a great responsibility and one makes such mistakes.'

Then come the infidelities. He takes up again with a woman he had known from before his marriage: (13)

A handsome woman with hair of that peculiar shade of deep red that suggests crimson...

This sounds like *La Belle Rousse* (The Beautiful Redhead), title of one of Sickert's paintings of Madam A. E. Villain, his Dieppe mistress. Further on, she is described as:

quite wonderful...stuck up in the middle of a sofa like a beautiful red idol with its hair combed into its eyes...

This is a painter's description of his model. Even the name given her in the novel, Mrs Ffrench, suggests Mrs French, - ie, French - woman. But how did Ellen know of her? It was not until after the break-up of their marriage that

Sickert settled with Madame Villain in her house. As the stall from which she sold her fish was on the quay at Dieppe, she may have been known to him from much earlier. If Ellen noticed his interest in this woman, it could account for what has been mentioned by his biographers, that Ellen did not seem much to enjoy their stays in Dieppe.

The next mistress, with whom Esther catches him in the library, is a titled woman, Lady Fanny. When they are alone, after the row, he assures her Fanny means nothing to him:

'Fanny is like a little idiot...she has the most abominable manners, like all her class. There's no moral and no intellectual difference, only a geographical and financial division, between Belgravia and Whitechapel.'

Whitechapel! That is peculiar. That particular district does not form the most natural opposite to Belgravia. Most people think of the East End, as opposed to the West End.

But amongst the seedy districts composing the East End, would Whitechapel be usual to pick out as the poorest or lowest? It is thought of as a foreign district. Limehouse is thought of as full of Chinese, Whitechapel as full of Jews. For the English poor, I should have thought Bow would better have exemplified the type. A Cockney is said to be one 'born within the sound of Bow Bells.' Or Billingsgate. Coarse, bad language is sometimes referred to as Billingsgate. Either would have made a more natural polar opposite to Belgravia, and beginning with B, alliterate more effectively. Why did 'Robin' say, or Ellen Sickert think of, Whitechapel?

Further on, Robin is reported as having said of his red-head: (16)

'She is - she is greedy and selfish and idle and a liar. She can't speak grammatically, and she has a Whitechapel accent that she tries to conceal, and she is absolutely divine.'

So Mrs Ffrench was not French after all. She came from Whitechapel. Perhaps that explains the earlier opposition of Whitechapel to Belgravia. He had a mistress from each. Ellen Sickert has perhaps fused the red hair of the Dieppe fishwife with the Whitechapel background of another of her husband's mistresses. There is no such thing as a Whitechapel accent. Not even Professor Higgins, (of whom I knew the part-original, Professor Daniel Jones) could have told the accent of one London East End district from another. One speaks of 'an East End Accent' or a 'Cockney Accent.' Whitechapel cannot have been chosen by the author as a district romantically poor, or romantically wicked - like the Apache district of Paris - or even dangerously poor, that would better be Limehouse or Dockland, with its wharfs and mists - as figured in the early Lillian Gish film, *Broken Blossoms*. Whitechapel is merely drab - notorious only as the scene of the Ripper murders. Whatever made Ellen Sickert produce one of her husband's mistresses from there? Did she meet Mary Kelly? During the time that he was employing her in Cleveland Street he could, conceivably, have brought her to the house, in Hampstead, but she would have had an Irish or Welsh accent and Mrs Sickert would not have associated her with Whitechapel.

Did Sickert have some other mistress who came from Whitechapel?

Or did Sickert maintain some sort of relationship with Mary Kelly after her removal to Whitechapel? Before he received the first blackmailing letter? How do we know there was a blackmailing letter? Florence took his word for it. But would he have taken Mary to his wife's house? Ellen got her divorce because he did bring his mistresses into the house.

The passage goes on:

> Of course Robin penetrated all the mysteries: 'What! Whisky and red herrings! How perfect! To walk in the park when the fashionable world that she did not know was there! How original! He would start off with her as if they were going on a voyage of adventure...but it didn't continue at that rate, and Ariadne, deserted as usual, consoled herself with Bacchus.'

In the park, means Hyde Park, which had its fashionable hour. But Mrs Sickert would not know whom he took to Hyde Park. Now if it was Dieppe...? Dieppe was certainly very fashionable, and small enough for people to bump into each other whom it had not been intended should meet. Joseph Sickert's mention of his father's having taken Mary Kelly to Dieppe has always been puzzling. He implies they went with Annie and Alice Margaret looking for all the world as though they were father, mother and child with nursemaid, but during his marriage, Sickert took his wife with him to Dieppe. Could he have asked Mary on the side, accommodated in different lodgings, where he could call on her when his wife bored him? That could explain why Mary did not enjoy the stay in Dieppe and returned alone. There is the hint at the girl's drinking problem.

The point is that with all this doubling, telescoping and transposing of elements of her real entourage in the fictional settings, there would be nothing surprising in her having fused the red hair of Sickert's Dieppe mistress, Madame Villain, with the Whitechapel background of Mary Kelly. The only question in my mind concerns the date and circumstances in which she met Mary. Did she know her name and learn of her having removed to Whitechapel from the newspapers reporting her death, or did Sickert's connection with her continue - even to the extent of inviting her to the matrimonial home - after her removal to Whitechapel?

That Ellen Cobden did ring the changes on elements which had a basis in her own experiences is confirmed when one reads her second novel, *Sylvia Saxon.* (This she published under her own maiden name, followed by her previous pseudonym in brackets). Richard Cobden, the statesman, Ellen's father, had been born in Sussex but by the time Ellen was growing up, his political work had taken the family to Lancashire. Ellen's mother was Welsh. In *Wistons,* the principle setting is Sussex. In *Sylvia Saxon,* it is Lancashire; one feels that the popular seaside resort, Rockpool, is meant to be Blackpool, and Blackhampton the Black having been transferred from pool to Hampton - an industrial town near to it. The Radical MP and considerable statesman who, in the novel, was the heroine's father-in-law, must, one feels, have been modelled on Ellen's own father, who was a Liberal MP. He is given a country house in Wales, which was in life Ellen's mother's country. Thus juggling with her personalities and locations, she is able to endow the personages and places with an exactly observed verisimilitude, whilst disguising them in fictionalized relationships. In the second novel, Sickert appears to figure twice, once as the tall, leonine man, twelve years her junior, whom Sylvia's moneyed mother chose for her husband (Ellen was twelve years older than Sickert and it was she who had the money), and (a different aspect of his personality being developed) the handsome, but ambitious and fundamentally bone-selfish man (this time a politician) with whom Sylvia falls in love. As in the first novel, the heroine is left, at the end, with the problem of facing life alone.

Both the novels have a murder, at almost the end, not of the heroine but of somebody near to her. In *Wistons*, it is her sister; in *Sylvia Saxon*, it is her adopted sister. The circumstances are not like those of the Ripper murders. Esther's sister, Rhoda, is stabbed by her lover, a character only introduced just before and not deeply characterized, because her self-sufficiency leads him into the incorrect supposition she has another love (it is not very convincing); Sylvia's adopted sister, Anne, is drowned by their former governess, to spare her the pain of having nothing to live for - a mad mercy killing. In both cases the murder coincides with the heroine's loss of her man, leaving her to be talked to - in both cases - by a stranger encountered by chance. One knows of no one close to Ellen Cobden who was murdered, yet the high autobiographical content of the novels, combined with the repetition of the theme, leave one wondering what was in her mind.

1 *Wistons*, Miles Amber [pseud Ellen Cobden] Fisher Unwin, 2 imp, 1902, p 97
2 Ibid, p 106
3 Ibid, p 99
4 Ibid, p 156
5 Ibid, p 158
6 Ibid, p 118
7 Ibid, p 132
8 Ibid, p 136
9 Ibid, p 140
10 Ibid, p 145
11 Ibid, p 180
12 Ibid, p 191
13 Ibid, p 150
14 Ibid, p 195
15 Ibid, p 183
16 Ibid, p 196
17 *Sylvia Saxon*, Ellen Milicent Cobden, (Miles Amber), Author of *Wistons* (T. Fisher Unwin, 1914)

Chapter 5
Eliminations

There is one group of attempts to identify the Ripper that I believe to be based upon misunderstanding. There is nothing to connect Montague Druitt with the crimes except that he was found drowned in the Thames shortly after they ceased. An unsuccessful barrister, he had been dismissed from the school at Blackheath where he taught, apparently without reason given, on 1 December, 1888, and was last seen alive on the 3rd. When his body was found in the river near Chiswick, there were stones in his pockets. It has struck more than one person his dismissal may have been for misconduct with a boy. There was no woman in his life, known of, save his mother, and he was McNaughton's suspect on the ground he was 'sexually insane' and that therefore his own family suspected him. Howells and Skinner, whose candidate he is, take 'sexually insane' to have been a euphemism for homosexual, and they are very likely right. But - quite apart from the consideration that Annie Chapman was murdered at close to 5.45 on the morning of Saturday 8 September, and he was by 10 o'clock in his white flannels and on the cricket-field at Blackheath, which is cutting it rather fine - aside from this timing, his possible homosexuality is a consideration that to my mind takes away from, rather than enhances, the likelihood he would have committed sadistic murders of women.

The whole point about homosexuals lies in that their sexual drive is towards their own sex, and not to the opposite. They are not men who are driven by a burning hatred of women. This is the fallacy which must have underlain the prostitutes' dancing for joy at the conviction of Oscar Wilde. They may have very kind relations with women, though not wishing to sleep with them. Sadism is a manifestation not of absence of sexual attraction, but of sexual attraction gone wrong. Homosexuals, if sadistic, murder boys - as Gilles de Rais or Dennis Neilsen. The sadistic murders of women are committed by men whose sexual interest is in women. This was not understood in the Victorian era, and judging from some of the books that appear, seems not widely to be understood today.

Admittedly, J K Stephen, another homosexual candidate, wrote anti-women poems, but they seem to me of a petulant, provoked nature.

The other theory I should say something about is that of Baroness Cremers. As one of the circle of young poets gathered around Victor B Neuburg before the war, I was present when an old friend of his came to visit him on her seventieth birthday. The conversation I listened to that day between the two was a very strange one, mainly about Aleister Crowley. It was dropped that she 'knew Jack the Ripper' - no, she did not mean Crowley, but I was not told whom she meant. I have related what I heard that day in my biography of Neuburg.(2)

When Mother told me Florence's story, I wondered if this and Baroness Cremers' story could be two ends of the same ball of string. Later again, while I was writing *The Magical Dilemma of Victor Neuburg* I interviewed a Mrs Joyce Saunders, whose mother had known both Neuburg and Baroness Cremers. She said, 'She knew Jack the Ripper very well, through her dear friend Mabel Collins', but would not elaborate. Then Gerald Yorke lent me a great pile of unpublished Crowley manuscripts, in which I did find what read as a most improbable story - doubtless heightened a good deal by the Crowlean imagination - about how Mabel Collins had confided to Baroness Cremers the trouble she was having with an ex-lover, a doctor, and of the strange events which led up to the two womens' becoming convinced he was the Ripper.(3)

But this was the man, calling himself Dr Rosalyn d'O Stephenson, who walked into Scotland Yard, said he had been a patient at the London Hospital and alleged that a Dr Morgan Davies on the staff there was the Ripper. He described with so much verve the manner in which he imagined Dr Davies to have committed the murders as to draw on himself some suspicion of having committed them himself. (4) Probably just a crank or hoaxer. I fear Baroness Cremers fell for his bluff.

Finally, I should like to dispose of a notion I first heard from Victor Neuburg's companion, 'Runia', that the location of the five murders marked the points of a reversed pentagram, and that the murders may have been committed as an evil occult ritual. I suspect Crowley of having been at the origin of this tale, but, as a glance at the map will show, the sites do not mark the points of a pentagram.

There are also a few outside contenders. In April, 1891, a Thomas Cutbrush was brought before the London County Sessions, charged with maliciously wounding one woman and attempting to wound another. Found insane, he was sent to an asylum. During some weeks previous to the incidents with which he was charged, there had been cases of stabbing or jabbing with a knife in the Kenington district of South London, where he lived, with his mother and aunt, and this caused some speculation whether he could have been the Ripper. A pause of over three years followed by a resumption on such a minor scale does, however, seem unlikely.

Sir Melville Macnaughton, making some notes at the Yard six years after the cessation of the crimes, place ahead of Cutbrush first Druitt, then Kosminski and third a Russian doctor, Michael Ostrog who was, at a later date, confined to a lunatic asylum on a homicidal charge and whose whereabouts at the time of the crimes it had never been possible to ascertain.

Ostrog has had no serious backer, but there was in the centenary year a brief article in a newspaper, which I did not think to keep, by a policeman, backing Aaron Kosminski, and this was followed by a telvision programme (unfortunately not shown on Anglia so I was unable to view it, but which was apparently based on the same). The primary document against Kosminski is Macnaughton's note:

> Kosminski - a Polish Jew - & resident in Whitechapel. This man became insane owing to many years indulgence in solitary vices. He had a great hatred of women, specially of the prostitute class, and had strong homicidal tendencies; he was removed to a lunatic asylum about March 1889. There were many circumstances connected with this man which made him a strong suspect.

The case against him seems to me parallel to the one against Druitt. He ceased to be in circulation some time after the crimes ceased, which could be made to account for their having done so, and he did not associate with women. Nevertheless, from the murder of Mary Kelly on 9 November until March is four months, which is longer than the Ripper left between his crimes. Further, whatever may have been his attitude towards women, I would have thought that someone who found his relief in solitary sex would be a shy type, either sexually inexperienced or, through failure to make relationships, withdrawn into himself, rather than given to pursuing them.

None of these characters has any link with any of the women murdered. That, only Sickert has.

1 *The Ripper Legacy*, Martin Howells and Keith Skinner (Sidgwick and Jackson, 1987), p 156
2 *The Magical Dilemma of Victor Neuburg*, Jean Overton Fuller, (Mandrake 1990)
3 *Ibid*, pp 166-7
4 *Jack the Ripper, the Bloody Truth*, Melvin Harris (Columbia, 1987) pp 180-3

Chapter 6
Sir William Gull

It is necessary to take an attitude to Gull. Sickert told his son Gull was the Ripper, yet it seems to me obvious he was not. Gull was born, at Colchester, on 31 December 1816. He was, therefore, seventy-one at the time of the murders, indeed only a few weeks short of seventy-two at the time of the last and most terrible of them.

Moreover, he had had a slight stroke in October of the previous year. He had been on holiday in Scotland and, while walking alone in the grounds of his house there, had been seized and fallen on one knee. He had been able to pick himself up and walk back to the house, but instead of resuming practice on his return to London as he had intended, he retired. The mutilations performed on the body of Mary Kelly would have required considerable physical strength and, it has been estimated, must have occupied at least two hours. Not work for a man of nearly seventy-two who had a stroke the previous year.

As we shall presently see, none of the statements made to the police by persons who had been about at the time of the crimes describe anyone looking to be of that age; neither do any of them speak of having seen or heard a coach in which he could have been conveyed.

So why did Sickert try to put the murders on to Gull's back? No man conceives against another a hatred so 'mineral' (to borrow a phrase from Sir Francis Bacon) without having met him? They must have come up against each other in some way.

Gull had a daughter, Caroline. She married another medical man, Theodore Dyke Acland, MD FRCP. One of Acland's students at St Thomas's Hospital was Dr T.E.S. Stowell, CBE, MD. He became a friend of Acland and his wife. He was later to write, 'I knew them both intimately and often enjoyed the hospitality of their home in Bryanston Square, over many years.' Sometimes Acland talked about the Ripper murders, upon which his wife Caroline's mind was apparently working.

Caroline told Stowell a very strange story, which she must have had from her mother. The Gull family were at their London home, 74 Brook Street, Mayfair, during the murders, and one night a police officer called without appointment, in company with a medium. It was Lady Gull who received them: (1)

> She was irritated by their impudence in asking her a number of questions which seemed to her impertinent. She answered their questions with non-committal replies such as 'I do not know,' 'I cannot tell you that,' 'I am afraid I cannot answer that question.'

Sir William Gull

Later Sir William himself came down and in answer to the questions said he occasionally suffered from 'lapses of memory since he had a slight stroke in 1887;' he said that he once discovered blood on his shirt. This is not surprising if he had medically examined the Ripper after one of the murders.

Jack the Ripper was obviously Sir William Gull's patient and Mrs Acland told me that she had seen in her father's diary an entry Informed Blank that his son was dying of syphilis of the brain'. The date of the entry was November, 1889....

What Caroline Acland told him, Stowell kept to himself - or practically to himself - for forty years, before publishing it in the article in the *Criminologist* of 1 November 1970 from which I quote.

Stowell's argument is that the Ripper was Gull's patient, whom he does not name but refers to as S. This is generally taken as S for Suspect. S was born the heir to power and wealth, of a family loved and admired...but resigned his commission 'after the raiding of some premises at Cleveland Street, off Tottenham Court Road, kept by a man named Hammond, which were frequented by various aristocrats and well-to-do homosexuals.' On the estates of his family in Scotland, S would have seen dressed the carcasses of deer, from which he would have gathered anatomical knowledge sufficient to perform mutilations, and when his mind became broken down by syphilitic poison it became directed towards murder; eventually he died of the disease.

Stowell seemed to be indicating Clarence, and several newspapers picked this up. He first let them go along with the idea then denied it, but before his denial appeared was dead. He was an elderly man and perhaps the furore had been too much for him. He died on 9 November, the anniversary of the death of Mary Kelly.

He had, however, told Colin Wilson some ten years earlier that he believed Clarence was the Ripper. (This was after reading something Wilson had written in 1960.) Wilson did not believe it. Clarence formed one of a hunting party at Balmoral on the morning of the murder of Elizabeth Stride and Catherine Eddowes, and on the night of Mary Kelly's murder was celebrating his father's birthday at Sandringham. This does not quite constitute a watertight alibi, since there was a good train service between London and Scotland and we do not know how late he stayed at his father's birthday party; nevertheless, it does seem to render his guilt unlikely - and syphilis does not render the sufferer murderous.

Furthermore I cannot believe Gull would have thought syphilitic softening of the brain rendered one murderous, or that Acland would have thought it - or Stowell, spontaneously. I believe this was the idea of Caroline Acland. I ask myself why she told this extraordinary story to Stowell. The medium who came with the police officer may well have been the Robert James Lees, medium who - it is part of Ripperologists' lore - led the police to a mansion in the West End of London, which proved to be home of a distinguished physician, whom they did indeed question. It does not matter whether it was Lees or not. The point is, this story had no credit-worthy backing until supplied by Gull's daughter, whose source can only have been her mother, unless Gull himself. Why did she not keep it to herself? Why did she tell Stowell? I think she told Stowell for the same reason Joseph Sickert told Knight his father's story. That is, she did not believe the Ripper was her father, but the call's having been made was unpleasing. She wanted an explanation of the affair that let him out. Clarence, she thought! That must be it. Her father had spoken of him as having frequented a bad house in Cleveland Street and having syphilis of the brain; it must be he who had gone mad and committed the murders, and her father, as a loyal servant of the crown, had covered up for him, as had her mother. This was how Caroline, putting herself in her mother's shoes, may have worked it out. Now that in any case makes her father accessory after the fact, and her mother too.

Two details are peculiar - blood on Sir William's shirt. I do not know why he should have had blood on his shirt, unless he cut himself - or perhaps indeed treated the Ripper, who need not have been Clarence.

As to the lapses of memory, it would seem not to his interest to have mentioned these, or the blood, but my mind goes back to a certain trial in France where the accused pled not guilty, but also pled abnormal condition of mind at the time - transparently so that if the verdict went against her she could appeal on grounds of diminished responsibility. I feel Caroline was hoping primarily to prove it was Clarence and not her father, but in case it should nevertheless turn out to have been her father, formed for him a defence, that when the crimes occurred he was unconscious of committing them.

Stowell's theme was taken up by Michael Harrison, who felt that where Stowell had gone wrong was in taking S to stand for Suspect. Surely it must be the first letter of the name of a man. He wrote a book *Clarence*, in which he put forward as the Ripper Clarence's former Cambridge tutor, James Kenneth Stephen. His only evidence against him, however, was that he wrote some anti-women poems, was possibly homosexual, once in foolery impaled a loaf of bread upon a sword, and in 1892 died in a mental home. This is really too thin.

Colin Wilson, seeing this, wrote:(2)

But if we dismiss Stephen, then who was S? There is one more obvious candidate - Sickert.

This he wrote after reading Knight's book. But then he adds:

Does this mean that Sickert was the Ripper? Almost certainly not. Artists and writers may become morbidly obsessed by certain murders but...no artist has ever been known to commit a premeditated murder. Sickert may have been Gull's suspect, and therefore the man who inadvertently caused suspicion to fall on the Duke of Clarence. But there is no evidence that he was capable of harming a fly.

Suppose he is wrong about this. Suppose Sickert could harm a fly. It is a mistake to think of artists as necessarily gentle. Van Gogh, sweetest, most loving and caring of men, once rushed at Gauguin with a razor, then turned and struck off his own ear to punish himself.

I said earlier I did not believe the Princess of Wales would have asked Sickert to take Clarence under his wing. Yet behind Sickert's tales there is the grain of truth to be discerned. Gull was Clarence's physician and she may have asked him to take Clarence under his wing - that is, to follow him to Cleveland Street and find out what the truth was with regard to matters concerning which very ugly rumours were reaching her.

This could all have brought Gull to Sickert's door. Where did Clarence and Annie sleep together? In her room? It would have been drab. In the brothel? Too sordid. At Sickert's would have been nicer. That is only my guess, but something is needed to bring Gull into collision with Sickert.

Sickert is unlikely to have been one of Gull's patients, but it is just possible he could have been injured during one of the killings. The four earlier victims were elderly and weak, but Mary Kelly was only twenty-five and could have fought back. Suppose he had got cut on his own knife? He might have felt he needed treatment yet been afraid to go to a doctor who might, on reading the papers next morning, feel it his duty to go to the police and report. How could he be sure even his own doctor would keep his confidence? He could have gone to Gull's, late at night - thinking to himself that Gull was the one person not in a position to ask questions such as 'How did you get this wound?'

I am not, of course, saying it has to have happened like this, but it could have. There has to have been a relation between Sickert and Gull such that Gull believed Sickert committed the murders, yet Sickert held Gull responsible for them.

If the idea was to protect the crown, Queen Victoria knew nothing of it. On the day after Mary Kelly's death, she wrote to Lord Salisbury: (3)

> This new most ghastly murder shows the absolute necessity for some very decided action.
> All the courts must be lit and our detectives improved. They are not what they should be. You promised when the first murder took place to consult with your colleagues about this.

And three days later she had a letter sent to her Home Secretary, Henry Matthews:

> 13 November, 1888
> The Queen fears that the detective department is not so efficient as it might be. No doubt the recent murders in Whitechapel were committed in circumstances which made detection difficult; still the Queen thinks that, in the small area where these horrible crimes have been perpetrated, a great number of detectives might be employed, and that every possible suggestion might be carefully examined, and, if practicable, followed.
> Have the cattle boats and passenger boats been examined?
> Has any investigation been made as to the number of single men occupying rooms to themselves?
> The murderer's clothes must be saturated with blood and must be kept somewhere. Is there sufficient surveillance at night?
> These are some of the questions that occur to the Queen on reading the accounts of

this horrible crime.

Poor Mary Kelly, who had failed to find a royal lover, as had Annie Crook, had in her death captured the attention of the Queen herself.

The point about the cattle boats is that they usually arrived on a Thursday, bringing cattle from the continent for slaughter at Aldgate, and left again on a Sunday. All the victims were found in the early hours of either a Friday morning, a Saturday morning or a Sunday morning. The Queen may have been thinking it could be one of the drovers. Her observations show at least as much penetration as do those of any of the police and detectives we shall later study.

1 'Jack the Ripper - a solution?' T.E.A Stowell, *Criminologist*, 1 November 1970
2 *Jack the Ripper, Summing Up and Verdict,* Colin Wilson (Bantam, 1987), p 201
3 *Ibid,* p 203
4 *Queen Victoria in Her letters and Journals,* selected by Christopher Hibbert (Murray, 1984), p 314

Chapter 7
The Pictures

(Publisher's note: The Sickert Trust: Patron Henry Lessore [The son of the sister of Sickert's third wife] has refused permission to reproduce some of the pictures analysed in this chapter)

Florence said there were pictures that contained the parts of a riddle and had to be read in conjunction, pictures also of his memory of the mutilated bleeding bodies, never exhibited, and too terrible ever to be exhibited, pictures she found unbearable to look at. I do not know whether there were pictures seen by Florence that have been destroyed, but there are a certain number which have seen exposure to the public, which look rather peculiar.

The strangest of all his pictures shows a woman looking up at a bust on the wall. He gave it alternative titles, *Amphitryon* and *X's Affiliation Order*. An Affiliation Order was a paper that could be served on a man, fixing his paternity of an illegitimate child and requiring him to pay maintenance. Amphitryon was a form taken by Zeus, the king of the gods, when descending to seduce a mortal, by whom he had a child. Orthodox Sickert scholars have hardly known what to think of the pair of titles, but with our clues we can see the idea: an august kingly or princely figure descended from his Olympian heights to seduce a common woman, and got her with child, and deserved to have been served with an Affiliation Order. Though she is looking up, presumably at the bust of her seducer, he looks not like a handsome young man, but a death's head. The implication is surely that her seduction brought the threat of death. Is the woman, then, Annie or Mary, or a composite figure representing all the women involved?

It was probably this and the *Ennui* with the gull on Queen Victoria's shoulder, in the picture within the picture, that Florence was thinking of when she said there were pictures that had to be taken together, as representing the parts of the riddle. The gull does not appear in the picture in the Tate, painted in 1913. It is in the version in the Ashmolean, painted in 1917 or 1918. In 1919 Sickert returned to Dieppe. It was, therefore, probably when Florence visited him in Dieppe in 1921 and he sat to her for his portrait, that he told her he was painting clues to the Ripper murders into his pictures, and that the supreme clue was a gull which he had placed on Queen Victoria's shoulder. This seems to me such an important self-disclosure that I wanted to date it as nearly as possible. Florence had told my mother that it was during her own and Sickert's widowhood, when she crossed the channel to execute a commission to make a pastel portrait of Saint Saëns, and she made one of Sickert at the same time. It had, therefore, to be between the deaths of Christine Sickert and Saint-Saëns.

I therefore wrote to Dr Stanley Sadie, Editor of *The New Grove Dictionary of Music and Musicians* asking if he could transmit some questions for me to anyone who knew of the French composer's movements between October 1920 and his death, in December, 1921. I received reply from Dr James Harding, telling me that Saint-Saëns returned from Algeria to Paris on 14 April 1921, so the portrait would have had to have been made between that date and 21 August, when he left Paris for Algeria, to die there. Dr Harding told me Saint-Saëns had on 6 August visited Dieppe, to give a farewell concert to the people who appreciated his work - the Château Musée of Dieppe had, he told me, a Saint-Saëns Room, and he suggested that it was one of the people of Dieppe who commissioned the portrait. I thought so too. That would explain what had always puzzled me. There were so many artists in France it had seemed strange they had to invite an English one who had to come from London. Probably they asked Sickert, and he recommended her.

The portrait, which is a very powerful one, gains in the intensity of its interest when it is realised that she made it during the visit on which he made the terrible disclosure, or perhaps one could call it confession - perhaps indeed, while he was sitting for her. As it does not seem possible Gull could have committed the crimes, I think his meaning must have been that, for setting him on this terrible course, he held Gull responsible. In the Tate version, the table is bare, the woman's blouse is plain and so is the wall behind her; Queen Victoria is there, in the picture within the picture, but without the gull. In the Ashmolean version, the table has been covered with a patterned cloth and the blouse and wallpaper endowed with pattern. If his sole reason for painting this version was to use Queen Victoria's shoulder to place a gull on, then the purpose of his busy patterning was to prevent it from being noticed at once.

The plaster cast in his self-portrait, *The Painter in his Studio*, is headless, but the appearance is not that of broken plaster but of a body with the head torn off. And what is that broad, ragged gash running from between the pubis and the navel to the throat? That is not a crack in plaster; that would flake. The raised edges suggest ripped flesh. Is not the artist standing beside a butchered woman's trunk? (Nobody who has reminisced about Sickert records having seen a cast in his studio - a lay figure, yes, but that is something different).

He did a series of paintings known as the Camden Town Murder series. On 12 September, 1907, a young woman, Emily Dimmock, known as Phyllis, was found with her throat deeply cut from ear to ear, in her bed at 29 St Paul's Road (now Agar Grove), Camden Town. She had been born in Walsall, but brought up in Wellingborough, Northamptonshire, where a job as a factory hand seemed too dull for her. She had answered an advertisement for a domestic servant in London, and, finding that again too dull, had drifted into prostitution. Her steady companion, Albert Shaw, a railwayman, was in Sheffield at the time, so suspicion fell on her clients. The one arrested was

The Pictures

Robert Wood, a young artist, of Scottish descent, who had been amongst the most recent. His case made legal history because he was the first to take advantage of a change in the law allowing the accused to take the oath and speak from the box. The prosecution disclosed, as the law required, that its researches had produced statements from two witnesses that they saw the accused on the 11th in the company of another man.

Marshall Hall defended him. No evidence was offered that Wood was with the deceased on the 11th and they found him 'not guilty.'

It is a pity that the other man was never described. As Sir John Napley has commented, the end of the case left one thing unsettled. 'Who, indeed, did kill Emily Dimmock?'(1)

Dr. Wendy Baron, whose *Sickert* is mainly concerned with the chronology of his work, and grew out of a PhD thesis on that subject, tells us his movements in 1907 are uncertain. He was addressing letters from 6, Mornington Crescent, Camden Town, where he painted his *Mornington Crescent Nude* and *Contre Jour Mornington Crescent Nude* - during the summer. He had hoped to go to Dieppe in July but had to put his visit off until the autumn. He did go, for there is a letter he wrote on the eve of crossing, but it is undated.(2) However, the case, which came to the Old Bailey on 12 December, received a good deal of newspaper coverage, with which no doubt Sickert familiarized himself.

It is generally taken that it was the mere proximity of the site of the *cause célébre* to where he lived - both scruffy little addresses were at the back of St Pancras Railway Station that caused his mind, for the first time, to dwell upon murder. However, he told his son the series was really founded on the murder of Mary Kelly.(3) Now if the murder of Mary Kelly was always on his mind, it would be quite possible for the recent affair, similar in that it was a throat cutting (though without other mutilation) to reanimate the memory. If these were the paintings Florence spoke of, she did not mention Camden Town in their connection.

Knight said the model used by Sickert for the man in his Camden Town Murder series was the defendant Robert Wood. He gave no evidence, so I supposed he had this from Joseph. According to Marjorie Lilly, the model for all these pictures, as well as for *Ennui*, was someone called 'Hubby.' Admittedly, there was something mysterious about Hubby. He arrived at Sickert's studio at 1, Granby Street, with a suitcase he had picked up at Euston. Sickert apparently took him in without question, which surprised her, because if there was one thing that shocked him, it was stealing. A couple had stolen some canvasses from one of the other studios and someone had pleaded for them not to be too harshly judged, saying, 'After all, everyone has a right to exist.'

Sickert had retorted, 'Not at all. Some people have no right to exist.'(4) This startlingly cold reply she attributed to his fun, but there was no doubt that he disapproved strongly. Yet Hubby with his stolen suitcase was accepted without criticism. Nobody was told his real name. She understood he was 'a broken down school fellow of Sickert's, now a casual vagrant.' Lillian Browse referred to 'Sickert's manservant Hubby - said to have been an ex-convict.' (5)

He does not look at all like Robert Wood, in the drawing by Joseph Simpson in Napley's book, which shows a sharp, aquiline face. Admittedly, one does not see much of the model's face in the murder pictures, but though it could have been induced by the beer, in *Ennui* it looks much puffier, as one sees it also in the picture *Hubby and Emily* - but Emily was the name of the woman murdered.

Dr. Baron writes, 'Sickert's model for the male figure is said to have been the commercial artist who was accused but finally acquitted of Emily Dimmock's murder,'(6) and gives as her source 'Information given to me by Mr Rex Nankivell who was told this by Sickert.'(7)

Strange, very strange. Could his appearance have changed so much in two years? Marjorie Lilly says, 'But Sickert was greatly relieved when Hubby took himself off, disappearing for good.'(8) That does sound as though he had felt he owed him something.

The picture, entitled simply *Camden Town Murder,* in which he sits glumly on the bed in which the woman lies prostrate, was done from a drawing reproduced by Emmons. The title of the drawing, however, is *What Shall We Do For The Rent?* Emily Dimmock was not behind with the rent. Mary Kelly was.

In *Summer Afternoon*, which belongs to the series, he sits perched on the edge of the bed, looking at her. There is something about her anatomy that puzzles me. Where is her navel? Where one would expect to find it, there is nothing. Its absence is cunningly blotted out by the way the light falls on the torso. What looks like a navel is much too far down, only just above the pubis. Indeed, one sees the v-shape of the groin just beneath it. In the police photographs of Catherine Eddowes, one can see that that was the position of the hole made by the knife as it first went in, before being dragged upwards. But Emily Dimmock was not mutilated in that part.

There is a drawing of a woman sleeping on a bed and a man standing looking at her. From behind the divide of his legs projects a knife, held in the hidden hand, and shaded dark. It is called *The Crisis*. The crisis is for the man.

Marjorie Lilly writes, of a visit to his studio: (9)

Alas, that I could see again, with the fuller knowledge that I now possess of his work, some of those drawings of long ago, which seem to have disappeared for ever! Their finer points escaped me but one black chalk sketch stabbed my spirit broad awake. A woman struggling on a bed, a faceless man with folded arms beside her lapped in shadow; a subject that Sickert had treated before and would treat again; but the terror conjured up by a few taut lines, the contrast of dark and light, were unforgettable. This was not a working note, to be squared up and enlarged as a picture afterwards, it was a drawing in its own right, the most dynamic Sickert sketch that I have seen. All the subsequent versions of it, such as *The Crisis* (circa 1909) seem clumsy by comparison. I thought of the sketch by David of Marie Antoinette in the tumbril on the way to the guillotine; this drawing had the same stark nightmare quality. It was a relief to turn for comfort to the quiet studio, the firelight and the kettle hissing on the hob, with a placid elderly gentlemen making the tea. Impossible to connect him with this savage explosion!

Yes indeed; that is the difficulty we all feel, Florence, Mother, Me.

The painting, *L'Affaire de Camden Town*, which, from the pose of the man, with folded arms, looks as though it had been made after the drawing, is frightening enough. What must the drawing have been like? Marjorie Lilly said he destroyed a lot of drawings and paintings while she knew him.

There are, however, pictures of earlier dates, dates preceding that of the Camden Town murder, which are peculiar. There is one called, *Le Journal*. A woman lies sprawling backwards against a sofa. A newspaper is in her hand; but she is not reading it. 'That woman is dead,' Sickert told his son, and pointed out to him that the paper is not being held by her above her head so that she could read it, but disappears behind her hair, which projects over it. Indeed, she looks dead, with her mouth open. [and a nurse says the skin colour is that of a corpse] It is perfectly obvious, yet has been missed by all the orthodox scholars, including Dr Wendy Baron, whose book appeared after Knight's, in which it was pointed out. Lillian Browse took it to have been painted in Venice, in 1904, because of its obvious resemblance to *Two Sketches of a Venetian Woman's head, 1903*. In the painting, *Le Journal*, the pose of the head resembles that of Catherine Eddowes in the police photograph, except that the line where her throat was cut has been replaced by a rope of pearls. In the two drawings, which seem to be of the same head, the line where the throat has been cut is un-camouflaged - especially in the lower one, where it is too nasty and jagged to permit of being taken for the edge of a lacy collar. Dr. Baron believes, because of the green and white striped sofa, that it was done in 1906, in Fitzroy Square, where (presumably because other pictures, known to have been done there, show it) there was a green and white striped sofa. That may be. He may, using the drawings of the two heads made in Venice, have built up the picture, later in Fitzroy Square. Wendy Baron says one of the difficulties with Sickert chronology is that a picture of a place was sometimes done after he had left it. It makes no difference. 1906 is still prior to the *Camden Town Murder*, and the heads three years prior to it. Wendy Baron said her friend Mrs Swinton the singer believed the picture to be of her. I cannot think he would have depicted a living woman as a dead one.

There are even some of the portraits of women I am not happy about. *The Lady in the Gondola*, leaning back with her eyes shut, is very beautiful, and may be asleep. But what are those two red weals on her cheeks? If they represent merely the angle of his brush-strokes, why are they not of the same sort of flesh-tone as the rest of the skin? Why are they red? Again, with *Giuseppina in a Lace Blouse*, there do seem to be weals on her cheek. Though less red, they are more lumpy, and have slight shadows to show the flesh raised. Guiseppina was not a professional model. On arrival in Venice Sickert asked his landlady to find a girl who would sit for him, but one feels she would have found one with better skin.

There is a disturbing nude, *La Hollandaise*. From the background of a darkened room, a heavily built woman sprawls across a bed and props herself up to look forwards. But she seems to have an enormous black moustache, or else animal's snout. As every artist knows the shadow beneath the nose is always important in any face, but the shape of it has to be observed carefully and the depth of the shadow estimated with regard to the depth of other shadows. Here, its intense brown-black exceeds that of the shadowed side of the face, and equals that of the darkest parts of the picture. Further, its shape is not that which would be cast by such a short nose, and it covers the whole of the upper lip, down to where one may presume the mouth to be, the mouth not being drawn, or the chin either. In the ear, and vertical high-light nearest to it, a faintly pink tone suffuses the putty which is the general colour of the flesh where it is in the light. The light on the lower jaw, however, seems to run too shallowly, so that the shadow that one would suppose to mark the underneath of the chin comes where one would expect the mouth to be, and no break in its formation is shown to indicate the fold, where the line from the base of the nose towards the corner of the mouth causes a change of plane. The effect is, therefore, that what seems to be shown is a dog's muzzle, the nose being, as dogs' noses are, black, and their chins almost nil.

If anybody says this effect must have been unintended, accidental, I would reply that we are dealing with a master of tonality. A half-trained student, lacking a good eye for tones, could, indeed, easily make the shadow beneath the nose so dark and huge as to create the impression either the lady had a moustache gummed to her upper lip, a moustache so long as to descend to cover the mouth (which would make it very difficult to eat), or, that she had been given the muzzle of a dog. But Sickert was a master craftsman; he insisted upon good drawing, as the *sine qua non* of a picture, and tonality was his forte. He could not make a mistake in the tonal values. It is as though one should say of a phrase in Shakespeare capable of conveying more than one meaning, that he could not have noticed it.

The eyes, too, are ambiguous. If the eyebrows are where they appear, then the oval lights should be the eyes, but not only have they no irises or pupils, they are not the greyish tints of the whites of the eyes in shadow, they are the light putty colour he uses for the flesh where fallen upon by the light. If it is meant to be the area between the cheekbone and the lower lid that has caught the light, there is no place for the eyeballs, for it goes up to the brows, and if it is meant to be the eyeballs, there is skin over them and she is - for all her alert expression - blind.

The Pictures

The near breast is of monstrous size, but where is the other? Looking at a black and white reproduction, one thinks that probably the bulbous thing on the left is the other breast, sticking out and away. In front of the original, in the Tate, one sees that his object is of the same bluish grey as the bolster, seen on the other side, and therefore part of it. Yet there is an eye-trick, for the markings on this part of the bolster are of a shape to suggest a nipple, although, when one looks closely, one sees that the further arm runs down between the body and this protuberance. In a nearby room in the Tate, a massive green *Woman* by Henry Moore shows a torso such that, by positioning oneself to view it from the angle *La Hollandaise* is viewed from, one can see where the other breast comes - high up, and of a volume proportionate to that of the near one. In *La Hollandaise*, the space taken up on the body by the one enormous breast is leaving no room for the other, and the lighting could not be as shown - could not pick it out so brightly and not lighten that deep shadow under the nose. Knight writes, '*La Hollandaise* is an abomination.' I find that word not too strong. It certainly is a hideous thing. Whether, as Knight believes, the nose has been cut off (but then it could not throw so deep a shadow) or it is a dogs', there is something else, which concerns the legs.

I mention their slashed appearance with some hesitancy, because it was a dictum of Sickert that when depicting a long narrow object, the strokes should run across and not along the form. This gives it strength and prevents a weedy look. On a limb, it emphasizes the rotundity at the expense of the length. Nevertheless, he has not done it on the arms of this figure. On the arm that is in the light, the strokes run along the form, not across it, and the result is enormously to emphasize the legs, which they do run across. There is a fine, rounded thigh, yes, but what worries is the lower leg, where, near the ankle, a shading-line goes right through it, so that not only is the foot separated from the leg but the line of the shin projects over the instep, as if there were a fold. One could think of the folds in rhinosceros-hide but what I cannot help being reminded of is the police photograph of Mary Kelly's remains, where one sees the great fold of the skin, flayed from the lower leg and rolled back. The white fold just above the knee, in the painting, is just at the point from which the folding back begins on the flayed limb.

Another picture, *Nuit d'Eté*, shows what is meant to be a luxurious nude sprawled on a bed. but her cheek and nose have been most cruelly slashed. And what is that line or slit running from above the pubis to the right of her throat? Can it be an opening in a bed-jacket or negligée? There are no folds to suggest the presence of any kind of clothing. That woman has nothing on. The opening is in her flesh. There was nothing like that in the Camden Town murder: Emily Dimmock's throat was cut and that was all. This looks like the police photograph of Catherine Eddowes, the cheek and nose slashed from the same direction, and the long slit from above the pubis to the right of the throat. Yet that photograph was not publicly available until reproduced in Daniel Farson's book, *Jack the Ripper*, in 1972. Both these nudes are dated by Wendy Baron c. 1906, that is, before the Camden Town murder. They are said to have been drawn from the same model, but how could breasts so enormous as in *La Hollandaise* have gone to nothing, as in *Nuit d'Eté*, unless they had been removed? In *La Belle Gatée,* the man is sitting on the bed, with the woman's upturned throat over his knees, his hands bearing down. He looks as though he is strangling her.

In all these bedroom pictures the man is clothed, the woman naked. Where both are clothed, as in *Preoccupation, Off to the Pub* and, of course, *Ennui,* they look away from each other. All these are presentations of non-relationships - the very opposite of Rodin's sculpted couples who so plainly delight in one another.

I also find disturbing the painting which used to be called *Girl Reading* but which Dr. Baron thinks ought to be called *Girl Doing Embroidery.* I think she is right, for there is no book and the attitudes of the hand would be more natural in embroidery. She is posed *contre jour*, and the white light from the window behind her falls upon the back of her chair and the top of her head. But what are all those patches of red? Lillian Browse seems to think they are just for fun. In any other artist it might be so. But in Sickert - red patches about the head and neck and over the breast, where they could be blood coming through the blouse? If one compares it with the justly admired portrait of *Victor Lecour*, also posed *contre jour*, the white light from the garden behind him falls on his dark blue suit, creating patches of light blue, and comes slightly round the other side of him. A patch of yellow may suggest afternoon sunlight. All that, though effective, is natural. But I do not believe in a red light, throwing patches of red on to that girl in such sinister patches, and what is that red around her feet. Is it the trimmed border to her skirt? The shape is that of intestines.

How did he get away with it? He got away with it under the label of Impressionism. Not that he was strictly an Impressionist. The Impressionists were a group of painters who believed in using only the colours that could be seen in the rainbow: no tertiary colours or black. They were more interested in catching the transient effects of the play of light than in the abiding form, and put on paint in little touches, so that the light danced in between, and the whole effect - as in Monet's *Impression, Soleil Levant* (which gave its name to the movement) or Sisley's *Misty Morning* - is atmospheric and shimmering. None of the strict Impressionists, Monet, Morrisot or Sisley, used lines. They felt that the eye did not see in lines. Sickert, following Degas, who was already doing something different, reintroduced lines. Both were essentially draughtsmen. But Sickert worked mainly in the tertiary colours, browns, greys, ochres, abhorred by the Impressionists. Yet he did keep with the Impressionists in applying his paint in very small touches - not in all of his pictures but in some of them, which gives to them a mottled look. But really his affinity is with Hogarth. He shares his zest for the vulgar. And Hogarth's *Shrimp Girl* is really a tonal study. Incidentally, the Impressionists were mainly landscapists. Their occasional nudes are decently posed. It is Sickert who gives us the lewd, open crotch studies.

He did three portraits entitled *Mrs Barrett*. Joseph Sickert told Knight his father had told him they were really of Mary Kelly, although she was long dead when they were done.

Lillian Browse refers to 'several of the charwoman, Mrs Barrett, of the Camden Town period.' All I can say is, she does not look like a charwoman to me. He may have called her that, to people who asked whom these paintings represented. It was unpleasing to notice, in Joseph Sickert's TV statement, that his father had referred to Mary Kelly as 'a servant.' The picture she reproduces is very beautiful, but I find it the most frightening portrait of a woman I know - the eyes, almost hidden within the deep shadow cast by the hat's large brim, just glinting out. Is this how the murderer saw her, in the second before he reduced her from a living, highly individual personality, to meat? Wendy Baron believes *Le Collier de Perles* also to represent her. If so, the upswept, massy hair reveals a good forehead, balancing the broad chin and strong nose. In the profile, Mrs Barrett the dark lashes, veiling her eyes, in the pale face, that are emphasized, the forehead being obscured by the hair's being combed forward in a bang - much as one sees it in the police portrait of Mary Kelly, put together by their artists from the verbal descriptions of her obtained from her neighbours in the East End.

In the pastel, entitled *Blackmail, Mrs Barrett*, she sits in a chair, the hair as in the *Le Collier de Perles*, combed out on the left in a wing, but one hand raised to her face, pensively, perhaps putting forward an idea. But there is something peculiar about the lower part of her face. That the mouth is not rendered, except for a few scratchy lines, I would not take as conclusively showing mutilation, in an artist who did often draw very sketchily. He could be just making a few shading lines to show that the lower part of the face recedes. It is rather the shape of the end of the nose and its distance from the mouth that seems sinister to me. It looks extremely short, the distance from the root of the nostrils to the mouth being much greater than that from the mouth to the chin which it could hardly be even if the head were tilted forward, almost as great as the distance from the tip of the nose to its junction with the forehead at the level of the corneas. Now that is not natural. It makes an extraordinarily long expanse of upper lip beneath the holes - of which surely one would not see so much, the head being tilted so as to show so much of the crown and so little of the chin - unless the real end to the nose, which would have obscured the nostrils, had been cut off, so that what one is seeing is not nostrils - in a short pig-snouted face - but the holes left by the dismemberment, higher up. As the other pictures of her show, she had a perfectly good nose, even a strong one. In a version in the Tate where the head is at almost the same tilt, the tip obscures the nostrils, as it would.

There is a small group of pictures of much later date that asks for some comment. All were painted in 1929. *The Raising of Lazarus*, according to the memory of Cicely Hey, the model for Lazarus's sister, was born of the spectacle presented when a lay figure he was given was being carried up the stairs one person at either end of it, holding it. He had photographs taken, with himself posing for both Lazarus and Christ. That seems clear.

But then, *Lazarus Breaks His Fast* seems to follow on from that. Again, he is the model for Lazarus, and had himself photographed for it. He is sitting at a table, raising a spoon to his mouth. According to Knight, who had it from Joseph Sickert, 'the painter said the picture was a veiled accusation of Gull, who had induced unconsciousness in the victims by feeding them poisoned grapes.'

This is very odd. I have already discarded the coach story, and I should have thought it would be almost more difficult to prevail upon a completely strange woman to eat grapes than to kill her outright. There is, indeed, a letter of Gull, reproduced by Knight, saying he did not eat cane sugar but found grape sugar a source of energy and so took raisins about with him. But what Lazarus is eating does not look like grapes. One does not, in any case, eat grapes with a spoon. If they are raisins, they are unusually large and plump, and one would not need a spoon to eat them with. They look to me like prunes. He is having breakfast - breaking his fast - with stewed prunes, which he is using a dessert spoon to raise from the bowl to his mouth. But Lazarus did not fast. He died. After he had been brought back to life, he would presumably resume the practice of eating, but one does of think of Lazarus as having fasted. That notion applies more to John the Baptist. Again, Lazarus did not sit in his shirt-sleeves at a modernly furnished table in a modernly furnished room. Lillian Browse writes: (16)

It is improbable that Sickert turned devout in his old age; the more likely explanation is that he saw himself in a patriarchal light...

She will be thinking here of the next picture, which she links with it. This is simply a self-portrait, but entitled *The Servant of Abraham*. Abraham was a patriarch. But Sickert was not. He was not the generator of a prodigious family, and had no legitimate children at all. Wendy Baron perhaps strikes deeper when she writes:(17)

It is possible his obsession with Lazarus reborn from the dead had something to do with the birth of Richard Sickert from the dead Walter.

This is something we first heard about from Sir Osbert Sitwell(18)

He began to like a square beard more than a pointed, in the same way that he altered his signature, suddenly convinced that Richard was a much more pleasing name than Walter, that there was thus reason in being Richard and none in being Walter.

The Pictures

For an established artist to change his persona with his signature is an impossibility, for everyone knows him under the old one. Sitwell, therefore, regarded this as a caprice. Wendy Baron, however, comments: (19)

His adoption of the name Richard in later life may not have been a mere caprice. It could evidence a deep desire to change his identity.

Yes. I think so. Wendy Baron had no inkling of anything in his past that was sinister. She thinks of it just that Sickert was fed up with Walter Sickert and his battles with paint and with the public. Richard Sickert was a new persona, the grand old man of English painting, well loved and respected...' (20)

Yes, now he was loved and respected, but I think he had more than his battles with paint and with the public - his battles to become established - to want to put behind him. One's name is very much part of one, and to want to change it seems to show a deep discontent with oneself. Mathilde Carré, former Resistant, sentenced by the Bench for having allowed herself to be 'turned around' by the Germans after they arrested her, born to non-believing parents had never been christened. During the twelve years she spent in prison, she came to long to be received into the church, and asked for baptism - but not with the name Mathilde, with the name, Lily. A new name, for a new born person, all innocent. I feel it may have been so with Sickert.

What else is there about Abraham? Abraham was dynastic, the father of all of us. One could hardly say Sickert was dynastic. All three of his marriages were childless. The only dynasty he cared about was that of the royal family.

I had better re-read my Bible. We finish with his being willing to sacrifice Isaac in Genesis XII. There was no servant in that. But in Genesis XIV, we do come to a servant of Abraham. The context is, moreover, very interesting. Abraham, being old and near to death, makes his servant swear to him that he will not marry his son Isaac to any of the daughters of the Canaanites, amongst whom they dwelt, but go to Mesopotamia and choose for him a worthy bride. The faithful servant does this, and brings back Rebekah, a virgin damsel of virtue, whom he presents to Isaac and she becomes by him the mother of thousands.

The servant, then, had a double role. He had firstly to negate the possibility of Isaac's marrying unworthily. Do we recognize something here? It was not Sickert who put aside Annie Crook. That was the role he ascribed to Gull, and yet he regarded himself as in some way acting as the servant of Gull, on behalf of the royal family.

To coincide with the opening of the exhibition of Sickert's works at the Tate Gallery of the North, in Liverpool, there was, on 28 September 1989, a feature on Sickert in 'The Late Show' on BBC2. The presenter, who appeared to regard this as Sickert's finest work, for he reserved it to the end, attempted to interpret the riddling title. Summarizing the role of the servant of Abraham, he said, 'He secured the succession.' Yes!

The speaker, attempting to apply this to the artist's role, said that having learnt from Degas to paint in the Impressionist style, he brought it to England, and thus ensured the succession of the Impressionist style of painting from France to England.

That is what I would call a brave try, by an art critic unaware of Sickert's obsession with the British Royal Family.

I think it is another of the riddling pictures Florence spoke of. In his mind, he had secured the succession, by putting aside Mary Kelly and those women friends of hers to whom she had imparted her knowledge of the scandalous liaison between the Heir Presumptive and a woman unfit to be Queen, which would have rocked England, and so cleared the way for his honourable engagement to Princess Mary of Teck (who, when because of his death she married his brother George, became our venerated Queen Mary).

He made a painting of *King George and Queen Mary* in the carriage in which they drove through he streets on their Jubilee procession. He did not see this. I did. It was in Oxford Street, and the crowds who had waited to see them pass afterwards broke from the pavements into the road, linked hands and forming into circles danced round and round, chanting, 'Knees up, knees up, knees up, Mother Brown!' I also saw the painting at its first exhibition, along with others to commemorate the Jubilee, in the Leicester Square Galleries. I went with my mother. It was very fine, but we were quite aware it had been done from a photograph, which he had seen, as we all had, in a newspaper. Half of Queen Mary's head was cut off by the frame holding the glass window panes of the carriage. Knight understood from Joseph Sickert that his father had said this was in memory of half of her still belonging to Clarence, to whom she had been first engaged. I think Knight imagined the symbolical composition had been the artist's own, not realizing he found it in a newspaper photograph. The fact that it was a 'found' composition does not, however, take away from the interest of what Sickert was reading into it. He was still thinking of the old drama, still feeling it was he who had paved the way for this worthy splendour.

In *The Servant of Abraham*, the great self-portrait - great in all senses, for it is much more than life-size - he is looking at himself critically and enquiringly. It is a very odd portrait, for the eyes are not properly aligned. Inability to align two eyes is a fault he attributes to Cezanne. Yet I cannot think of a picture by the French artist in which they are so conspicuously out of alignment as here. Moreover they are not looking in the same direction. The one on the left is rolled upwards, which the one on the right is not. I am not pointing to these inexactitudes in the drawing as faults. In a way that is difficult to describe, they add to the undoubted power of the picture. It is uncomfortable, as well as being great. It is not a hostile self-portrait. It think that he is, in all sincerity, trying to assess what he had done in his life and to weigh his deserts with an even hand: he had painted many pictures, some of them good, he had

The Pictures

taught innumerable students, he had killed five women, protected the honour of the royal family and secured the succession.

That this was never in danger, that Clarence had no intention of marrying Annie Crook and that whatever Mary Kelly had gone about saying would have made no difference whatever to the Royal Family and certainly not have brought the succession to an end, is irrelevant.

It was so in his mind, in that deepest and most private part of his mind that he could share with no one. He had dealt with a situation; encapsulating it, he said he was the Servant of Abraham.

And yet, how far was that service pure and not the excuse for indulgence of a personal urge? The murders were not sexual in the strict sense, for in no case were the parts between the legs the focus of attack. Yet the taste for blood is addictive. The sadistic murderer repeats.

How did he manage to stop himself? I think there are two factors; he was of a sufficient intellectual and moral calibre to want to; and, because he was an artist, when the urges to re-live the old excitement came upon him, he was able to transfer them to canvas.

1 *The Camden Town Murder,* Sir John Napley (Weidenfeld, 1987), p 140
2 *Sickert,* Wendy Baron (Phaidon, 1973), p 114, n4
3 Knight, p 255
4 Lilly, p 47
5 Browse, p 76
6 Baron, pp 110-111
7 Baron, p 115, n. 26
8 Lilly, p 47
9 Ibid p 16
10 Knight, p 257
11 Baron, p 340
12 Baron, p 338
13 Knight, p 255-256
14 Baron, p 347-348
15 Knight, p 250
16 Browse, p 61
17 Baron, p 171
18 Sitwell, p xix
19 Baron, p 170
20 Baron, pp 120-121

Chapter 8
The Writings

None of those who have written about Sickert knew him deeply. Neither is that their fault. Emmons wrote:(1)

> He approached the denizens of both his worlds with the same gentle courtesy; but there was always a limit beyond which he never stepped, nor would allow others to step. An underlying reserve prevented anyone who might have been inclined from taking liberties with his friendship. An unwarranted demand would be met in a flash of coldness, even of harshness. The 'serpent lay dormant in the basket of figs.' Sometimes, when a mood of depression or misanthropy caught him, he would remain invisible for weeks at a time, then suddenly reappear, as gay and debonnair as ever: entertaining his friends...overflowing with cordiality...

And again: (2)

> That it pleased him to lead double or even treble lives may be admitted; that he was often undependable, flippant and inconsistent, likewise; and that an apparent courtesy sometimes covered a masked but grinning snare.

When Emmons speaks of his double or treble worlds or lives, he means to refer only to his commutations between people of his own educational background and the uneducated working people of London and Dieppe, but 'grinning snare' is strong and strange.

And again: (3)

> Sickert, so generous in every other respect, of time, of attentions, of things, yet retained one thing he could not give - himself.

Emmons attributes it to 'the kind of selfishness peculiar to some artists...in which everything is sacrificed to the art.' An artist - or a writer, poet or composer - needs, obviously, to be left alone while in the throes of creativity, but such a bottling up of the emotions as not to be able to give of the self, is not a usual hallmark of artists. Van Gogh, for all his rages, gave of himself, and gave and gave.

Emmons writes of the peculiarly insulting manner in which Sickert tendered his resignation from the Royal Academy, asking the President to spend the day with him at a place where he was staying in the country and saying nothing about it, but posting it from the station after seeing him off: 'the serpent in the basket of figs - Boreas after Zephyr'.(4)

That serpent in those figs haunted Emmons, for he brings them in for a third time:(5)

> Always smiling, brotherly and paying compliments, as if he were addressing women of great charm. But he kept his distance, there was an impenetrable zone created by his politeness - the serpent lay dormant in the basket of figs.

This is the man seen from the outside. He had - for what I think are obvious reasons - no confidant, and feared any kind of relationship in which an exchange of confidences was expected, or which, by holing his armour plating of superficial courtesy, let out emotions of a violence he would not be able to stop.

Hoping to strike upon some deeper traits, I read through the whole of his art criticism, collected by Sitwell. It is not that one expects to find a confession of a murder in a review of an exhibition, but, in the way he reviews the work of others, a man discloses much of himself. Also, imagery can be revealing. Would there be any imagery?

It was not time wasted, for I did come, to a considerable degree, to know him through these writings. On the whole, he strove to be fair to his contemporaries and rivals, even when he did not like them, though there were a good many serpents among the figs.

As I read, I marked a few things with which I agreed or disagreed. It opens with his reaction against Whistler, whose apprentice and pupil he had been: His *Miss Alexander* is 'A bad picture, *Lachons le mot,* badly composed, badly drawn, badly painted.'(6) I have always thought so! In spite of having taken an incredible seventy sittings. All the same, Whistler's *Old Battersea Bridge* was one of the things I fell in love with on my first visit to the Tate, when I was sixteen, and I still think of it as one of the loveliest of all pictures. This and the other *Nocturnes*, Sickert tells us, were not done on the river bank, but after long looking, from memory, back in the studio. That may explain that atmospheric simplification of the pattern that is so effective, the elimination of inessentials.

Sickert was very much against the revolution of Monet and Cezanne in taking their easels out into the open air - where the sun moves and the shapes of the lights and shadows alters all the time (though the *plein-airists* had their ways of coping with this). His idols were Millet and Degas. He deplores several times the English pronunciation of his name as DAY-gas; it should be deGAS'. Also, he greatly admires Pissaro. That he seems to prefer him to Monet is probably because he is a little more solid. He also admired Gauguin for his sculptural quality.

He appreciated the classical draughtsmanship of Ingres. But:(7)

The nude corresponds to nothing in our modern habit of life. With all his powers of draughtsmanship, when Ingres essayed, in *Le bain turc*, a composition consisting entirely of nude figures, the effect is trivial, and a little absurd.

Yes, that is just it - and the art schools (as he says) make one spend so much time drawing from the nude, which is wasted - though he found his own, hideous use for it.

He stresses the historical continuity of art:(8)

We who know Poussin, can see how Degas follows on, normally, naturally, in most conservative order. We can see Camille Pissaro evolve from Corot gradually...

Yes, but these reflections lead him to assert, 'There is no modern art.' I disagree. I feel the exhibition of 1874 launched something new, and that it is not by coincidence that while Monet was teaching himself and others to work only with the colours of the spectrum and apply in small particles so that the light danced between, Madame Blavatsky, far away, was explaining, to a different group of people, the auric colours, the seven rays and the insubstantiality of matter. In a period when science was at its most materialistic, it was suddenly the moment for teaching there was no such thing as solid matter, that all was moving atoms, vibrations, living colour that was the spiritual side of things.

Has Sickert any special attitude to women? Not as regards women artists. Berthe Morrisot is appreciated by him. Her *Bords de Rivière* has 'sacred atmosphere of delicate intensity...exquisite illumination..'(9) Courbet's storm points the contrast. Berthe Morrisot is strong because she is penetrated by the beauty of the scene, while Courbet's *Storm* makes an impression of lamentable weakness.

His praise of Thérèse Lessore's work seems almost exaggerated - and was written years before she became his third wife.

When he thinks of women, who are not artists, as evaluators of art, he begins however, to get chauvinistic: (10)

Women are interested in art when it ministers to their vanity, as in the flattering portrait...Women are interested in landscapes that represent scenes where they would like to be, alone, or in sympathetic society. They are interested in optimistic presentations of life, in which the figures represented are given sympathetic parts, in which they 'look nice'...

As a matter of fact, there is a grain of truth in this. The preference of women for landscape - of which he complains not here alone but elsewhere as well - possibly derives in part from their being so confined by housework as to want some reminder of the sweet fresh air of out of doors in open spaces - hence the popularity of prints of Cezanne's *Mont St. Victoire* for the house. Of course, he is complaining that they do not buy genre pictures of the sort that he paints. But why should they?

It is only fair to mention that he considers the language of art as tending to be unintelligible not only to women but to young men, for: (11)

The appreciation of art is a matter of long preparation, of many preludes, that it comes as a cumulative revelation...There is no *coup de foudre*, in the understanding of art, no love at first sight.

Here I disagree totally. It has always been the *coup de foudre* with me, with the Botticelli *Venus*, with the Van Gogh *Cornfields* with the Franz Marc *Red Horses*, with the Paul Nash *Wood on the Downs*, Durer's *Large Piece of Turf*. It is love at first sight, or it is nothing.

Whoever loved but loved not at first sight?

One can, subsequently to the first sight, learn things about the painter, his times, his forerunners, the influences that played upon him or against which he reacted but can that increase the love of the picture which is total at first impact? It can add interest, but of a different order, biographical or historical, academic. It has nothing to do with the fact that the picture succeeds for one or it does not.

The Writings

Sickert's mind is indeed very literary, linear, conservative. He feels the continuum. He has spoken with an elderly person who spoke, when very young, with a then elderly figure from a world that now seems to have receded into history, yet is present, as all the ages are present through such chains of contact...

He does become resentful of, even spiteful about, women as non-buyers of what he considers the best work, He has even invented a character: supergoose: (12)

Painters...my brothers...Cease to look to the super-goose for your bread. To begin with, she is always overdrawn. Look in the chophouses of the city for some pearl of an elderly business man...

That is good humoured. This is less so:(13)

...we occidentals have already long been living under a goosocracy. A walk through the Royal Academy or any of the exhibitions brings this fact home to us pretty clearly. An appreciable fraction of the painters of the day wear the livery of this fair despotism. It is a government of beings in matinée hats, that hates art as it hates all realities, as it hates work, childhood, home, maturity, literature, thought, and for which of course, pain, old age and death do not exist.

Yes, he means women.

A number of fashionable portrait painters, he alleges, have: (14)

taken the goose's shilling. The required ideal...is a ravishing hat, for the description of which I must refer you to abler and more *sächverstandig* pens. A little face, for the description of which I am forced reluctantly into the French - museau...

Museau means literally, muzzle. Does that explain *La Hollandaise* - the woman's apparent dog's muzzle?

He is irritated that women commission pictures by Sargeant:

At the Royal Academy he observed: (15)

A radiant supergoose standing in front of a sketch by Mr Sargeant entitled *Cypresses*. Standing quite close...and peering into some slabs of white paint that at a proper distance resolve themselves into a spirited *pocharde* of bullocks, she murmured with conviction and pathos, 'Marvellous! Simply marvellous!' That there might be no mistake, I wrote those words down on the spot in the margin of my catalogue. Now I am quite convinced that at the distance at which your ladyship was standing from the wall the painting can have conveyed nothing at all to her untutored intelligence.

And, still on the subject of Sargeant: (16)

When the supergoose pays the piper, she has a right to call the tune. In the duel between the painter and the supergoose, it is the supergoose who comes out top dog.

Well yes, Some artists prefer not to undertake portraits, for that reason.

He even invents opinions for the supergoose attributing to her an attack upon what is good. After averring (*New Age*, 14 March 1914), that modern painters will have to learn to draw again a head like Millet's of Theodore Rousseau, he adds: (17)

I can hear the objection that the devil's advocate, always most admirably represented in the most perfect, and therefore the most slipshod, form by the supergoose of the tea-table, will put forward: 'But, Mr Sickert, is not Millet's *Head of Rousseau* uncommonly like many bad and smudgy art-school drawings...have you not for years been recommending to all your students the purchase of Mr Neville Lytton's half-crown book on water-colour? Surely the most important water-colour paints of both Prout and Gallow are at variance with such recommendation!' (I have had, for reasons of space, to make my supergoose talk intelligently. I admit that she is, for once, dramatically a failure).

'Madame, Millet's *Head of Rousseau* is, at first glance, astonishingly reminiscent of the worst type of dull art-school head. But some of us have time for more than a first glance...'

There has been no progress, only decadence in water-colour art since the early Turners and the early Gertins...I will make this the subject of a future essay. Meanwhile, Mr. Neville Lytton's book continues the perfect and complete statement of our case.

Half a crown! Will she buy it? Not she!

Note that woman, here, is hated not as artistically uneducated - she knows the names - but because she will not appreciate and will not buy what he wills she should. And seven years later, in the *Burlington Magazine*, of October 1922: (18)

Protestantism and the increasing jealousy of women have killed both classic figure subjects and conversation pieces. The walls of the house beautiful have been blasted by the fair sex. Herself bedaubed, she has successfully driven her painted rivals from the canvas, and a mediatised army of occupation, called by courtesy 'landscape', holds a melancholy and transitional sway. Not ever, be it noted, landscape with figures, as in the Caracci or Turner. If the subject be Venetian, not only is the gondolier songless, he isn't there at all....

Come to think of it, Cezanne's *Mont St Victoire*, Van Gogh's *Cornfield with Cypresses* and even Hobbema's forever graceful and gracious *Avenue at Midelharnis*, prints of which have found their way onto the walls of many homes, by the woman's introduction or by her permission, are landscapes without figures.

It is a new offence, I did not know women were blamed for.

They probably do not go much for Sickert's interiors with figures.

There is a strange little etching reproduced by Sitwell, entitled *Café Royal - the Barnacle*. At first sight, one sees only what appears to be a woman seated at a table, leaning and craning her neck somewhat forward, her raised hand ending in two pincers. But what is that dark, beak-shaped thing that projects from behind her face? Can it be something accidental in the background? It is too dark and definite for that. Is it the far side of the brim of her hat, as it curves round her face? No, it is so much blacker than the near side. And why is the picture called *The Barnacle*? Has she got a prodigiously large barnacle fitted over her forehead and nose? The effect is that of a bird's beak, and her face, dominated by it, seems to fall away to nothing. The strange case that must be meant to represent a hat, stretches so far back as to give the impression of not being fitted to the head, or that the head and neck continue in one unbroken line. The whole effect is that she has not a human but a long-necked bird's head and neck. A goose's. That is it. She is super-goose. Sitwell, who has been at pains to choose his illustrations from among Sickert's least offensive, cannot have understood - nor Thérèse Lessore, who passed the proofs of the illustrations. (Neither Browse nor Baron has anything to say about it).

It will be noticed that in all these references the woman is not a frail figure but a dominating one: beneath her reign he feels dominated by brute stupidity.

Dislike of womens' judgment in art hardly renders murderous. I did, however, find one thing that startled me. It comes in his review, for the *New Age*, of 28 May 1914, of the Exhibition of Twentieth-Century Art at the Whitechapel Art Gallery. To this there was, apparently, an informative catalogue, which advised visitors how to view the artists in groups:(19)

Influences being mutual and reagent in their nature, I am not even called upon to protest against the classification of a whole group of moderns as influenced by myself and Lucien Pissaro. That whole group might, perhaps, more correctly, be described as being students of the great Impressionist group.

He had taught Gore one thing, which he himself had been taught by Whistler, not to block out the 'general idea' of a picture first, but to start from the point that most interests one, a selected focus, and work outwards from that.(20) But Gore (he had earlier remarked) had learned from Steer, who had learned from Monet. To have been a pupil of Whistler meant, to have been at one remove of a pupil of Courbet, and at two removes from Corot, while there had been interaction between the two Pissaros, Camille and Lucien.

For these reasons, he modestly declined having been of so much importance in the formation of this new group of British artists. Furthermore, he adds a caution concerning the wisdom of following so closely in the wake of any others, as merely to be copying his style instead of from the real world of nature: (21)

The realist has over the derivative painter this advantage. The realist is incessantly provisioning himself from the inexhaustible and comfortable cupboard of nature. The derivative romantic, on the other hand, can hardly expect such varied and nutritious fare if he restricts himself to the mummies he can find in another man's Blue-Beard closet.

Blue-Beard's closet! Blue-Beard was Gilles de Rais, in whose castle were found the remains of his victims, murdered long ago. Even the meaning of the sentence is not instantly transparent. If it is, that the pictures of his upon which the moderns are modelling their style are in a style he himself had abandoned, long ago, - as, for instance, when he jettisoned the influence of Whistler for that of Degas - that could have been said more clearly. Blue-Beard suggests something unpleasant and why 'mummies'? That suggests long dead corpses, wrapped up and not meant to be seen again. The exhibition was in Whitechapel. To review it, he had had to go back there, where the sight of streets he knew too well re-opened the door of his own Blue-Beard closet.

1 Emmons, p 79
2 Ibid, p 85

3 Ibid, p 86
4 Ibid, p 289
5 ibid, p 290
6 Sitwell, p 17
7 Ibid, p 113
8 Ibid, p 27
9 Ibid, p 160
10 Ibid, pp 90-1
11 Ibid, p 91
12 Ibid, p 35
13 Ibid, p 69
14 Ibid, p 70
15 Ibid, p 73
16 Ibid, p 76
17 Ibid, p 121
18 Ibid, p 251
19 Ibid, p 278
20 Ibid, p 4
21 Ibid, p 280

Chapter 9

Excursus Concerning Art

Does my suspicion concerning Sickert alter my estimation of his art, and should it do? These are two questions I have been asking myself. There is a school that says a work of art is a thing in itself, to be valued purely aesthetically, without reference to any meaning in it, and that one should not need or wish to know anything about its creator. I have been trying to trace the lineage of this idea, and find two main rootstocks. The earliest is Théophile Gautier, in numerous of his writings, but perhaps radically in his poem, 'L'Art', 1852,(1) implying that as an ancient sculpted head survives the civilization in which lived the artist who produced it, so art should be pursued not for any social aim but simply for art's sake. He did not come out with this unprovoked. It was his counter-blast to the moralizing tendency of Victor Hugo, in particular to his suggestion that the drama - and by extension of the idea, any art - should be the vehicle of a national, social and human mission.(2) It was Gautier's counter-declaration which was accepted by the French group of symbolist poets, and, through Baudelaire, and Stéphane Mallarmé, came to influence artists. It crossed the channel to enjoy a flowering in the expressed attitudes of Pater, Wilde, Beerbohm and their circle, and again spilled into the visual arts. The other rootstock, which may have been a subsidiary of the first, seems to have been Roger Fry's prescription, in 1912, when presenting the second of his exhibitions introducing the work of the great French Post Impressionists (a term coined by him) to the English, that art should concern itself with colour, mass, volume rhythm and space, and not be 'literary' or seek to tell a story.(3) This dictum seems to have had an effect on artists out of all proportion to what might have been expected. I think it must have been after the Second World War that these same dicta were being relayed by John Farley to students at the Central School of Arts and Crafts. It was, of course, a trend annoying to Sickert, whose art was always literary and story-telling and who mocked the notion that art should not be of or about anything.

Where do I stand? A work of art is a thing in itself, yes. When I was first taken to the Louvre, by my mother, when I was thirteen, and we came to a flight of wide stairs, atop which was unexpectedly a marble statue with wings thrown back - the *Winged Victory of Samothrace*. I was so breath-taken by the glory, by the movement of the wind in those wings, that - no more than if the missing head had been found and stuck on - could anything I might be told about it have added to my exultation. A work of art makes its own impact; but in the case of a sculpture of antiquity, perforce, because we do not know anything about who sculpted it. Should some incredible archaeological find endow the sculptor with a name and biography, it would be difficult not to take that into account. Where something is known of the author, we feel our understanding to be enriched.

I agree that a painter must be concerned with colour and rhythm. However good the intention, poor composition, poor colour and absence of rhythm will not allow a work to come over well. Yet I do not want those things alone. Mondrian and Ben Nicholson are pleasing enough, yet, because their abstracts are not of or about anything they do not really stir us. Deliberate attempts to make art bear a message, moral or social, so falsify the springs of creation as to end in sentimentality or bathos, however.

Yet it is a fact that works of art have *pari passu* resonance with one plane or another. I have heard Hélène Bouvard - whose clairvoyant perceptions transpire through her poems - say that the music of Manuel de Falla vibrates to the highest spiritual levels, but that that of Wagner, despite its pull, has a certain linkage to the underworld, that can make it dangerous. There was a piece of Grieg's incidental music to *Peer Gynt* - which I did not altogether dislike - which my mother used to play, but with caution, as it was known to have lowered some peoples' temperature to below normal. I do not know that she actually believed in trolls, but while she played there was a suspension of disbelief to the extent that she did not want to bring them into the room. The first time I heard Bach, I felt there were choirs of angels in the stream of sound.

Pictures, though the seeing takes only an instant, can affect for a lifetime. I was sixteen when, on a visit to Florence, in the Uffizi galleries, I left my mother sitting down for a while on a bench and wandered on, and found myself alone in a small room, in which there was only one picture, of a girl, who looked no older than me, yet whose eyes held all wisdom, as she stood, naked in candour and grace, in an enormous cockle shell. Alone with this surprising and wonderful thing, the breath was so nearly taken out of me that, though marvelling and puzzling at the strangeness of the concept, it was some moments before I could sufficiently collect myself to step up near enough to read the words beneath that might give the answer: *La nascita di Venere* da Sandro Botticelli. I had never seen it in reproduction before thus finding myself alone with the original, and almost taken out of myself. Literal comprehension came only secondarily: Venus - Aphrodite - was born from the sea, that must be why the artist set her feet amongst waves.

Later I learned that my experience had been paralleled by that of Victor Neuburg, poet and mystic. He was only six when he saw, hanging in a house he had been taken to visit, a reproduction of Botticelli's *Primavera* and so nearly came out of himself that it seemed to connect him with something that happened before he was born. This experience was renewed when he was twelve, sitting in a doctor's waiting-room and turning the pages of a magazine on the table, wherein he came for the second time on a reproduction of this incredible picture. The impact on him was so profound that it affected his whole life, for the painted girl strewing the flowers breathed to him of something he was never able to find in any flesh and blood woman.

Notice that though his experience and mine related to different pictures, both were painted by the same artist, and neither of us knew, at the time of the first encounter, that Botticelli had belonged to the circle of Marsilio Ficino, the scholar and mystic who taught the philosophy of Plato to the Renaissance, and therefore certainly intended in his pictures to convey what Plato meant by the higher love.(4)

Turner's and Monet's last paintings - the Turners in which sun, sea and mist seem to be almost all that there is and all boundaries lost, and *Les nymphes*, in which there is practically nothing but the sunlight reflected in the surface of his water-lily pool in which Monet gazed until he went blind - seem to belong to that threshold at which, from the plane of higher intellectual mentation there is a craving to pass - a passing - to the Buddhic plane and the state of nirvana, into which, consciously or unconsciously, both artists must have hoped the death of their bodies would give them entry. Both are in the spiritual key of Wordsworth's 'Ode on Intimations of Immortality'. For Turner the sun was God. For Monet it was the light of the sun; for Van Gogh the sun and the moon and the stars.

Lady Emily Lutyens has told us of an occasion the eighteen year old Krishnamurti was, on coming upon a picture of Buddha in *Myths of the Hindus and Buddhists*, so affected that, as if unable to stand it, he rushed from the room, but then came back again, saying he had had a vision of Buddha.(5) Now this interested me, because there are two paintings of Buddha in that book,(6) both by Abanindro Nath Tagore, one, *The Victory of Buddha*, the frontispiece, and one, *Buddha as Mendicant,* and Vilyat Inayat Khan, son of the Sufi teacher, told me during the war that he was profoundly affected by both, but chiefly by the latter, which he scarcely dared to look at, as it always made him feel as though he were going to faint.

Pictures have, then, like music and poetry, enormous powers to affect us. Where does that leave Sickert?

I said Sickert was not my favourite artist, but neither is he my particular abomination. That title would have to go to Hieronymus Bosch. Amongst the Moderns, the Surrealists seem - with a few honourable exceptions - each to live isolated from the outside world within his own particular private hell. The only Surrealist picture I really admire is that magnificent eagle which is also a mountain and a wave, by René Magritte, perplexingly entitled *The Domain of Arnheim* - 1962, and perhaps one or two of Max Ernst's, but he had been under the influence of the healthier *Blaue Reiter* (Blue Rider) school. When I went to the 1936 Surrealist Exhibition at Burlington House, I felt it was in the main diseased. When I came to a large, greenish portrait of a woman, beautiful except that where her mouth should be were only insects, I withdrew from it as a thing of evil. Why is it that the Dali, even after all these years - for I have never seen it in reproduction - seems to me more quintessentially evil than Sickert's murder pictures? I am asking myself that question. I think it is because in the Dali, the woman is corrupted from within, which is a worse thing than to be murdered by the Ripper, which is only violence from without.

The Dali is the opposite of Monet's dissolution of light into Nirvana; it is dissolution into putrefaction. The same is true of that melting watch of his in the same exhibition - at least I suppose it was his - I have forgotten its title - for there are four or five of them in his later *Christ of St John of the Cross*, 1951, which contains no Christ or Saint but only the melting watches. A watch is not an organic being, but yet is an organized thing put together by a being in organized form, and its melting is putrefaction.

Sickert's art is not putrefactive. The murder pictures give us an insight into the mood that produced murder. Perhaps they are the work of a man struggling out of it, and therefore in the uphill process of redeeming himself. As the theme of this book obliges me to concentrate attention upon those of his pictures that have to do with murder, I should like to say that many of his pictures are in no way sinister. He could even be in some respects underrated. His several paintings of the Eglise de Saint-Jacques at Dieppe seem to me better than Monet's series of the Cathedral at Rouen. The Monets are done from too close up, so that there is no context, of street, pavings or other buildings, to give scale or compositional interest. One seems to be looking at an almost all-over rough fabric with projections that catch the light, though the absence of dark tones denies much sense of depth. One is not shown, and can hardly guess, anything of the over-all shape of the Cathedral, and there seems to be no attempt to make a composition with pattern. Sickert's *Facade of Saint Jacques* loses nothing in mystery, but rather gains it, from the area of shaded cobbled square, pavements, and huddle of houses round about, from some of which a shadow falls on the lowest part of the church. Colour and light are subtle, composition interesting. In his *Rue Pecquet*, the narrowness of the street limits the view we have of the church, but it is there, in all its weight and depth and age; venerable.

I have never seen any comment on his *Dieppe Races*, c 1924-6, the only picture I know that really conveys the rush of the horses in a confused blur that is all that one sees as one is standing close up to the rails at the side of the course as they go by. The Italian Futurist painter Giacomo Balla gave us in 1912 *Dynamism of a Dog on a Leash*, his merry little dachshund running along on as many legs as a centipede, but that was perhaps done as something of a joke, whereas Sickert is using the same diffusion of the limbs more naturally, casually, as part of a whole picture. The only other artist I know who has really presented horses galloping convincingly is Elizabeth Butler. Her *Scotland Forever*, 1881, takes one's breath in the way that only a master work can. They are all coming towards one, nostrils and eyes dilated. But she was not an Impressionist. Degas is thought of as the great impressionist painter of horses and their jockeys, but his (at least in any that I can recall) only amble about in paddocks; they do not gallop.

When I read in Lillian Browse a reference to Degas as 'the older and greater master,'(7) I wonder if she is not selling our man short. Sickert was younger, and when he showed his early townscapes to Degas, allowed himself to be told, 'But they all look a bit as though they were painted at night,'(8) and made himself use some lighter colours. But when we come to the theatre, Degas gave just the dancers on the stage, but Sickert gave us the audience as well, and they add a lot to the atmosphere and interest. There is something really very clever in the way in which, in a picture such as *That Old Fashioned Mother of Mine*, amidst swirls of blue light, Impressionist in the best sense, he has, by the double shadows cast by the singer, told us all we need to know about the lighting.

His portrait of *Aubrey Beardsley*, though half turned away from us, catches in the whole attitude of the long, lanky man, what we feel we need to know about the aesthete. His *Victor Lecour* confers upon a fat man who kept a restaurant in Dieppe an immortal dignity, in which everything is owed to the artist and the way in which he makes a rotund light from behind play about his form.

These, then, would be my happier choice of his pictures, though his most powerful still seems to be that heavy brooding man with folded arms who looks down at the woman in the sordid bedroom, *L'Affaire de Camden Town*.

1 'L'Art' in *Emaux et Camées*, Théophile Gautier, 1852; but see also the chapter 'Art for Art's sake' in *From Gautier to Eliot, the Influence of France on English Literature 1851-1939*, Enid Starkie (Hutchinson, 1960)
2 'Preface' to *Lucrèce Borgia*, Victor Hugo, 1833
3 *Five Woman Painters*, Teresa Grimes, Judith Collins and Oriana Addeley (Phaidon, 1989), p 21
4 *Il sognio nostalgico di Botticelli*, Piero Bargelini (Del Turco, Roma, 1946), pp 63-4 See also *Botticelli*, D.E. Baconsky (Meridiani, Bucharest, 1975) pp 7-9
5 *Candles in the Sun*, Lady Emily Lutyens (Hart-Davis, 1957) p 63
6 *Myths of the Hindus and Buddhists*, Sister Nivedita and Ananda Coomarswami (Harrap, 1913), frontispiece and plate facing p 276
7 Browse, p 17
8 Sutton, p 43

A Close Look at the Murders

Chapter 10
Mary Nichols

There are two ways in which one can begin research into a mystery. One can start with an idea, postulate it true, and then look to see whether the evidence bears it out. This is not a bad method. Cosmologists use it. It has, however, the danger that one may become attached to the idea, interpret evidence so as to fit it, overlooking details that do not conduce to it. Also, in presenting points as they become relevant to an argument, chronological order tends to be lost. That is something to which I attach importance. I felt, therefore, that as I had started with an idea, that the murderer might be Sickert, I should at this juncture make a second start, by the other method, which is more pedestrian. What I now wanted was to take a close look at the murders, through the eyes, not of later people, but of those involved at the time, the policemen who were called out, the doctors who were summoned, the first finders of the bodies.

Scotland Yard has been helpful, but the case papers of all the Ripper Murders are now at the Public Record Office.(1)

The first, on 31 August, was of Mary Ann ('Polly') Nichols, in Buck's Row, now Durward Street, a small one, parallel with the Whitechapel Road, on its north or Spitalfields side. The earliest report is that of Inspector J. Sprattling:

P.C. 97J Neil reports that at 3.45am on 31st inst he found the dead body of a woman lying on her back with her clothes a little above her knees, with her throat cut from ear to ear on a yard crossing at Buck's row, Whitechapel. P.C. [Neil] obtained the assistance of P.C.s 55H Mizen and 96J Thain. The latter called Dr. Llewellyn, of 152 Whitechapel Road. He arrived quickly, and pronounced life to be extinct, but a few minutes. He directed her removal to the mortuary, saying he would make a further examination there, which was done on the ambulance.

Upon my arrival there and taking a description I found that she had been disembowelled, and at once sent to inform the doctor of it. He arrived quickly and on further examination stated that her throat had been cut from left to right, two distinct cuts being on the left side. The windpipe, gullet and spinal cord having been cut through, a bruise apparently of a thumb being on the right lower jaw, also one on the left cheek. The abdomen had been cut open from centre of bottom of ribs on right side, under pelvis to left of the stomach; there the wound was jagged. The omentum or coating of the stomach was also cut in several places, and two small stabs to private parts appeared done with a strong bladed knife, supposed to have been done by some left-handed person, death being instantaneous.

Description: Age about 45; length 5 ft 2 or 3; complexion dark; hair dark brown turning grey, eyes brown; bruise on lower right jaw and left cheek, slight laceration of tongue; one tooth deficient front of upper jaw, two on left of lower.

Dress: brown ulster, 7 large brass buttons figure of a female riding on a horse and a man at side thereon, brown linsey frock, grey woollen petticoat, flannel drawers, white chest flannel, brown stays, black ribbed woollen stockings, man's spring-soled boots,

Mary Nichols

cut on uppers, tips on heels, black straw bonnet, trimmed black velvet.

I made enquiries and was informed by Mrs Emma Green a widow of New Cottage, adjoining, and Mrs Walter Purkis, of Eagle Wharf, opposite, also William Louis, night watchman of Messrs Brown & Eagle at Bucks Row and at wharf near, none of whom had heard any screams during the night, or anything to lead them to believe that the murder had been committed there.

The station and premises of the East London and District Railways, also the wharves and enclosures in the vicinity have been searched but no trace of any weapons could be found there. P.C. states that he passed through the Row at 3.15am. and P.S. 10 Kirby about the same time, but the woman was not there then and is not known to them.

Scotland Yard was informed at once, and Detective Inspector George Frederick Abberline of the Criminal Investigation Department (CID) came to take charge of the investigation - as he would of that into the murders yet to come. Unfortunately the blood on the spot where Mrs Nichols was found had been washed off before he arrived, so we are denied what he might have been able to tell us about the exact extent and position of it. We do, however, have Abberline's report.

It differs in one or two particulars from Inspector Sprattling's. It now appears that it was not a policeman who had been the first finder of the body.

Abberline says:

At about 3.40am, 31st ult, as Charles Cross, of 22 Doveton street, Cambridge Row, Bethnal Green, was passing through Bucks Row, Whitechapel on his way to work he noticed a woman lying on her back on the footway against some gates into a stable yard. He stopped to look at the woman when another carman (also on his way to work) named Robert Paul, of 30 Fosters Street, Bethnal Green, came up and Cross called his attention to the woman, but being dark they did not notice any blood, and passed on with the intention of informing the first constable they met. On arriving at the corner of Hanbury Street and Old Montague Street, they met P.C. 55 Mizen, and acquainted him of what they had seen and on the constable proceeding towards the spot he found that P.C. 97J Neil (who was on the beat) had found the woman and was calling for assistance.

P.C. Neil had turned on his light and discovered that the woman's throat was severely cut. P.C. 96 J Thain was also called and sent at once for Dr. Llewellyn of 152 Whitechapel Road, who quickly arrived on the scene and pronounced life extinct and ordered the removal of the body to the Mortuary. In the meantime P.C. Mizen had been sent for the ambulance and assistance from Bethnal Green Station, and on Inspector Sprattling and other officers arriving, the body was removed to the Mortuary. On arriving there the Inspector made a further examination and found the abdomen had been severely cut in several places, exposing the intestines. The Inspector acquainted Dr. Llewellyn who afterwards made a more minute examination and found that the wounds in the abdomen were in themselves sufficient to cause instant death, and he expressed an opinion that they were inflicted before the throat was cut.

The body was not then identified. On the clothing being carefully examined by Inspector Helston he found some of the underclothing bore the mark of Lambeth Workhouse which led to the body being identified as that of a former inmate named Mary Ann Nichols, and by that means we were able to trace the relatives and complete the identity. It was found she was the wife of William Nichols, of 37 Coburg Street, Old Kent Road, a printer in the employ of Messrs. Perkins, Bacon and Co, Whitefriars Street, City, from whom she had ben separated about nine years, through her drunken immoral habits, and that for several years past she had from time to time been an inmate of various workhouses. In May of this year she left Lambeth Workhouse and entered the service of Mr. Cowdry, Ingleside, Rose Hill Road, Wandsworth. She remained there until the 12 July when she absconded stealing various articles of wearing apparel. A day or two after she became a lodger of 18 Thrawl Street, Spitalfields, a common lodging house, and at another common lodging house, at 56 Flower & Dean Street up to the night of the murder.

About 1.40am that morning she was seen in the kitchen at 18 Thrawl Street, when she informed the deputy of the lodging house that she had no money to pay her lodgings. She requested that her bed might be kept for her and left stating that she would soon get the money. At this time she was drunk. She was next seen at 2.30am at the corner of Osborn Street and Whitechapel Road by Ellen Holland, a lodger in the same house, who seeing she was very drunk requested her to return with her to the lodging house. She however refused, remarking she would soon be back and walked away down the Whitechapel Road in the direction of the place where the body was found. There can be no doubt with regard to the time because the Whitechapel Church clock chimed 2.30 and Holland called the attention of the deceased to the time.

We have been unable to find any person who saw her alive after Holland left her. The distance from Osborn Street to Bucks Row would be about half a mile. Enquiries were made in every conceivable quarter with a view to trace the murderer but not the slightest clue can at present be obtained...

So, we are left with a period of an hour and ten minutes between the last sighting of her alive, at 2.30 and the discovery of her body, dead, at 3.40, and no one saw a man where she would have been standing about.

Dr Llewellyn's suggestion that two of the smaller stabs could have been made by a left-handed person is against all of the candidates. Abberline does not, however, say anything about left-handedness; neither do any of the doctors who would be called in to examine the subsequent Ripper victims.

The police did well to trace so much of Mrs Nichols' history, but it does not help us - except in that her last two lodging-houses in which she had been residing since her arrival in the Spitalfield area, in July, were in Flower & Dean Street and Thrawl Street. Both these small, grimy streets, off Commercial Street to the east, we shall find named again as we pursue our enquiries.

The striking feature of the Nichols case is that although Inspector Sprattling questioned people around, including the night watchmen, none of them had heard anything.

This was taken by Knight as support for the story of the murders having been committed in a coach, and indeed he was able to cite the words of Inspector Helston to *The Times* of the morning after the murder, 'viewing the spot where the body was found it seems difficult to believe that the woman received her death wounds there.' This refers to the paucity of blood.

Rumbelow, a writer who had been a policeman, had, however, already drawn attention to two things. If the first injury is strangulation or cutting of the windpipe, there is no cry and very little blood. It spurts three feet if cutting of one of the carotid arteries (the big ones on either side of the throat) is the cause of death, but, if the windpipe has previously been cut or strangled, only seeps out slowly, so that only a little would be on the ground beneath the body, most of it being absorbed by the clothes. This would meet not only the absence of cries but Dr Llewellyn's evidence at the inquest that little blood was found in the gutter, 'not more than would fill two wineglasses.' (2) Knight objects to this, because it was not stated in the evidence that the clothes were full of blood.

On the other hand, James Hatfield, who helped undress the body at the Mortuary, told the Coroner:

Her dress was loose, so I didn't have to cut it, but I cut the bands on her petticoats and peeled 'em down with my hands, the petticoats that it. She was wearing a shirt-waist, and I cut that down the front.

Now, why did he have to cut them? If it was because the body was already stiff that it was difficult to get clothes off it, that would have applied to the dress, with its sleeves. If it was the tight-lacing at the back that was the trouble, could he not have turned the body over so as to be able to undo lacing or hooks at the back? The word 'peeled' suggests to me layers of clothing stuck together by blood. This would go to support Rumbelow.

Dr Llewellyn, at the inquest, rejected the suggestion that the attack might have been from behind, saying that in his opinion the right hand had been placed across her mouth to prevent her from crying out, and that the knife wounds had been made from left to right, as by a left-handed person.

That assumes the murderer to have been standing in front of his victim. If, however, as Rumbelow urges, he was standing behind her, the opposite would have been the case. He would have put his left hand round from behind and over her face and mouth, not only to silence her but to hold her head conveniently back, and put his right arm round from behind to draw his knife across her windpipe from left to right.

A word needs to be said about the common lodging-houses in which not only Mrs Nichols, but every one of the Ripper's victims lived. They were privately owned. The landlord did not, in most cases, live on the premises. He might live in a house nearby, or, if richer, might live in a better part of London and own half a dozen of these miserable houses in Spitalfields and Whitechapel. To manage them, he employed a deputy, who did live in the lodging house, took the rent, in most cases daily in advance, and did some cleaning, though they were usually pretty dirty. The rooms, as originally built, had in many cases been partitioned, so as to make smaller rooms. In some cases the partitions did not extend even from floor to ceiling. The rooms were 'furnished,' but barely, with just a bed, table and chair, no wardrobe and needless to say no washing facilities. On the ground floor there was a kitchen, to which the lodgers would bring their own food, to cook and eat, sitting at benches or on the floor. Beneath the taps to the kitchen sink, lodgers might wash themselves and their clothes. As the rest of the house was often very cold, lodgers would sometimes remain sitting in the common kitchen-wash-house just for warmth, and so became the lodgers' meeting place. In nice weather, they would sit on the pavement, outside. The lodging-houses were of three types, for men only, for women only, and common. For obvious reasons, the women who became the Ripper's victims were in the common lodging houses. They were not brothels. Some of the rooms were occupied by respectably living couples. Women in prostitution did, however, sometimes bring their clients back with them (though usually they merely withdrew with them from the lighted thoroughfares into the dark, tiny courts, with which the district abounded).

Though it is usual to refer to the Ripper's victims as prostitutes, yet the term can be misleading to people of today. They were not what, until the Street Offences Act, used to be seen standing about in the West End. They had not (at any rate in the majority of cases) chosen that way of life. They were not professionals; they were occasionals. Their average age was forty-five (except for Mary Kelly, who was younger). They were women who had come adrift from husband or family, who had had menial employments but lost them or were unable to make ends meet. It was when they were unable to pay the rent of their wretched accommodation, that they went out on the streets to make up the deficit in the only way they knew. Some of them had a steady man friend, who was not a pimp, but forgave them, knowing their straits. All of them had a drinking problem. What I cannot make out is whether they drank to drown the misery of having to prostitute themselves, or prostituted themselves to buy the drink. Probably it was a vicious circle. They drank what they had made for the rent, and so had to go out again. They owned nothing save what they wore. They were in no conceivable sense of the term, gay. The Victorian use of the word 'unfortunate' to mean prostitute is now referred to as a euphemism. In the case of these poor women, it was not a euphemism.

1 *The Public Record Office,* Kew; MEPO/3/140
2 *The Complete Jack the Ripper,* Donald Rumbelow (W.H. Allen, 1975) pp 173-5

Chapter 11

Rings off her Fingers:

Annie Chapman

In the early morning of Saturday, 8 September, it was Inspector Joseph Chandler who was on duty at the Commercial Street police station when a man came in and said there was a body in the back yard of 29 Hanbury Street. The man was John Davis, a porter in the Spitalfields market, and lodged in Mrs Richardson's house, 29 Hanbury Street, in the room above the cellar at the back. When he heard the clock strike 6am he got up and made some tea, then left the house by the back door, meaning to go to his work in the market, when he saw the body, in the back yard, against the palings. He could see the woman's throat was cut and so had come straight to the police. Inspector Chandler noted that it was 6.10 when Davis arrived, reporting the body. Chandler's response is best given in the words of his own official report:

I at once proceeded to 29 Hanbury Street and in the back yard found a woman lying on her back, dead, left arm resting on left breast, legs drawn up, abducted, small intestines and flap of abdomen lying on right side above shoulder, attached by a cord with the rest of the intestines inside the body two flaps of skin from the lower part of the abdomen lying in a large quantity of blood above the left shoulder, throat cut deeply from the left and back in a jagged manner right around the throat.

I sent at once for Dr. Phillips, divisional surgeon, and to the station for the ambulance and assistance. The doctor pronounced life extinct and stated the woman had been dead at least two hours. The body was then removed on the police ambulance to the Whitechapel Mortuary.

On examining the yard I found on the back wall of the house (at the head of the body) and about 18 inches from the ground about six patches of blood varying in size from a sixpenny piece to a point, and on the wooden paling on left of the body near the head patches and smears of blood about fourteen inches from the ground.

The woman has been identified by Timothy Donovan, deputy of Crossingham's lodging house at 35 Dorset Street, Spitalfields, who states he has known her about 16 months as a prostitute, and for past 4 months she has lodged at above house and at 1.45am 8th instant she was in the kitchen, the worse for liquor and eating potatoes. He, Donovan, sent to her for the money for her bed, which she said she had not got, and asked him to trust her, which he declined to do. She then left stating that she would not be gone long; she saw no man in her company.

Description: Annie Siffey, age 45, length 5 ft; complexion fair, hair wavy, dark brown, eyes blue; two teeth deficient in lower jaw, large thick nose.

Dress: black figured jacket, brown bodice, black skirt, lace boots, all old and dirty.

A description of the woman has been circulated by wire to all stations and a special enquiry called for at lodging houses etc, to ascertain if any man of a suspicious character or having blood on his clothing entered after 2am 8 inst.

Inspector Chandler sent a telegram to Abberline, who hastened from

Florence Pash by W R Sickert from the collection of Dr David Coombe, Cambridge

Florence Pash by Jacques-Emile Blanche painted at Dieppe in the summer of 1885, Stanford University Museum of Art

Mrs A A Humphrey (Florence Pash) by Charles Conder, Etching, The British
Museum

Walter Sickert by Florence Pash, Pastel executed in Dieppe in August 1921, Islington Public library

Ennui by W R Sickert, The Asmolean Museum, Oxford

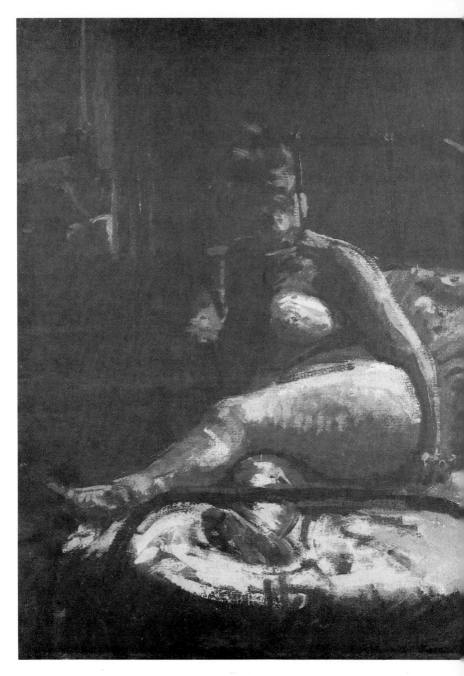

La Hollandaise by W R Sickert, The Tate Gallery

Blackmail, Mrs Barrett by W R Sickert Pastel 1903-1904, The National
Gallery of Canada

Mrs Barrett by W R Sickert, The Courtauld Institute Galleries, London

The Servant of Abraham by W R Sickert,The Tate Gallery, London

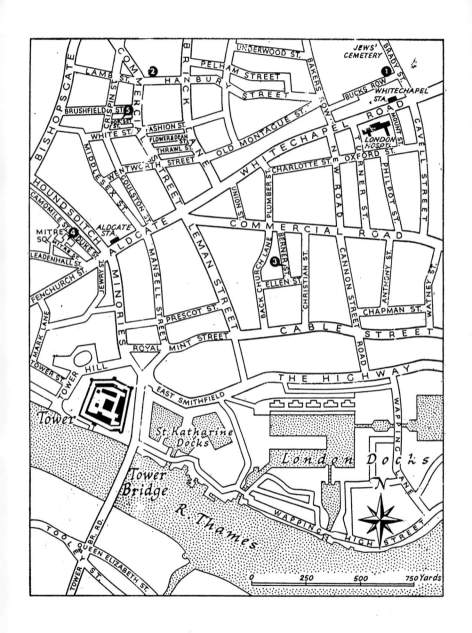

Map of Whitechapel

Police photographes of the victims

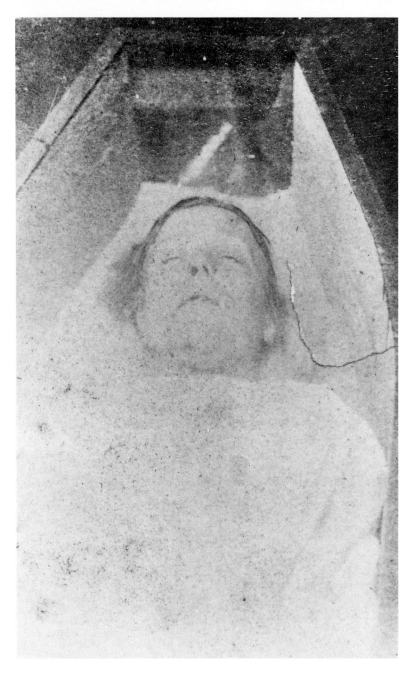

Mary Nichols

Annie Chapman

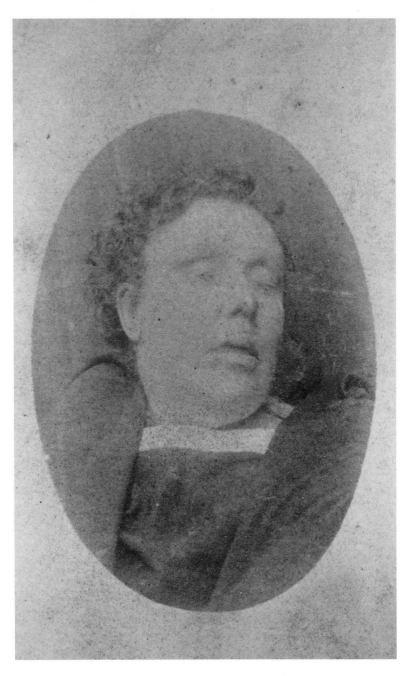

Elizabeth Stride

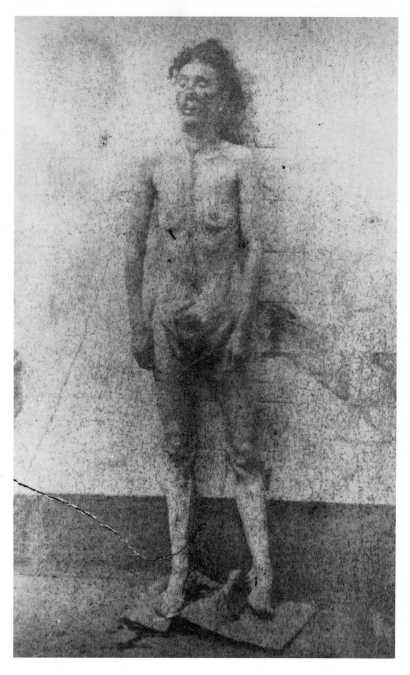

Catherine Eddowes

Mary Kelly

Annie Chapman

Gravesend. It is from Abberline's report we learn the victim was subsequently identified as the widow of:

A coachman named Chapman who died at Windsor some 18 months since from whom she had been separated several years previously through her drunken habits, and who up to the time of his death made her an allowance of 10s per week. For some years past she has been a frequenter of common lodging houses in the neighbourhood of Spitalfields, and for some time previous to her death she had resided at 35 Dorset Street where she was seen alive at 2 am on the morning of the murder ...From then until her body was found no reliable information can be obtained as to her movements.

The inquest was opened on 10 September at the Working Lad's Institute in Whitechapel Road. The Coroner was Wynne E. Baxter. There was some friction between him and the divisional surgeon, George Bagster Phillips, because the latter said, 'I think I had better not go into further details of these mutilations which can only be painful to the feelings of the jury and the public.'

The Coroner did not agree, and said the details, however painful, were necessary in the interest of justice. How long would it take to perform the incisions found on the body?

Dr. Phillips replied,'I myself could not have performed all the injuries I saw on that woman, and effect them, even without a struggle, under a quarter of an hour. I still think it is a very great pity to make this evidence public. These details are fit only for yourself, sir, and the jury.'

Coroner Baxter suggested that the ladies and boys in the room should leave.

Dr. Phillips said, 'I still feel that in giving these details to the public you are thwarting the ends of justice.'

Knight, of course, takes it that Dr. Phillips must have been a Freemason and was witholding evidence that might incriminate the Brotherhood. There is a tendency in all of us who are trying to investigate the crimes, at a remove in time and without responsibility, to feel vexed at the suppression of any details that could help us, but it seems to me unnecessary and perhaps unfair to suspect Dr. Phillips' motives. I seem to remember that while the police were trying to catch the Yorkshire Ripper some details of the mutilations were withheld, on the ground they could prejudice the hunt. It is not always good to tell the killer just how much detail has been noticed and treated as significant. There is also something else I would have thought of, in Dr. Phillips' shoes; one does not want to inspire imitative murders.

Knight's point is that in the Mason's symbolic story, the three murderers of Hiram Abiff are punished by having their heart and vitals taken out and thrown over their left shoulder. He supposes it was because the murderer was confused in his hurry or the perpetration of the deed was entrusted to Netley, who was not a Mason, that Mrs Chapman's entrails were thrown over the wrong shoulder by mistake.

At the same time, if the cuts were being made from left to right, by a man squatting near the right of the head or shoulder, would not the entrails, being ripped up from the abdomen, come towards him and slide to the ground around the right shoulder?

The medical evidence was given in the *Lancet*. The woman's face and tongue were swollen, and there were bruises on her face and chest. There were abrasions on her ring finger, where her rings had been pulled off. The incisions in her throat were made from the left side. There were two distinct cuts, parallel, about an inch apart. From the worrying of the muscle, it was Dr Phillips' opinion the killer had been trying to cut through the spine and sever her head from the trunk:

The abdomen had been entirely laid open and the intestines severed from their mesmeric attachments which had been lifted out and placed on the shoulder of the corpse; whilst from the pelvis, and uterus and its appendages with the upper portion of the vagina and the posterior two thirds of the bladder had been entirely removed. Obviously the work was that of an expert - or one, at least, who had such knowledge of anatomical or pathological examinations as to be enabled to secure the pelvic organs with one sweep of the knife.

He thought the murder weapon must have been a very sharp knife, with a thin, narrow blade, at least six to eight inches long, probably longer; the wounds could not have been inflicted with a sword or sword-bayonet or bayonet. They could best have been inflicted with a post mortem knife, which might not be contained in an ordinary surgical case. The knife of a slaughterman, well ground, would be a possible alternative.

The Coroner introduced into his summing up his own belief, that the murderer was no stranger to the post mortem room. 'There was a market for that missing organ.' He said he had received a letter from the sub-curator of the Pathological Museum telling him that an American student had been trying to procure specimens to illustrate a thesis.

Inspector Chandler's report said nothing about rings and Abberline, though he had gathered the deceased wore two brass rings, a wedding-ring and a keeper and that 'the finger bore the mark of their having been removed,' thought of them as missing. An issue of the *Pall Mall Gazette,* published within hours of the murder, carried, however, the information:

A curious feature of the crime is the murderer had pulled off some brass rings which the victim had been wearing and these, together with some trumpery articles which had been taken from her pockets, were placed carefully at the victim's feet.

Where did the reporter get this? To Knight, the two brass rings suggested the two brass pillars of Solomon's Temple seen in section, and he recalled that all metals, including rings, were removed from the candidate before he is made a Mason. On this basis, he accused Dr. Phillips of having stolen the rings, to remove the traces of a Masonic killing, which, as a Mason himself, he recognized. This seemed to me illogical. After John Davies had stumbled on the body and informed the police, it was Chandler who was the first on the scene, and Chandler who called Dr. Phillips. Dr. Phillips could not, therefore, have hidden them from Chandler. I wrote to New Scotland Yard about this, and had a reply from their W. Waddell, Curator of the Black Museum, informing me it was Dr. Phillips who noticed the rings. So, far from secreting them, he was the one who had drawn them to attention.

Indeed, Rumbelow had written:

Phillips made a thorough search of the yard, which yielded several clues. Several items had been deliberately placed or scattered about the yard. The woman's clothing had not been torn but the pocket that she carried under her skirt had been cut open at the front and at the side. A piece of muslin and a comb and a paper case were lying close to the body. As if he was taking part in some elaborate ritual the killer had laid two brass rings he had torn from her fingers, some pennies and two farthings at the woman's feet. Near her head was a part of an envelope and a piece of paper containing two pills. On the back of the envelope was the seal of the Sussex regiment and on the other side the letter 'M' and a post office stamp 'London, 8 Aug, 1888.'

Dr. Phillips, so far from stealing them, must have made for the police a memorandum of the things he had noticed.

Farson felt the setting out of the objects was significant, though he confessed himself unable to think in what way. The coins could have been from the man's pocket. Yet the cutting open of the woman's purse suggests it was from that he took the coins which he laid out. If it was a pocket she had sewn on to the inside of her skirt, why did he have to cut it open? She would have needed to be able to slip her hand into it, unless it contained things but rarely needed. Perhaps it did, and the coins came from a purse, not found, or from the man.

What can it mean? Only one association comes into my mind, probably inappropriately, and that is with Danaë, to seduce whom Zeus descended in a shower of gold. That, however, would suit Annie Crook better than Annie Chapman. Perhaps I am thinking less of the original Greek legend than of Dante Gabriel Rossetti's allusion to it in his poem 'Jenny.' The poet has gone with a prostitute to her room, but as they sit on the bed she falls straight asleep. Realizing how tired she must be, he has not the heart to wake her up for the purpose for which he had come. He sits for a while, lost in long thoughts. Then he rises, and, before slipping out, plants coins about her:

I think I see you when you wake,
And rub your eyes for me, and shake
My gold, in rising, from your hair,
A Danaë for a moment there.

In that case it was the man who, moved by compassion, gave something for nothing. To have intended a hideous reversal and parody of the poet's beautiful image would suppose a murderer who had read Rossetti, and it is too long a shot.

Apart from the police and Dr. Phillips, a number of witnesses appeared, whose evidence I will present in the chronological order of the times to which they relate.

Amelia Farmer came forward to say she had seen the deceased two or three times in the week before she died. There was a man whom Annie referred to as 'The Pensioner,' with whom she spent an occasional weekend. She had borrowed from Liza Cooper, another prostitute, whom she had known for fifteen years, a bar of soap, for the Pensioner to wash with. On Monday, 2 September, at 'Ringer's,' Liza taxed Annie with not having returned this bar of soap. (That a bar of soap was so important, lets us glimpse the desperate poverty in which these women and their friends lived). The quarrel which had started at Ringer's continued after they had all returned to the kitchen of the lodging house at 35 Dorset Street. Liza kicked and mauled Annie, and bruised her eye and chest. The next day, Tuesday 3rd, Amelia Farmer met Annie by the side of Spitalfields Church. Annie looked and complained of being very unwell. She had had nothing to eat or drink save a cup of tea and was wondering if she would go to the hospital and ask to be taken in at the casual ward for a day or two.

In conjunction with this it will be helpful to view a passage in a later report of Abberline:

I beg to add that at 11am on 15th inst William Stevens, a painter, of 35 Dorset Street, Spitalfields Common Lodging House, came to Commercial Street Station, and made the following statement: I know Annie Chapman as a lodger in this same house. I know that on Friday 7th inst the day before the murder she came into the Lodging House and said she had been to the hospital, and intended going into the infirmary next day. I saw that she had a bottle of medicine, a bottle of lotion and a box with two pills and as she was handling the box it came to pieces, she then took out the pills and picked up a piece of paper from the kitchen floor near the firplace, and wrapped the pills up in it. I believe the piece of paper with the Sussex Regiment thereon to be the same.

That explains the pills found by her body and also the Sussex Regiment paper; not part of a letter addressed to herself but just something she had picked up. Enquiry at the Regimental headquarters revealed nothing.

To return to Annie Chapman's movements as established at the Inquest: The afternoon and evening of Friday 7th were spent at Ringer's and in the kitchen of 35 Dorset Street, until, at about 1.45 on the morning of the 8th, the deputy, Timothy Donovan, asked her for the money for her bed, which sent her out to solicit, in the hope of making it.

Mrs Emilia Richardson, a widow, said she rented 29 Hanbury Street, lived in it and let out the rest of the house in rooms. She had sixteen lodgers. In the ground floor front room, she had a mother and daughter, Hardman, who sold cats' meat from it, as well as lived and slept in it. The front door opened on to a passage which went straight through to the yard at the back, as well as giving access to the stairs, and, so that her lodgers could get in and out, she kept both the front and the back doors open day and night. On Saturday the 8th, she was awake by 3.00am, and heard nothing unusual. At 4.00am she went up the stairs to give a call to a carman, Thompson, who occupied the second floor front with his wife and daughter. At no time did she see or hear anything unusual.

John Richardson, her son, a Spitalfields market porter, of 2 John Street, said he called at his mother's just before 5.00am and, as he always did on market days, looked into the yard to make sure she had padlocked the cellar in which he kept tools. There were steps down from the passage to the yard, which was about four feet lower. One of his boots was hurting him, so he sat down on the steps, and cut away a piece of the leather. There was already enough light to see, and had the body been there then, his feet must practically have been resting on it. It could not have been there at that time.

The reference to a knife interested Coroner Baxter. Why was Richardson outside the house with a knife?

To slice carrots for his rabbit. He had afterwards slipped it into his pocket.

He was required to fetch it, which he did, and it was handed to the police. It was not the kind of knife to interest them.

There was also some interest taken in a leather apron which Dr. Phillips had, during his inspection of the yard on Saturday afternoon, found lying half in and half out of a pan of water in the yard. John Richardson agreed that it was his. He used it when working in the cellar or shed. His mother explained that on Thursday she had taken it from him, washed it for him and hung it on the palings to dry.

John Richardson further said that although his mother was not afraid to sleep with both the front and back doors open, because she trusted her neighbours, he had on some occasions found prostitutes with their clients in her back yard, and even inside the house, on the first floor, in the passage, and he had always chased them out.

At 5.00am, approximately, a Mrs Darrell was passing and saw in the back yard of 29 Hanbury Street a woman, whom she had identified at the mortuary, and a man, aged about 37, height about 5 ft 7; rather dark beard and moustache, dark clothes, black scarf and black soft hat.

Shortly after her must have been Elizabeth Long, wife of a park keeper, of 195 Church Row, Whitechapel. She was on her way to Spitalfields Market, walking along the northern side of the road, going westwards, when she noticed in the back yard of 29 Hanbury Street a man and a woman. The man asked, 'Will you?' and the woman said, 'Yes.' The woman she had identified at the mortuary. The man had had his back to her but she thought he was about forty, a little taller than the woman, in a dark coat, 'shabby genteel appearance.' She thought he spoke like a foreigner. She had heard the Brewer's clock strike 5.30.

Next, Albert Cadosh, Cadoche or Cadosch, carpenter, said he lived at 27 Hanbury Street, adjoining 29, from which its yard was separated only by the palings. It was at 5.15 he got out of his bed. He dressed and went out, by the back, and, from the other side of the palings, heard a woman's voice, cry 'No, No!' He heard a scuffle, and a sound as though someone had fallen against the palings. They were about 5ft 6in high, and he did not look over. It was 5.30 when he passed Spitalfields Church.

There appears a slight discrepancy in timing between his and Mrs Long's account, for the bit of dialogue she overheard must surely have preceded what he heard, which must have been the falling of Mrs Chapman's body, as she was murdered. Why did he not see the man's head above the palings? Perhaps, the murderer was already bending down as he forced her to the ground.

I have checked that on 8 September the sun would have risen at 5.20. It would, therefore, have been light, but not yet strongly light, at the time of the crime, if one takes this as 5.30. One can, of course, see in the early dawn. What surprises me is that Mrs Darrell and Mrs Long could attempt a description of a man seen only passingly from the street, a man seen through a narrow dark passage, in the back yard to one of the houses. The palings against which the pair stood were on the west side of the yard, so would catch the sun's rays if high enough, but the disk would hardly have been visible over the houses, so that it is unlikely the faces would have been illuminated. One is grateful to the two women for what they were able to say, though I doubt if we should take their descriptions to the letter.

There is a further statement of Abberline, dated 14 September:

I beg to report that the man Stanley who occasionally cohabited with the deceased Annie Chapman and referred to by witnesses at the inquest as the pensioner called at Commercial St Station this evening and gave a satisfactory account of himself, and will attend the adjourned inquest on 19 inst. Inquiries have been made at the London Hospitals and other places but no useful information has been obtained. With regard to Commissioner's memorandum of 13th inst I have submitted special report. A man named Edward McKenna is now detained for identification supposed same as described in Evening papers and special memo from C.O. that evening as having been seen at Heath St, and other places with a knife.

F.G. Abberline.

Edward Stanley, 'the Pensioner,' of 1 Osborn Place, Whitechapel, had been in bed at his lodging house until an hour after Mrs Chapman's body was discovered, and on the date of the earlier murder had been in Gosport.

The principal suspects were slaughterers, butchers and surgeons; any people who had professional access to knives. The police had more than one knife handed to them, one found on a doorstep, but not of the right kind. It had to be a special kind of knife; those used in the leather trade not being capable of inflicting the injuries. They were enquiring at hospitals, in the hope of hearing of some medical man or student who was acting suspiciously, and enquiring at slaughterhouses and butchers' shops, of which there were many in the neighbourhood. Abberline had also been making enquiries of prostitutes, to whether there was any man they feared. They told him of one whom they called 'Leather apron,' who exacted protection money and ill-used them if they refused it. Abberline identified this man as Jack Pizer, a Polish Jewish boot-finisher, aged 38. On 10 December, Pizer was arrested, at 22 Mulberry Street and taken to the Leman Street Police Station. However, he had alibis for the times of both the murders, so amply corroborated, that he had to be released.

Annie Chapman

At the Chapman inquest, he appeared in order to answer questions and so clear himself from suspicion.

Abberline, by this time, had another suspect, Joseph Isenschmid, a Swiss. He and his wife had had a pork butcher's shop at 59 Elthone Road, Upper Holloway, but the business had failed and he had spent some time in Colney Hatch asylum. Now he was out, but lodging at 60 Milford Road, Holloway, where a fellow lodger informed on him that he was often out very early in the morning. This was to buy sheep's heads, kidneys and feet which he dressed and sold to restaurants. His wife had not seen him for two months and said that when he left, he took with him two of his butcher's knives. Abberline tried very hard to establish the movements of this man at the time of the murders, and, ironically, most of the photostats sent me from Kew concern Isenschmid. He was arrested, on 12 September, but as there was no evidence against him, he was not charged but sent to the Bow Infirmary Asylum, Fairfield Row, where he was certified insane. Abberline wanted to confront him with a Mrs Fiddymont, landlady of the Prince Albert Public House, Brushfield Street, who said a man had come into the bar with blood on him very close to the time of Annie Chapman's murder, that is, at 7.0am on the day, but the doctor at the Bow Asylum would not let his patient be confronted or interrogated, as it would be injurious to his condition. On 18 September, Abberline ended one of his long reports after returning from the Bow Asylum:

> Although at present we are unable to procure any evidence to connect him with the murders he appears to be the most likely person that has come under our notice to have committed the crimes, and every effort will be made to account for his movements on the dates in question.
>
> F.G. Abberline.

At least, in the Bow Asylum, he was safely under restraint and supervision. He was there when the Ripper struck again.

1 Rumbelow, p 61

Chapter 12:

Grapes

Or the Circumstances of the Murder of Elizabeth Stride

Some people do not regard the murder of Elizabeth Stride as one of the Ripper's, because, apart from her throat having been cut, she was not mutilated. Others regard it as especially important, the one Ripper murder actually witnessed. That he did not stay, this school avers, was because he was interrupted, by the witness.

The scene was Berner Street, a small one running down from Commercial Road to a small railway station, of the London, Tilbury and Southend Railway. Back from the pavement was a small court known as Dutfield's Yard. This had gates, which were open. The witness was Israel Schwarz. At 12.45am on Sunday 30 September, according to his statement as taken down by Inspector Swanson, Schwarz was turning from Commercial Road into Berner Street when, just at the spot where later the body was found, 'he saw a man stop and speak to a woman, who was standing in the gateway. The man tried to pull the woman into the street, but turned her round and threw her down on the footway, and the woman screamed three times, but not very loudly. On crossing to the opposite side of the street, he saw a second man standing lighting his pipe. The man who threw the woman down then called out, apparently to the man on the opposite side of the road, "Lipski!" and then Schwarz walked away, but finding he was followed by the second man he ran as far as the railway arch, but the man did not follow so far. Schwarz cannot say whether the two men were together or known to each other. Upon being taken to the mortuary, Schwarz identified the body as that of the woman he had seen and he thus describes the first man who threw her down:- age about 30, 5ft 5in, complexion fair, hair dark, small brown moustache, full face, broad shouldered: dress dark jacket and trousers, black cap with peak, had nothing in his hands. Second man age 35, ht 5ft 11in, complexion fresh, hair light brown; dress: dark overcoat, old, black hard felt hat, with brim, had a clay pipe in his hand.

There were, however, earlier sightings of Mrs Stride that night.

William Marshall, labourer in an indigo warehouse, identified her at the mortuary as the woman he had seen at about 11.45, about three doors from where he was living in Berner Street. She was talking to a man. They were not near enough to a lamp for him to see his face, but 'He had on a small black coat and dark trousers. He seemed to me to be a middle aged man.'

Answering questions to the Coroner, he said the cap was 'a round cap with a small peak to it - something like what a sailor would wear. ' He was 'about five feet six inches and he was stout. He was decently dressed, and I should say he worked at some light business and had more the appearance of a clerk than anything else...He was not wearing gloves and he had no stick or anything in his hand.' The coat was 'a cutaway one...I was standing at my door and what attracted my attention first was her standing there some time and he was kissing her. I heard the man say to the deceased, "You would say anything but your prayers." He was mild speaking and appeared to be an educated man. They went down the street.'

At 12.30 P.C. 452H William Smith patrolled Berner Street on his beat. He saw a man and a woman, whom he had since identified in the mortuary, talking together. The man 'had a newspaper parcel in his hand'. It was about eighteen inches in length and six or eight inches in width. He was about five feet seven inches...He had on a hard felt deerstalker hat of dark colour and dark clothes... an overcoat. He wore dark trousers... About twenty-eight years... he was of respectable appearance.'

A quarter of an hour after this, at about 12.45, a boxmaker, James Brown, went out to buy something for his supper from a chandler's shop. A chandler's was a shop selling candles, groceries and the like.

From more than one of these testimonies one gathers, incidentally, that not only were a good many people about late at night, but that small shops, at which one could buy something to eat, were open much later than they would be today.

The chandler's was in Berner Street and Brown saw a man and a woman standing against the wall by the Board School. He heard the woman say, 'Not tonight, some other night.' This is not the admonition one would have expected to hear used by a prostitute soliciting. Perhaps the man was not so much a client as a pal, hoping to be received for nothing. Brown said the man was leaning over the woman, with his arm on the wall. He was wearing a long dark overcoat, long to his heels. Brown took home the provisions he had bought at the chandler's and 'When I had almost finished my supper I heard screams and shouts for the police - that would have been in about a quarter of an hour.'

Although both Brown and Schwarz give 12.45 as the time they went into Berner Street, it is obvious Brown went there earlier, as he did not see the man throw the woman over. Neither did he see the tall man, with the pipe, who could only have arrived just before Schwarz did.

Note that neither the tall man nor Schwarz reacted as though they had seen a murder. Neither rushed forward to help the woman. It was a rough district, and it was common to see people pulling, pushing or throwing each other about. It was not until the next day, when he heard that there had been a murder, that Schwarz thought to go to the police and say what he had seen.

Yet why had Schwarz run from the scene, why had the tall man followed him and what was the meaning of Lipski?

The answer to all these questions appears in a statement made by Abberline precisely to explain them, which came with the photostats sent me from the Public Record Office. It has not been produced before:

Metropolitan Police, Criminal Investigation Department,
Scotland Yard
Object: Whitechapel Murders
Reference to Papers 52983
1119
1st September, 1888

With reference to the annexed Copy extract from Home Office letters.
I beg to report that since a jew named Lipski was hanged for the murder of a jewess in 1887 the name had very frequently been used by persons as a mere ejaculation by way of endeavouring to insult the Jew to whom it had been addressed, and as Schwarz had a very strong jewish appearance I am of opinion it was addressed to him as he stopped to look at the man he saw apparently illusing the deceased woman.
I questioned Israel Schwarz very closely at the time he made the statement as to whom the man addressed when he called Lipski, but he was unable to say.
There was only one other person to be seen in the street, and that was a man on the opposite side of the road in the act of lighting his pipe.
Schwarz being a foreigner and unable to speak English became alarmed and ran away. The man whom he had seen lighting his pipe also ran in the same direction as himself, but whether this man was running after him or not he could not tell, he might have been alarmed the same as himself and run away.
A house to house enquiry was made in Berner Street with a view to ascertain whether any person was seen acting suspiciously or any noise heard on the night in question but without result.
Enquiries have also been made in the neighbourhood but no person named Lipski could be found
With regard to the second question.
I beg to report that searching enquiries were made by Sergt Troest in Aberdeen Place St John's Wood the last known address of the insane medical student named John Sanders, but the only information that could be obtained was that a lady named Sanders resided with her son at no 20, but left there to go abroad about 2 years ago.
F.G. Abberline
Inspect. Supt.

An insane doctor or medical student was one of the ideas being floated around.

I also found amongst the photostats sent me a draft letter to HM Home Office

With ref to yr letter I have to inform you that the opinion arrived at in this dept upon the evidence of Schwarz at the inquest in Eliz Stride's case is that the name Lipski which he alleges was used by a man whom he saw assaulting the woman in Berner Street on the night of the murder, was not addressed to the supposed accomplice but to Schwarz himself. It appears that since the Lipski case, it has come to be used as an epithet in addressing or speaking of jews.

With regard to the latter question of yr letter I have to state that [copy passage in the report as marked in blue]. C.W.

The initials appear to be those of Sir Charles Warren, Commissioner of the Police of London. The brackets surrounding the instructions to copy the passage he had marked in blue, are Sir Charles', but drawn square by him.

One sees, now, why Schwarz ran. He thought they were after him, because of his being Jewish. In a district such as Whitechapel where the proportion of Jewish residents was especially high, there was probably a good deal of racial tension.

But there is something neither Abberline or Sir Charles remarks upon. I find it very difficult to conceive that a man in the middle of committing a murder would have so little concentration as to have attention to spare for a passing Jew. In calling out to him, he would increase the likelihood that the Jew could pick him out, later, at any identity parade.

The man who threw Elizabeth Stride down had breath to spare. Does he have to be the murderer?

A Mrs Fanny Mortimer, of 36 Berner Street, said she opened her front door between 12.30 and 1.00 for a breath of air:

I was standing at the door of my house nearly the whole time between half past twelve and one o'clock this morning and did not notice anything unusual. I had just gone indoors and was preparing to go to bed when I heard a commotion outside and immediately ran out thinking that there was another row at the Socialist Club close by. I went to see what was the matter and was informed that another dreadful murder had been committed in the yard adjoining the clubhouse, and on going inside saw the body of a woman lying huddled up just inside the gate with her throat cut from ear to ear. A man touched her face and said it was quite warm, so that the deed must have been done while I was standing at the door of my house. There was certainly no noise made and I did not observe anyone enter the gates. It was soon after 1 o'clock when I went out, and the only man whom I had seen pass was a young man carrying a black shiny bag who walked very fast down the street from the Commercial Road. He looked up at the Club, and then went round the corner by the Board School.

The young man whom Mrs Mortimer saw was probably Leon Goldstein, aged twenty-two, who, after the murder, called, of his own accord, at Leman Street police station, to report that he had walked down Berner Street at that time, carrying a black bag. The police eliminated him from their enquiries.

Elizabeth Stride's body was found at 1.00am by Louis Diemschutz, Secretary of the Socialist Club. He was returning from selling his jewellery from his costermonger's barrow and tried to drive his pony and trap into Dutfield's Yard, as usual. The pony shied, as if avoiding something, and his cart touched something. Diemschutz got down from it, struck a match and saw the body. He informed P.C. 252 Lamb, who proceeded with him to the spot, and Doctors Frederick Blackwell and George Bagster Phillips were sent for.

Blackwell, who was the first to arrive at the scene, looked at his watch as he did so. It said 1.10. He found the victim's windpipe and throat had been cut right through, from left to right.

Schwarz had seen no knife. In his statement, he particularized that the man he saw throw the woman over had nothing in his hands. Therefore, he was not witness to the murder. The murderer was, then, not interrupted in his task, and, if the Ripper, could have proceeded to his usual mutilations, after Schwarz had gone.

Dr.Blackwell estimated that, when he arrived, at 1.10, the woman had been dead from twenty minutes to half an hour. Half an hour would place the murder before both Brown and Schwarz saw her alive. Bearing in mind the estimated times that they give, the later time of 1.50 seems more appropriate.

We cannot, therefore, eliminate the possibility that a man, other than the one with whom she had been seen in company - perhaps seeing her on the ground and so at a disadvantage, took out his knife and finished her off.

Unlike Schwarz, the man who smoked a clay pipe and was 5ft 11in height did not come forward to make a statement to the police.

The inquest brought out something of Elizabeth Stride's background. The Revd. Sven Olsson, pastor of the Swedish Church in Trinity Square, said he had known her for about seventeen years. She had told him she was born on 27 November, 1843, which would make her just short of forty-five, that her maiden name had been Gustaafsdotter, and that she was married in July, 1866, to a carpenter at Sherness, John Thomas Stride. He had, she said, been one of those drowned in the 'Princess Alice' disaster (but when Rumbelow checked he did not find that name amongst those on board, so perhaps she had just drifted apart from him).

A Mrs Tanner, who kept a common lodging house at 32 Flower and Dean Street, said the deceased was lodging with her, but only since Thursday. She had known her on and off, but only as 'Long Liz.' There was a man whom she lived with.

He came forward. He was Michael Kidney, a waterside labourer, of 35 Dorset Street, and his testimony is touching:

I have seen the body. It is Long Liz. I have known her for about three years and she has been living with me nearly all that time. I left her in Commercial Street as I was going to work. I expected her to be at home but when I got home I found she had been in and gone out. She was subject to going away whenever she thought she would. During the three years I've known her she has been away from me altogether about five months. I've cautioned her the same as I would a wife. It was drink that made her go. But she would always come back again. I think she liked me better than any other man. I didn't see her again until I identified the body in the mortuary.

There is a question as to what Stride was holding, and whether any significance is to be attached to it. Probably to make the point that she was not using it to defend herself, the Coroner said in his summing up, 'She was still holding in her hand a packet of cachous.' Cachous were breath sweeteners. In *The Times* of Monday 1 October, it was said that in her right hand she had grapes, and in her left, sweetmeats. The *Evening News* also said Stride was holding grapes in her right hand and that there was a witness who claimed to have sold grapes to a man he had seen with Stride. I would prefer what was told the coroner by the doctors called to the body, but Stephen Knight had a particular reason to be interested in grapes. Joseph Sickert had told him he had it from his father that Sir William Gull fed poisoned grapes to the women invited into the coach, so as to render them unconscious before he cut their throats. As an elderly man, he might have found it difficult to do this had they been conscious and struggling. Of the four victims found in the street, according to the Sickert story, Stride had been the only one who had refused to get into the coach. Therefore, Netley concealed the vehicle in a dark thoroughfare south of Commercial Road. Anderson and Netley followed Stride to Berner Street. I would interpose, here, that the horses were, then, apparently left without anyone in charge of them. A horse is not like a car, that can just be parked and left. It did not apparently concern the coachman that, having left them, the horses might move off, carrying the helpless Gull goodness knows where. Having let go of the horses, in Knight's theory, Netley followed Stride up Berner Street.

Grapes were, therefore, in Knight's mind when he went through the case papers, then still at Scotland Yard, and he was electrified when he found they did indeed contain reference to grapes - in a statement by Police Sergeant Stephen White. Because he makes something rather strange out of it, as evincing foul play by the police or some higher authority, I will copy it from the photostats and then we can look at it coolly:

Metropolitan Police
H Division
4th Day of October, 1888

Subject Whitechapel Murders
(Berner Street)

With reference to attached extract from Evening News of 4th inst.
I beg to report that acting under the instructions of Inspector Abberline, in company with P.C. Dolden, C.J Dept, I made enquiries at every house in Berner Street, Commercial Road, on 30th inst, with a view to obtain information regarding the Murder. Any information that I could obtain I noted in a book supplied to me for that purpose. About 9am I called at 44 Berner Street, and saw Matthew Packer, Fruiterer in a small way of business, and asked him what time he closed his shop on the previous night. He replied *half past twelve*, in consequence of the rain it was not good for me to keep open. I asked him if he saw anything of a man or woman going into Dutfield's Yard, or saw anyone standing about the *street about the time he was closing his shop. He replied No, I saw no one standing about neither did I see anyone go up the yard*. I never

saw anything suspicious or heard the slightest noise and knew nothing about the murder until I heard of it this morning.

I also saw Mrs Packer, Sarah Harrison and Harry Douglas residing in the same house but none of them could give the slightest information regarding the matter. On 4th inst I was directed by Inspector Moore to make further enquiry and if necessary see Packer and take him to the Mortuary.

I then went to 44 Berner St and saw Mrs Packer who informed me that two detectives had called and taken her husband to the Mortuary. I then went towards the Mortuary when I met Packer with a man. I asked him where he had been. He said this detective asked him to go to see if I could identify the woman. I said have you done so. He said 'Yes.' *I believe* she bought some grapes at my shop about 12 o'clock on Saturday. Shortly afterwards they were joined by another man I asked the man what they were doing with Packer and they both said that they were Detectives. I asked for their Authority one of the men produced a card from a pocket book but would not allow me to take it. They then said they were private detectives. They then induced Packer to go away with them. About 4pm I saw Packer at his shop and while talking to him the two men drove up in a Hansom Cab and after going into the shop they induced Packer to enter the cab stating that they would take him to Scotland Yard to see Charles Warren.

From inquiry I have made there is no doubt that these are the two men referred to in attached newspaper cutting who examined the drain in Dutfield Yard on 2 inst. One of the men had a letter in his hand addressed to Le Grand and Co, Strand.

Stephen White Sergt

Extract from 'Star' newspaper attached
Respectfully submitted.

F.G. Abberline Inspector
F. Arnold Supt

Now I can understand that Knight was excited, for it is obvious that Stephen White, having been told by Inspector Moore that he should, if necessary, take Packer to the mortuary, was surprised and slightly annoyed to find that Packer had been taken there by two other men, and it is evident he was not altogether satisfied that they were detectives, despite their saying they were taking Packer to Sir Charles Warren at Scotland Yard.

What seems to me unwarranted - and typical of Knight's tendency to leap - is his conclusion that they were agents of the government conspiracy. What seems to me more likely is that Sir Charles Warren, becoming anxious because of the lack of success in catching the murderer, had sent two men of his own, to investigate, and to fetch Packer to him, without notifying the Officers routinely on the job. It would not be the only occasion in which Sir Charles, though zealous, was maladroit. Knight, however, suspects his motive in sending the two men. Knight writes:(1)

They had just two functions. The first was to pre-empt Packer's evidence about selling grapes to the Ripper. The second was to remove all trace of grapes from the drain in Dutfield's Yard.

If Warren had employed these men in the cause of justice he would have made sure

that Packer's evidence was heard. But...his knowledge was suppressed.
Why should Warren have wanted to conceal the facts about the grapes...? (1)

Now, that is not quite right. The two men did take Packer to Sir Charles Warren. Indeed, Knight presents as an illustration the first page of the statement Warren took down from him, without transcribing it or saying what it was about. Warren's writing is in places hard to read, which is doubtless why Knight did not attempt to copy it out. I, too, find it difficult, yet, because I believe the matter important, I will do my best, even though I have to leave a few uncertainties. The first thing one will see is that Sir Charles Warren, so far from trying to conceal and suppress grapes, alludes to them in his opening line:

Matthew Packer
Kept a small shop in Berner St - has a few grapes in window black & white. On Sat night about 1pm a young man from 25-30 - about 5.7. with long black coat buttoned up, soft felt hat, kind of [?] hat, rather broad shoulders - rather quick in speaking - rough voice. I sold him half pound of grapes 3d. A woman came up with him from Back Church end (the lower end of street), black frock & jacket, fur round bottom of jacket, she was [?] playing with a flower like a geranium'[?] white outside red inside. I identify the woman at St George's Mortuary as the one I saw that night.
They passed by me as though they were going up Com Road, but, - instead of going up they crossed to the other side of the road to the Board School and were there for about half an hour till I'd say 11.30, talking [or 'telling'] to me nothing. I then put up my shutters. Again they passed on opposite to my shop. They went near to the club for a few minutes apparently listening to the music.
I saw no more of them after I shut up my shutters.
I put the man down as a young clerk.
He had a frock coat on - no gloves
He was about [5ft] 11/2[sic] inches or 2 or 3 inches - a little bit higher than she was.

C.W.
4.10.88

Despite the occasionally unclear words, there are enough here that emerge clearly to bring out a point which no previous writer has made and which seems to me important - that Packer saw the couple not just once, only, but several times. They were moving backwards and forwards in the street, meandering, over half an hour, listening to music. Why has no one ever noticed they were listening to music?

The point seems to me important because - to my mind at least - it weakens the picture of this being the man on murder deadly bent. It is quite incongruous with Knight's thesis, that this woman was despatched very quickly, by the coachman, Netley, after administration of poisoned grapes - all while Gull waited in the carriage parked nearby. Half an hour passed. There is a slight discrepancy between the statements made to White and to Warren as to the time at which Packer shut up shop, after 12 or at 11.30, but that does not matter. It would be natural to be uncertain of the exact time. What is important is that the couple were more or less in his view over a considerable period, appearing friendly and relaxed listening to music. It does not sound to me like a prostitute with her client, any more than a murderer with his victim; more like two friends with nothing to do and nowhere to go, just spending a little time in each other's company.

Knight also found a note by Inspector Swanson that amongst the rubbish swept up in Dutfield's Yard was found a grape stem. I do not find this document in what is supposed to be the complete set sent to me in photostat, but I suppose it was once there. A paper or two can have got lost in the transfer from Scotland Yard to Kew. Dr Phillips told the Coroner that he found fruit stains on the handkerchief of the deceased, but he also said, 'I am convinced that the deceased had not swallowed either seed or skin of grape within many hours of her death.'

I do not think Knight should have accused Dr. Phillips of lying to the Coroner. Dr Phillips did not perform the post mortem alone. He and Dr Blackwell performed it together, in the presence of two other doctors.

Though it must have been tempting to Knight to tie up the grapes he found mentioned in the police files with the grapes in the story he had from Joseph Sickert, they do not fit into it in a natural manner. Stride was the one woman (of those murdered in the street) who, according to Sickert, refused to get into the coach (in the existence of which I do not believe at all) to be fed therein by Gull with grapes previously poisoned, so Netley followed her down Berner Street.

How is poison supposed to have been got into the grapes sold by Packer? If they were not poisoned, how can Packer's evidence be read as corroboration of Sickert's story (which I must say seems to me in this part completely fanciful). These are points Knight has not thought out.

I can see the way Knight's thought was running. Grapes were sold to a man seen with Stride. A grape stem was found in Dutfield's Yard. Where were the grapes off it? Somehow poisoned, they must have gone into Stride's stomach. Therefore, Dr. Phillips was lying when he said he did not find them there.

There is another possible explanation, which occurs to me. The grapes were eaten by the man who bought them, and he dropped the stem.

Inspector Swanson's note that a grape stem was found in Dutfield's Yard was, however, worthwhile. I see it as evidence tending to corroborate that the man who bought the grapes was the same man subsequently seen standing with Stride in Dutfield's Yard.

There were a number of sightings of Stride with a man in Berner Street or Dutfield's Yard, by Packer, Marshall, Smith, Brown and Schwarz (Knight mentions neither Marshall nor Brown). The man was variously described by them. His height was estimated by Schwarz as 5.5, by Marshall as 5.6 and by both Packer and Smith as 5.7. That is a variation within only two inches, and both Packer and Schwarz say he had broad shoulders. All said his clothes were dark. Marshall and Schwarz said his coat was cutaway; Packer and Brown said it was very long. Marshall and Schwarz said he wore a cap with a peak; Smith that he wore a deerstalker: that is a cap with two peaks, one behind as well as one in front. In the dim light, the one behind could easily have been hidden by the collar of the coat. Only Smith mentions his carrying a large parcel, but that, if heavy, could sometimes have been put down.

The question has always been whether all these sightings related to the same man or to a series of different men. I think that the evidence of the second page of Sir Charles Warren's taking down of Packer's evidence - the page not reproduced or referred to by Knight - weighs the balance of probability very strongly in favour of all the sightings having been of the same man. Packer saw them passing up and down for about half an hour. If, as he first said, this was from the purchase of the grapes at 12.00, half an hour would bring us to 12.30 and the sighting by P.C. Smith at 12.30, and through the sighting by Marshall at 11.45. Even if the purchase of the grapes was nearer to the revised time of 11.00, half an hour (all times being approximate) would bring us practically to 11.45, the time of the sighting by Marshall.

It was worthwhile my having obtained the photostats from Kew. I think by their inspection, to have resolved at last one of the factual questions of the case. Elizabeth Stride was seen that night not with a succession of different men, but several times with the same man, with whom she had walked up and down and stood about for some considerable while.

It also puts out of court Joseph Sickert's and Knight's contention that this was the man who went after and despatched her very quickly, while Gull waited in his carriage, parked as briefly as possible.

I also feel that this man, seen by Packer, Marshall, P.C. Smith, Brown and Schwarz, was not the murderer. It would have been imprudent to kill after having been seen with his victim by so many people, and his behaviour was too relaxed, he would not so have dawdled with her, buying the grapes which he ate himself, talking, spooning, listening to music and exchanging chat with her - until suddenly they had a tiff, and he threw her down and walked off.

I feel that I have eliminated a suspect.

That leaves the 5ft 11in man.

1 Knight, p 243

Chapter 13:

The Trail from Mitre Square: Catherine Eddowes

The City Police were, then as now, separately organized from the Metropolitan Police, each Force having its own Commissioner. With one exception, all the murders fell within the area of the Metropolitan Police, but Mitre Square, so near to the other sites yet slightly to the West of them, was just within the city.

Major (later Lieut. Colonel Sir Henry) Smith, Acting Commissioner of the City Police, had, on the night of 29 September, gone to bed, at the Cloak Lane Station. In the small hours of the 30th, he was wakened by the bell near his head, and a voice said through the tube, 'Another murder, sir, this time in the City,'(1)

He was dressed, in the street and in a hansom within a couple of minutes, a Superintendent with him and three detectives hanging on behind, so that the vehicle rolled. In Mitre Square Smith found City Police, Metropolitan Police and Doctors gathered around the mutilated remains of a woman.

We can follow what had been happening from the report made later (on 6 November) for the Home Office by Chief Inspector Donald Swanson, of the Metropolitan Police.

I beg to report that the facts concerning the murder in Mitre Square which came to the knowledge of the Metropolitan Police are as follows:

At 1.45am 30th Sept Police Constable Watkins of the City Police discovered in Mitre Square the body of a woman, with her face mutilated almost beyond identity, portion of the nose being cut off, the lobe of the right ear nearly severed, the face cut, the throat cut, and disembowelled. The P.C. called to his assistance a Mr Morris, a night watchman and pensioner from the Metropolitan Police, from premises looking on the Square, and surgical aid was subsequently called in, short details of which will be given further on in this report.

The City Police having been made acquainted with the facts by P.C. Watkins the following are the results of their enquires so far as known to Met. Police:-

At 1.30am the P.C. passed the spot where the body was found at 1.45am and there was nothing to be seen there at that time.

1.35am three Jews, one of whom is named Mr. Lewin [sic], saw a man talking to a woman in Church Passage which leads directly to Mitre Square. The other two took but little notice and said that they could not identify the man or the woman, and even Mr Lawende states that he could not identify the man; but as the woman stood with her back to him, with her hand on the man's breast, he could not identify the body mutilated as it was, as that of the woman he had seen, but to the best of his belief the clothing of the deceased, which was black, was similar to that worn by the woman whom he had seen, and that was the full extent of his identity.

2.30am P.C. 245A Long (the P.C. was drafted from A Division temporarily to assist H Division) stated that at the hour mentioned he visited Goldstone [sic] Street Buildings, and there was nothing there at that time, but at 2.55am he found in the bottom of a common stairs leading to Nos. 108 to 119 Goldstone Street Buildings, a piece of a bloodstained apron, and above it written in chalk the words, 'The Juwes are the men who will not be blamed for nothing', which he reported, and the City Police were subsequently acquainted at the earliest moment, when it was found that beyond doubt the piece of apron found corresponded exactly with the part missing from the body of the murdered woman.

The surgeon, Dr. Brown, called by the City Police and Dr. Phillips who had been called by the Metropolitan Police in the cases of Hanbury Street and Berner Street, having made a *post mortem* examination of the body reported that there were missing the left kidney and the uterus, and that the mutilation so far gave no evidence of anatomical knowledge in the sense that it evidenced the hand of a qualified surgeon, so that the police could narrow their enquires into certain classes of persons. On the other hand as in the Metropolitan Police cases, the medical evidence shewed that the murder could have been committted by a person who had been a hunter, a butcher, a slaughterman, as well as student in surgery or a properly qualified surgeon.

The result of the City Police enquires were as follows:- beside the body were found some pawn tickets in a tin box, but upon tracing them they were found to relate to pledges made by the deceased, who was separated from her husband, and was living in adultery with a man named John Kelly, respecting whom enquiry was at once made by the Metropolitan and City Police, the result of which was to show clearly that he was not the murderer. Further, it showed that the deceased's name was Catherine Eddowes, or Conway, who had been locked up for drunkenness at Bishopsgate Street Police station at 8.45pm 29th, and being sober was discharged at 1am 30th.

Enquiry was also made by the City and Metropolitan Police conjointly into her antecedents, and it was found that there did not exist amongst her relations or friends the slightest pretext for a motive to commit the murder.

At the Golston [sic] Street Buildings where the portion of the bloodstained apron was found the City Police made enquiries, but unsuccessfully and their subsequent enquiries into matters affecting persons suspected by correspondence or by statements of individuals at Police Stations, as yet without success, have been carried on with the knowledge of the Metropolitan Police, who on the other hand have daily acquainted the City Police with the subjects and nature of their enquiries.

Upon the discovery of the blurred chalk writing on the wall, written - although mis-spelled in the second word - in an ordinary hand in the midst of a locality principally inhabited by Jews of all nationalities as well as English, and upon the wall of a common stairs leading to a number of tenements occupied almost exclusively by Jews, and the purpose of the writing being to throw blame on the Jews, the Commissioner deemed it advisable to have it rubbed out. Apart from this there was the fact that during police enquires into the Bucks Row and Hanbury Street murders a certain section of the Press cast a great amount of suspicion upon a Jew named John Pizer, alias 'Leather Apron', as having been the murderer, whose movements at the dates of those murders have been satisfactorily enquired into by Metropolitan Police, clearing him of any connection, there was also the fact that on the same morning another murder had been committed in the immediate vicinity of a Socialist Club in Berner Street, frequented by Jews, considerations which, weighed in the balance with the evidence of chalk writing on the wall to bring home guilt to any person, were deemed the weightier of the two. To those police officers who saw the chalk writing, the handwriting of the now notorious letters to a newspaper agency bears no resemblance at all.

Rewards were offered by the City Police and by Mr Montague [M.P. for Whitechapel] and a Vigilance Committee formed, presided over by Mr Lusk of Alderny Road, Mile

End, and it is to be regretted that the combined result has been that no information leading to the murderer has been forthcoming. On the 11 October Mr Lusk brought a parcel which had been addressed to him to Leman Street Police Station. The parcel contained what appeared to be a portion of a kidney. He received it on October 15 and submitted it for examination eventually to Dr Openshaw, curator of London Hospital Museum, who pronounced it to be a human kidney. The kidney was at once handed over to the City Police, and the result of the combined medical opinion that they have taken upon it is that it is the kidney of a human adult, not charged with fluid, as it would have been in a case of a body handed over for dissection to an hospital, but rather as it would be in the case where it was taken from a body not so destined. In other words similar kidneys might and could be obtained from any dead person upon whom a post mortem had been made from any cause, by students or a dissecting room porter. The kidney, or a rather portion of the kidney, was accompanied by a letter couched as follows:

From Hell

Mr Lusk

Sir

I send you half the kidne I took from one woman presarved it for you tother piece i fried and ate it was very nise. I may send you the bloody knif that took it out if you only wate a while longer.

signed

Catch me when

you can

misther Lusk

The postmarks upon the parcel are so indistinct that it cannot be said whether the parcel was posted in the E or EC district, and there is no envelope to the letter, and the City Police are therefore unable to prosecute any enquiries upon it.

The remaining enquiries of the City Police are merged into those of the Metropolitan Police, each force cordially communicating to the other daily the nature and subject of their enquires.

The foregoing are the facts so far known to Metropolitan Police, relating to the murder in Mitre Square.

The kidney, or rather half-kidney, Sir Henry Smith, as Acting Commissioner of the City Police, would later write was made over by himself to the City Police Surgeon, Dr. Gordon Brown, with instructions to call in to assist him the most eminent men in the medical profession. The examination of it was made with the help of a Dr. Openshaw and a Mr. Sutton, the latter being senior surgeon at the London Hospital and 'one of the greatest authorities living on the kidney and its diseases.'(2)

The combined opinion of the medical men who examined the object which had been sent in the post was that it was part of the kidney of a human being, in an advanced stage of Bright's disease, a 'ginny' kidney, in all respects matching the one remaining in the body of the deceased Catherine Eddowes. There was about an inch of renal artery attached. The renal artery is about three inches long, and two inches remained in the body of the deceased, where the kidney had been removed. Sutton said he would stake his reputation that the piece of kidney they were examining 'had been put in spirits within a few hours of its removal from the body.' (3)

Who keeps spirits at home? They are used in making pickles, and in making artists' varnishes. Sickert used varnishes, though I do not know if he made his own. I have reserved to a separate chapter my analysis of the handwriting and spelling of the letter, upon which I base my opinion it cannot be the product of a genuine illiterate.

Catherine Eddowes was identified by her sister, Liza Gold, of Thrawl Street. She said Catherine was forty-three. She and John Kelly had just returned on Thursday from hop-picking in Kent.(4)

Here again, one sees that these women were not wholly prostitutes. Hop-picking is hard work. To city dwellers, the fresh air and scenes of the countryside may have been an annual treat - it is usually the same people who go down each year, and of course they cannot be people with normal jobs that would prevent their absence. Once back in London, she returned to her sad beat.

Smith said it was a small beat, well known to the police. He was furious when he learned that, in the Bishopsgate Police Station, which was under his jurisdiction, they had had her in custody as drunk, and let her go out, as sober, without following her. His orders had been that women in such circumstances should be shadowed, for their own protection. Had she been, the murderer would have been caught, in Mitre Square.(5)

At the inquest, on 4 October, in the Golden Lane Mortuary, P.C. 881 Watkins, told the coroner, Mr S.F. Langham, that he had walked through Mitre Square at 1.30am shining his bull's eye lamp into all corners, and there was nothing there. When he came back at 1.40am there was the body, 'like a pig in the market', her entrails 'flung about her neck.' This timing, if accurate, would have allowed the murderer only 14 minutes within which to do everything - and he would have had still less time if the three Jews were right in saying it was at 1.35 they saw her standing with her hand on the breast of a man. It is a pity the three could not describe him, as he was probably the murderer.

Nevertheless, a description appeared in the *Police Gazette*, in the issue that carried two descriptions of the man seen with Elizabeth Stride. The *Police Gazette* does not give the names of the witnesses to whom it owes descriptions. In the Stride case I could recognize those taken from the statements of P.C. William Smith and Schwarz. I had no means to recognize the source of the description of the man seen with Eddowes. This ran:

At 1.35am, 30 September, with Catherine Eddowes, in Church Street, leading to Mitre Square, where she was found murdered at 1.45am, same date, a man, age 30, height 5ft 7 or 8 inches, complexion fair, moustache fair medium build, dress pepper and salt coloured loose jacket, grey cloth cap with peak of same material, reddish neckerchief tied in a knot; appearance of a sailor. Information respecting this man to be forwarded to inspector MacWilliam of Old Jewry, London, E.

I wrote to New Scotland Yard, asking if I might be furnished with the name of the witness - was it Levin or Lawende (alternatively spelt by Inspector Swanson) who had amplified his first statement, or somebody else? I received a reply from W. Waddell, Curator of the Black Museum; the above description was provided not by Lawende but by P.C. White.

This was very interesting and tied up with something else. More than thirty years later, after his retirement from the force, Stephen White wrote an article, which appeared in the *People's Journal* of 26 September, 1919:

For five nights we had been watching a certain alley just behind the Whitechapel Road. It could only be entered from where we had two men posted in hiding, and persons entering the alley were under observation by the other two men. It was a bitter cold night when I arrived at the scene to take a report of the two men in hiding. I was turning away when I saw a man coming out of the alley. He was walking quickly but noiselessly, apparently wearing rubber shoes, which were rather rare in those days. I stood aside to let the man pass. And as he came under the wall lamp I got a good look at him.

He was about five feet ten inches in height, and was dressed rather shabbily, though it was obvious that the material of his clothes was good. Evidently a man who had seen better days, I thought, but men who have seen better days are common enough down East, and that of itself was not sufficient to justify me in stopping him. His face was long and thin, nostrils rather delicate, and his hair was jet black. His complexion was inclined to be sallow, and altogether the man was foreign in appearance. The most striking thing about him, however, was the extraordinary brilliance of his eyes. They looked like two luminous glow worms coming through the darkness. The man was slightly bent at the shoulders, though he was obviously quite young - about 33 at the most - and gave one the idea of having been a student or professional man. His hands were snow white, and the fingers long and tapering.

As the man passed me at the lamp, I had an uneasy feeling that there was something more than usually sinister about him, and I was strongly moved to find some pretext for detaining him; but the more I thought it over, the more was I forced to the conclusion that it was not in keeping with British Police methods that I should do so. My only excuse for interfering with the passage of this man would have been his association with the man we were looking for, and I had no real grounds for connecting him with the murder. It is true I had a sort of intuition that the man was not quite right. Still, if one acted on one's intuition in the police force, there would be more frequent outcries about interference with the liberty of subjects, and at that time the police were criticized enough to make it undesirable to take risks.

The man stumbled a few feet away from me, and I made an excuse for engaging him in conversation. He turned sharply at the sound of my voice, and scowled at me in surly fashion, but he said 'Good-night', and agreed with me that it was cold.

His voice was a surprise to me. It was soft and musical, with just a tinge of melancholy in it, and it was the voice of a man of culture - a voice altogether out of keeping with the squalid surroundings of the East End.

As he turned away, one of the police officers came out of the house he had been in, and walked a few paces into the darkness of the alley. 'Hello! What is this?' he cried. And then he called in startled tones to me to come along.

In the East End we are used to shocking sights, but the sight I saw made the blood in my veins turn to ice. At the end of the cul-de-sac, huddled against the wall, there was the body of a woman, and a pool of blood was streaming along the gutter from her body. It was clearly another of those terrible murders. I remembered the man I had seen, and I started after him as fast as I could run, but he was lost in the dark labyrinth of the East End mean streets.

Comparison of the detail within these two accounts shows the variation which can occur not only in descriptions of the same man by different witnesses, but of the same man by the same witness after an interval of time. In the report White made on his return to the Station that night, the man was 5ft 7 or 8in in the article thirty years later, 5ft 10in. In the formal, immediate official report, the man had 'complexion fair, moustache fair'; in the article for the public 'His complexion was inclined to be sallow' and 'his hair was jet black.' It would be very unusual for a man whose complexion and moustache were fair to have hair jet black, and a complexion surely cannot be at once fair and sallow. Would much of his hair have been seen under the 'grey cloth cap with peak'? I prefer the formal report, written immediately P.C. White got back to the Station. The 'reddish neckerchief' which features in it has, in the article, disappeared. All the same, it is interesting that, in the article, his fingers are remembered as 'long and tapering,' and his voice as 'the voice of a man of culture.'

I do not understand P.C. White's excess of thoughtfulness which prevented him from detaining this man. Without having ground sufficient to justify an arrest, surely it is in order for a policeman to stop a person and ask for his identity and reason for being at a particular time and place? Too thoughtful or too scared?

Only ten minutes elapse between 1.35 when the three Jews saw Catherine Eddowes standing with her hand on a man's breast, and 1.45 when she was found dead, just after White had seen this man go by, so one feels he must have been the murderer.

Dr. Frederick Gordon Brown, surgeon to the City of London Police, who had been called to the body at Mitre Square, made a full statement to the Coroner:

The throat was cut across to the extent of about 6 inches or 7 inches. The sterno cleido mastoid muscle was divided: cricoid cartilage below the vocal chords was severed through the middle; the large vessels on each side of the neck were severed to the bone, the knife marking the intervertebral cartilage. The sheath of the vessels on the right side just open; the carotid artery had a pin-hole opening; the internal jugular vein was open to the extent of an inch and a half - not divided. All the injuries were made with some very sharp instrument, like a knife, and pointed. The cause of death was haemorrhage from the left carotid artery. The death was immediate. The mutilations were inflicted after death. They examined the injuries to the abdomen, the walls of the abdomen were laid open, from the breast downwards. The cut commenced opposite the ensiform cartilage, in the centre to the body. The incision went upwards, not penetrating the skin that was over the sternum; it then divided the ensiform cartilage, and being gristle they could not tell how the knife had made the cut. It was held so that the point was towards the left side and the handle towards the right. The cut was made obliquely. The liver was stabbed as if by the point of a sharp knife. There was another incision in the liver, about 2 1/2in and below the left lobe of the liver was slit through by a vertical cut. Two cuts were shown by a jag of skin on the left side. The abdominal walls were divided vertically in the middle line to within a quarter of an inch of the navel; the cut then took a horizontal course for 2 1/2in to the right side. It then divided the navel on the left side - round it - and made an incision parallel to the former horizontal incision, leaving the navel on a tongue of skin. Attached to the navel was 2 1/2in of the lower part of the rectus muscle of the left side of the abdomen. The incision then took an oblique course to the right. There was a stab of about an inch in the left groin, penetrating the skin in superficial fashion. Below that was a cut of 3in going through all tissues, wounding the peritoneum to about the same extent. There had not been appreciable bleeding from the vessels.

Mr Crawford, City of London Solicitor: What conclusion do you draw from that?

Dr Brown: That the cut in the abdomen was made after death, and that there would not be much blood left to escape on the hands of the murderer. The way in which the mutilation had been effected showed that the perpetrator of the crime possessed some anatomical knowledge.

Mr Crawford: I think I understood you to say that in your opinion the cause of death was the cut in the throat?

Dr Brown: Loss of blood from the throat, caused by the cut. That was the first wound inflicted.

Mr Crawford: Have you formed an opinion that the woman was standing when that wound was inflicted?

Dr Brown: My opinion is that she was on the ground.

Mr Crawford: Does the nature of the wounds lead you to any conclusion as to the kind of instrument with which they were inflicted?

Dr Brown: With a sharp knife, and it must have been pointed; from the cut in the abdomen I should say the knife was at least six inches long.

Mr Crawford: Would you consider that the person who inflicted the wounds possessed great anatomical skill?

Dr Brown: A good deal of knowledge as to the position of the organs in the abdominal cavity and the way of removing them.

Mr Crawford: Could the organs removed be used for any professional purpose?

Dr Brown: They would be of no use for a professional purpose.

Mr Crawford: You have spoken of the extraction of the left kidney. Would it require great skill and knowledge to remove it?

Dr Brown: It would require a great deal of knowledge as to its position to remove it. It is easily overlooked. It is covered by a membrane.

Mr Crawford: Would not such a knowledge be likely to be possessed by one accustomed to cutting up animals?

Dr Brown: Yes.

Mr Crawford: Have you been able to form any opinion as to whether the perpetrator of this act was disturbed when performing it?

Dr Brown: I think he had sufficient time. My reason is that he would not have nicked the lower eyelids if he had been in a great hurry.

Mr Crawford: About how long do you think it would take to inflict all the wounds and perpetrate such a deed?

Dr Brown: At least five minutes would be required.

Mr Crawford: Can you as a professional man assign any reason for the removal of certain organs from the body?

Dr Brown: I cannot.

Mr Crawford: Have you any doubt in your mind that there was no struggle?

Dr Brown: I feel sure that there was no struggle.

Mr Crawford: Are you equally of the opinion that the act would be that of one man, one person only?

Dr Brown: I think so. I see no reason for any other opinion.

Mr Crawford: Can you as a professional man account for the fact of no noise being heard by those in the immediate neighbourhood?
Dr Brown: The throat would be so instantaneously severed that I do not suppose there would be any time for the least sound being emitted.
Mr Crawford: Would you expect to find much blood on the person who inflicted the wounds?
Dr Brown: No, I should not.

Dr. George Sequiera, Divisional Police Surgeon, mentioned that he had been on the scene at Mitre Square within ten minutes of the body's discovery, so perhaps he was the first of the doctors to arrive. He differed from Dr. Brown in that he did not think a great deal of anatomical knowledge would have been required. Neither did the two doctors, Dr. McKellar and Dr. William Saunders, who had like Dr. Sequiera assisted Dr. Brown at the post mortem. A curious point is contributed by Dr. Brown:

Dr Brown: The abdomen was all exposed, the intestines were drawn out to a large extent and placed over the right shoulder; a piece of the intestine was quite detached from the body and placed between the left arm and the body.
Mr Crawford: By 'placed' do you mean put there by design?
Dr Brown: Yes.
Mr Crawford: Would that also apply to the intestines that were over the right shoulder?
Dr Brown: Yes.

So, here we have, as in the Chapman case, the imputation of an arrangement. One piece of intestine had been, of intent, placed between the left arm and the body. I am not able - at any rate not yet able - to interpret this but think it should be noted.

Dr. Brown also said:

A triangular flap of skin had been reflected from each cheek...

There is, in that detail, as in the nicking of both the lower lids, the idea of a symmetrical design, as in the placing of Annie Chapman's rings at her feet.

Crawford's question as to whether the cutting up of animals would have provided sufficient knowledge will have been directed to the possibility that the killer was a butcher.

My friend Timothy d'Arch Smith suggested to me that carving a joint could provide it. A saddle of mutton would come with the kidney still in it, and though it would be removed because it cooked at a different rate, a pater familias might have seen it in the kitchen. Carving was the man's job. There was a chapter on it in Mrs Beeton's *Household Management*. Artists, of course, study anatomy. Leonardo da Vinci was very keen on it and George Stubbs went to the length of dissecting a horse. Nevertheless, this is not a point I would press, as their concern is more with the skeleton and things that would show through to the surface, such as muscles and tendons, rather than anything so deep-seated as a kidney.

Stowell's argument against Clarence was that having taken part in deer-hunting he could carve the carcass, but Michael Harrison, defending the Heir Presumptive, said it was hard on the poor lad to make him into the Ripper because he knew how to gralloch a stag. (6)

What was more likely in Crawford's mind was that there were a great many slaughterhouses and butchers in the district. Indeed, the Jewish slaughterhouse at Aldgate was the starting point of Odell's theory the Ripper could be a shochet (Jewish ritual slaughterman), though Rumbelow quotes a letter he found amongst the many received by the police, that came from an ordinary family butcher, saying he was sure he could do it from his experience in cutting up a pig, and so could any man of his trade.(7)

There were a great many butchers around Aldgate, in the Spitalfields and Whitechapel area, some of which did their own slaughtering on their own premises. In such a district, a man with blood on his hands and clothes would attract less attention than in any other. Also, it meant a lot of knives about.

There is one passage in Inspector Swanson's report we have not taken up yet. It is important and connects what was found in Goulston Street (misspelled Goldstone Street); the missing half of Catherine Eddowes' apron, bloodstained, and the writing on the wall. The apron had been folded, said Smith, and the writing was directly above it. Smith told an Inspector McWilliam to fetch a photographer, but though Mitre Square was in the City, Goulston Street was in Whitechapel, East London, and so in the Metropolitan jurisdiction, and therefore Sir Charles Warren, Commissioner of the Metropolitan Police was informed. On arriving, he ordered the writing to the rubbed off. This, Smith thought, 'was a fatal mistake.' One understands Warren's fear, that the apparent meaning, that the Jews did it, could provoke a breach of the peace, yet it is a cardinal rule of investigation that one does not obliterate evidence. Knight compounds the issues by asserting that 'Juwes' was not a mis-spelling of Jews but a masonic term, for 'the Juwes were the three apprentice masons who killed Hiram Abiff.' (8)

I thought it prudent to check on this with a friend I knew was a Freemason. I rang him and asked, 'Does the word Juwes, spelt JUWES mean anything in Masonry?'

He had read Knight's book (and also) his critique of Freemasonry *The Brotherhood* and found much of it interesting, but could not follow the argument of the 'Juwes' passage.

Indeed, a recent scholarly study by John Robinson, *Born in Blood*, (Century 1990) traces the origins of the word to Old French *Jubés*, places of punishment for villains, and amongst Masons, for the murderers of their hero. This does not help Knight at all.

I still think Juwes probably was a genuine mis-spelling of Jews.

At the entrance to a lodging house commonly used by Jews, the motive of the writer would have been to insult them, or, if the writer was the murderer, to put the blame on them, or sow a false trail. Warren would surely have been better to wait until the words had been photographed, in case the hand was the killer's, but I do feel his motive was to prevent violence against the Jews.

If the Ripper wrote the words, he would have had to set out carrying not only his knife but his chalk, so there would have been premeditation. Who carried chalk naturally? It is used chiefly for writing things on blackboards in a classroom. Most chalk graffiti are by children. I would say it was the work of children, but that a P.C. passing only shortly before had noticed nothing. Or just someone who did not like Jews. Seeing the writing could have given the killer the idea of folding and placing the half apron there.

I visited Goulston Street. It was at mid-day on 24 December 1988. The street was very depressing, very dirty, with unswept rubbish and a general air of decay. I found the doorway. It was blocked up with lumber and leading to nowhere - and covered with graffiti. I took some dismal photographs, and, as I looked at it, felt it would have attracted the same sort of graffiti then, when it was inhabited.

Cullen, arguing the case for Montague Druitt, urges that he would not have had to go all the way back to his home in Blackheath in bloodstained clothing, since he had still his chambers at no 9 King's Bench Walk in the Inner Temple, which he could have reached on foot either via Fleet Street or the Embankment.(9) If so, he was going in the wrong direction. Goulston Street is east of Mitre Square. To reach it, he would have had to go down to Aldgate, turn east, crossing Houndsditch and Middlesex Street ('Petticoat Lane') to take the next one north. He was heading not south-west but north-east.

This direction seems not good for any of the named candidates. James Kenneth Stephen, it is pointed out by Michael Harrison, as his proposer, lived during the time of the crimes with his parents at 32 de Vere Gardens, Kensington, and could therefore have taken the underground from Kensington High Street to Aldgate East - and presumably returned the same way.

Sickert would by this time have lost his old studio in 15 Cleveland Street when the house was pulled down, along with several others, to allow for the extension of the Middlesex Hospital. His claim to have witnessed a raid on a premises in the street, that was probably Hammond's, in 1889, does, however, suggest that he had moved not very far, and that too would have meant setting out from and returning to the west. Neither would Goulston Street lead to his home in Hampstead.

The Ripper disappeared into East End slums. Perhaps the murderer really was just some East End butcher. Goulston Street leads nowhere - except to

Catherine Eddowes

Mary Kelly.

Smith tells us the murderer had washed his hands in Dorset Street, 'at a sink up a close, not more than six yards from the street. I arrived there in time to see the blood-stained water.' (10)

Dorset Street did not strike Smith as significant because he could not know where the next murder was going to be committed. But Dorset Street is a very short, small one. Washing his hands in Dorset Street - or in any part of Dorset Street - he would have been in ear-shot of Mary Kelly's entrance and must have been seen by her if she had been standing in it.

No, I am not saying that Sickert, having murdered Stride and Eddowes went on - after washing his hands to make himself respectable - to spend what remained of the night with Mary Kelly. He would have found Joe Barnett there. But it is odd, very odd.

1 *From Constable to Commissioner, the Story of Sixty Years, Most of them Misspent,* by Sir Henry Smith, K.C.B. (Chatto, 1910) pp 149-50
2 Smith, pp 154-5
3 Smith, p 155
4 *The Identity of Jack the Ripper,* Donald McCormick (Jarrolds, 1953)
5 Smith, p 152
6 *Clarence,* Michael Harrison (W.H. Allen, 1972) p 139
7 *The Complete Jack the Ripper,* Donald Rumbelow (W.H. Allen, 1975) p 133
8 Knight, p 178
9 *Autumn of Terror, Jack the Ripper, His Crimes and Times,* Tom Cullen, (Bodley Head, 1965) p 237
10 Smith, p 153
11 Smith, ibid.

Chapter 14:

The Spelling and Handwriting of the Ripper's Letter

It is probably too late to dissociate the name Jack from the Ripper, but the only letters to the police actually signed Jack the Ripper are generally considered to be amongst the time-wasting hoaxes. One of them was a postcard promising 'tomorrow double event this time.' This was received just after the 'double' murder of Elizabeth Stride and Catherine Eddowes, both found in the early morning of Sunday 30 September. The police published it, asking for anyone who recognized the handwriting to come forward, and the press rushed to the conclusion that it showed foreknowledge of the two latest murders and therefore must be by the murderer. Sir Robert Anderson regarded it, however, as 'the creation of an enterprising journalist.' (1)

Indeed, someone working in a newspaper office would know the news that was to be carried in next morning's paper during the hours of darkness in which it was being printed. Knight observed that the postcard was postmarked Oc 1. The bodies of Stride and Eddowes were found at 1am and 1.43 on 30 September. To show foreknowlege that there would be two, the postcard would have had to be posted on the 29 September. That was a Saturday, but in those days, when both collections and deliveries were so much more frequent than nowadays, there was always a Sunday collection, so that even if it missed the last post on the 29th, it must have borne a 30 September postmark. It was posted after the bodies had been found.

That leaves only the one letter, the letter, in quite a different writing, that came in the parcel wrapped up with part of Mrs Eddowes' kidney:

From Hell
Mr Lusk
Sir
I send you half the kidne I took from one woman presarved it for you tother piece i fried and ate it was very nise. I may send you the bloody knif that took it out if you only wate a while longer.

signed
Catch me when
you can
misther Lusk

The Ripper's Handwriting

I believe the apparent illiteracy of this letter to be feigned.

'Kidne' is not a natural misspelling for 'kidney.' No English word ends in 'e' that is sounded, except for the unusual personal name, 'Brontë,' where two dots are necessary to indicate this peculiarity. A much more natural misspelling would be 'kidny', since many words end with a 'y' that has not an 'e' before it. Some foreign words, notably German and Italian end in a sounded 'e', but there is no indication the writer of this letter was foreign. 'tother' for 'the other', is North country, but nothing else is. There used to be an old fashioned, aristocratic pronunciation of 'preserved' as 'presarved' - the 'er' being sounded as 'ar' as in 'Derby,' 'clerk,' 'sergeant,' etc. The person accustomed to the 'presarved' pronunciation would not have written 'tother' or 'kidne.'

'nise' is not a likely misspelling for 'nice.' Natural misspellings generally have behind them a reason, albeit a fallacious one - the commonest cause of error being false analogy between words of similar sound but different orthography .

The words ending in 'ise' are all pronounced as though ending in 'ize;' eg. 'rise,' 'prise,' 'wise,' 'surmise,' 'demise,' all rhyming with 'prize,' The words in which 's' is sounded in this position are uniformly spelt with a 'c': 'dice,' 'lice,', 'mice,' 'rice,' 'twice,' 'trice,', 'entice,' 'vice,' so that 'nice' falls naturally into this group. Not even the least educated put it into the wrong one.

The silent 'l' in 'half' and the silent 'k' in 'knife' have been observed, but whereas 'nife' might be a natural naive misspelling, 'knif' and 'whil' are both unnatural, because words having that sound do not end that way. 'Life,' 'rife,' 'strife,' and 'wife' all teach the addition of the final 'e' in this position and no example teaches to the contrary; 'bile,' 'file,' 'mile,' 'pile,' 'rile' and 'tile' all teach the use of the correct final 'e' in 'while', and there is no contrary example, the words ending simply in 'il' - 'evil,' 'peril,' 'devil,' 'pupil,' all having it in unstressed positions, of pronunciation too different to conduce to a misspelling: 'whil'. The silent 'h' was observed. A more natural naive misspelling would be 'wile.'

'Waite' for 'wait' is, because of the many words that end in 'ate,' a spelling mistake that is possible; but it is the only one that is.

'Misther' for 'Mister' is impossible. 'Misther' is found only in novels and stories in which an attempt to imitate cockney pronunciation is made by an author without knowledge of phonetics. Such authors will also represent the Cockney as saying 'wot', as though we did not all put the 'a' in that word into our short 'o' phoneme - ie rhyming 'wot' with 'cot,' not with 'cat.' The untrained tend to imagine their own pronunciation and that of others. The study of phonetics which I undertook at the suggestion of Professor Daniel Jones, included a course in Phonetics of English for teachers of English, given by Miss Marguerite Chappalaz - a subject I later taught for a year to other teachers of English at the Speech Fellowship. This course included regional pronunciations, including Cockney, or as we called it more politely, East London. The consonant 's' and the combination 'st' are pronounced by East London speakers exactly as by standard English (RP, ie Received Pronunciation) ones. Where East London differs markedly from RP is in what it does with the 't,' finally and in some medial positions as before 'le' or 'en' and intervocally. The interruption of the air-flow, breath, is by the East Londoner made not by bringing the tongue into contact with the alveolar ridge but by constricting the glottis to form a glossal stop, in place of the RP lateral or nasal plosion as in 'kettle' or 'kitten.'(2)

Initial 't' is pronounced as by RP speakers, excepting that in stressed positions it (and 'd') may be slightly afflicted.

None of these peculiarities are ever carried over by the east Londoner into his spelling, because he is unconscious of them. He is thinking the correct letter.

'Mister' is pronounced 'mister,' exactly as in RP - and it is never written out, but contracted, as by everybody, 'Mr.'

The writer of the 'From Hell' letter does it correctly at the beginning 'Dear Mr Lusk.' The 'Misther Lusk' at the end signs it a forged style.

The vulgar convoluted flourish to the capital L for 'Lusk' and 'S' for Sir', executed shakily, seem to me the work of a man pretending to have been taught copperplate at school but unaccustomed to using it. It is at variance with the swift confidence betrayed in the execution of the bare 'h' of hell, which characterizes education.

Feeling that I should have an opinion more experienced that my own with regard to the handwriting, I wrote to Dr Vernon Harrison. He is a handwriting expert, whose opinion is sought as to whether some piece of handwriting of legal import is truly in the hand of the person whose hand it purports to be, or the imitation of that hand by someone else. I wrote to Dr Harrison (whom I had met only briefly at a lecture by somebody else), enclosing photostats of the 'From hell' letter and of the few words in Sickert's hand at the bottom right-hand corner of the Ashmolean *Ennui*. (3) I chose those because they were the only specimen of Sickert's writing I possessed which did not give away his identity, either by his signature or some reference in the text to art, and I felt sure Dr Harrison would prefer not to know the identity of the writer. I asked him how much he would charge for a professional opinion whether the writers were the same or different, and gave him my own opinion (not at such length as I have given it here) hoping he would at least tell me if he thought me mistaken. He replied, saying his usual professional charge was in three figures, which he might waive in a case of exceptional interest, but he would not give an opinion on photostats, or even on good photographs, but only on inspection of the original papers. Nevertheless, two things he would tell me, immediately and free of charge: he agreed with my opinion that the appearance of illiteracy offered in both the spelling and the handwriting of the 'from hell' letter was 'contrived,' and that, with regard to the snippet from the document of origin not disclosed to him (that is, the lines written by Sickert on a corner of the Ashmolean *Ennui*), whilst obviously he would not chance an opinion on so small a sample, in photostat, he saw 'some points of resemblance between the two.'

The handwriting of the snippet is hard to read. I wrote to the Ashmolean, Oxford, to ask if they could decipher it, but they were able to make out only what I could, that the starting and ending phrases were 'O I Say.' They suggested, however, that the lines were from some popular song of the day, and I feel sure they are right. Probably they are from a music hall hit by some loved entertainer.

Dr Harrison did not specify the points of resemblance between this and the Ripper's hand perceived by him; I will therefore point to two that appeared to me, before I wrote to him. The third word of the second line is certainly 'her' and the small 'h' is made in exactly the same neat, print-like form as the small 'h' for hell in the Ripper's letter - that neat, print-like form of that small 'h' having been the first thing to strike me, in the Ripper's letter, as incongruous with the wobbling-ornate flourishes of the vulgar hand affected. It is only the highly-educated that make these neat print-like forms that seem to imitate those of printed books.

In both hands, one sometimes finds the small 'a' in the form of a 'u,' open at the top, the roofing curve not attempted. This is not a rarity, yet a point common to both.

1 *The Lighter Side of my Official Life* Sir Robert Anderson (Hodder and Stoughton, 1910)
2 See *The Phonetics of English*, Ida Ward, D. Lit (Heffers, Cambridge, 1941), 1948 ed., pp 135-136, and *An Introduction to the Phonetics of English*, A.C. Gimson, Professor of Phonetics, University College, London (Edward Arnold, 1962) ed 1976, pp 163, 167-171
3 That is, their drawing, squared up by him for their painting.

Chapter 15
Room 13 Mary Kelly

The murder of Mary Kelly was the only one committed within the victim's own room. This was in 26 Dorset Street (today Duval Street), a common lodging-house, owned by John McCarthy, who lived next door at 27. The room she had had been part of what must have been intended as the back parlour, partitioned off. As it did not communicate with the rest of the house, it had been given its own special entrance, into the alley-way leading to Miller's Court. This was a tiny little courtyard at the back, on to which her window looked. The sole entrance to the alley-way to Miller's Court was from Dorset Street, under a narrow, tunnel-like arch. Though there were some other houses on Miller's Court, it was thus, a dark pokey place, oversecluded and dangerously cut off. Room 13 was in her name, as Marie Jeanette Kelly and she paid 4s 6d a week for it, but during most of the time she had been there she had Joseph Barnett living with her.

Barnett appears to have been a decent sort of man, and emerges as by far the best man friend Mary Kelly ever had. He had tried to get her off the streets. Some writers have inclined to treat as fantasy her claim to have been taken by a gentleman to France and the Frenchification of her name. I am certain there was nothing French sounding in her name as it was given me by my mother from Florence. It was just plain English Mary, and one Christian name only. She may have heard these double-barrelled Christian names so common in France and fancied a transformation from plain Mary to Marie Jeanette, to give herself a bit of glamour. If it is correct as Joseph Sickert said, that his father had taken her to Dieppe in the summer of 1886, and Joe Barnett had lived with her for eighteen months, that is from about May 1887, that leaves us with just about a year during which she would have lived with these other two men. That these two could be named, as companions of a certain duration, makes me wonder if I was correct in my understanding she left Sickert's employ in order to become a prostitute, on a professional basis. It sounds more as though she had been trying to find a steady man, with whom she could live, resorting to prostitution when let down. And yet Barnett says she did tell him she was in a West End gay house before coming to the East End; and that supports the story as I thought I had it from my mother and Florence. Perhaps she had discovered prostitution was no fun, repented a bad decision, and was trying to find again just one man to whom she could be a wife. She was back on the streets when Barnett found her; he got her off them, tried to rehabilitate her, but then he lost his work, so that there was nothing coming in but what she brought home. He did not want to live on her earnings and so moved out, without withdrawing his friendship for her. There had, however, been a quarrel between them on the night he moved out, he told the inquest, a quarrel in which the window had got broken. It was because she had brought another prostitute, Maria Harvey, in to share their room.

This has caused some modern writers to speculate that she was a lesbian. I do not think so. I do not think these writers realize the depths of the poverty and squalor in which all these people lived. There was a good deal of sub-letting of the room space. It was not uncommon for the bed to be occupied by the main tenant, a couple or two lying on the floor. Mary and Joe, having a whole room to themselves, were living a little above the standard of the neighbourhood, which, when he lost his work, they could no longer afford. To keep on the room would be economically viable only if there was a sub-let.

She had lost her key. It must have been after the breaking of her window on 30 October, for she was able to put her arm through the hole in order to bolt the door on the inside.

Abberline took a statement from Maria Harvey, of 3 Newcourt, Dorset Street

I slept two nights with Mary Jane Kelly, Monday and Tuesday last. I then took a room at the above house. I saw her last about five minutes to seven last night in her own room, when Barnett called. I then left. They seemed to be on the best of terms. I left an overcoat, two dirty cotton shirts, a boy's shirt and a girl's white petticoat and black crêpe bonnet in the room. The overcoat shown me by the police is the one I left there.

So Mrs Harvey had retired discreetly, and after Joe Barnett left, Mary Kelly was, on this the last night of her life, alone.

There are statements taken by Abberline of witness as to what she was doing later:

Statement of Mary Ann Cox, No 5 Room, Millers Court, Dorset Street, Spitalfields.
I am a widow and an unfortunate. I have known the female occupying No 13 Room, Miller's Court, about 8 months. I knew her by the name of Mary Jane. About a quarter to twelve last night I came into Dorset Street from Commercial Street, and I saw walking in front of me Mary Jane with a man. They turned into the court and as I entered the court they went indoors. As they were going into her room, I said good night Mary Jane. She was very drunk and could hardly answer me, but said good night. The man was carrying a quart can of beer. I shortly afterwards heard her singing. I went out again shortly after twelve and returned about one o'clock and she was still singing in her room. I went out again shortly after one o'clock and came in at 3 o'clock. There was no light in her room then and all was quiet, and I heard no noise all night.
The man whom I saw was about 36 years old, about 5ft 4in high, complexion fresh and I believe he had blotches on his face, small side whiskers and a thick carroty moustache, dressed in shabby dark clothes, dark overcoat and thick felt hat.
Mary Jane was dressed I think last night when I saw her, in a linsey frock, red knitted cross-over around her shoulders, had no hat or bonnet on.

One feels it unlikely a man with a knife concealed would come with a quart can of beer, and probably this was not the murderer. Abberline took down a statement from another man, who came forward, voluntarily, George Hutchinson:

Metropolitan Police
H Division
12 November, 1888
Re Murder
At 6 pm 12th George Hutchinson of the Victoria Home, Commercial Street, came to this station and made the following statement.

about 2 am 9th I was coming by Thrawl Street, Commercial Street, and just before I got to Flower and Dean Street, I met the murdered woman Kelly and she said to me, Hutchinson will you lend me sixpence. I said I can't I have spent all my money down at Romford, she said good morning I must go and find some money. She went towards Thrawl Street. A man coming in the opposite direction to Kelly tapped her on the shoulder and said something to her, they both burst our laughing. I heard her say alright to him and the man said you will be alright for what I have told you. He then placed his right hand around her shoulder. He also had a kind of small parcel in his left hand with a kind of strap round it. I stood against the lamp of the Queen's Head Public House and watched him. They both then came past me and the man hung down his head with his hat over his eyes. I stooped down and looked him in the face. He looked at me stern. They both went into Dorset Street. I followed them. They both stood at the corner of the court for about 3 minutes. He said something to her. She said alright my dear come along you will be comfortable. He then placed his arm on her shoulder and she gave him a kiss. She said she had lost her handkerchief. He then pulled his handkerchief a red one out and gave it to her. They both then went up the Court together. I then went to the court to see if I could see them but I could not. I stood there for about three quarters of an hour to see if they came out. They did not so I went away.
Circulated to A[ll] S[tations]
Description, age about 34 or 35, height 5 ft 6, complexion pale. Dark eyes and eyelashes.Slight moustache curled up each end and hair dark. Very surly looking. Dress, long dark coat, collar and cuffs trimmed astrakhan and dark jacket under, light waistcoat, dark trousers, dark felt hat turned down in the middle, button boots and gaiters with white buttons, wore a thick gold chain with linen collar, black tie with horse shoe pin, respectable appearance, walked very sharp, Jewish appearance. Can be identified.

George Hutchinson

Was this the murderer? Can we trust Hutchinson's statement? According to it, he seems to have been inordinately curious, following the couple and standing outside the door. He could have made it all up. Yet there is another statement taken by Abberline, from a Mrs Sarah Lewis, which lends it confirmation in as much as she saw a man standing outside the premises:

Statement of Sarah Lewis, 24 Great Pearl Street, Spitalfields, a laundress.
Between 2 and 3 o'clock this morning I came to stop with the Keylers at 2 Miller's Court as I had a few words with my husband. When I came up the court there was a man standing over against the lodging house on the opposite side in Dorset Street but I cannot describe him. Shortly before 4 o'clock I heard a scream like that of a young woman, and seemed to be not far away. She screamed out murder. I only heard it once. I did not look out of the window. I did not know the deceased.
Sarah Lewis further said that when in company with another female on Wednesday evening last in Bethnal Green, a suspicious man accosted her. He carried a black bag.

Although Mrs Lewis said she could not describe the man she saw, one wishes Abberline would have let her see Hutchinson, and asked her if he looked like the man she saw. When he took her statement, of course, Hutchinson had not yet appeared.

Another statement that was taken confirms Mrs Lewis's with regard to the time of the scream:

Elizabeth Prater, wife of William Prater of No 20 Room, 27 Dorset Street:
I went out at about 9 pm on the 8th and stood at the bottom of Miller's Court until about 1.30. I was speaking for a short time to a Mr McCarthy who keeps a chandler's shop at the corner of the court. I then went up to bed. About 3.30 or 4 am I was awakened by a kitten walking across my neck, and just then I heard screams of murder two or three times in a female voice. I did not take much notice of the cries as I frequently hear such cries from the back of the lodging-house where the windows look into Miller's Court. From 1 am to 1.30 am no one passed up the court, if they did I should have seen them. I was up again and downstairs in the court at 5.30am but saw no one except one or two carmen harnessing their horses in Dorset Street. I went to the 'Ten Bells' p.h. at the corner of Church street and had some rum. I then returned and went to bed again without undressing until about 11am.

We have, therefore, two testimonies to screams having been heard shortly before 4 o'clock. Of course, all these times are only approximate, but if it was at 2.00 that Hutchinson saw Mary meet the man off Thrawl Street, and it took them about ten minutes to walk to Dorset Street and Miller's Court, and Hutchinson stood watching for about three quarters of an hour, as he says, that would bring us to about 3.00 when he left, just after the arrival of Sarah Lewis.

Did the man with whom Hutchinson saw Mary Kelly remain until between 3.30 and 4.00, when he murdered her? Or did he leave, after Hutchinson ceased his vigil, and another man enter?

That there had been a murder was discovered on the morning of Friday 9th November when McCarthy sent his man, Bowyer, to try to collect the rent owing. Abberline took statements from both man and master:

John McCarthy, Lodging house Keeper, 27 Dorset Street, Spitalfields.

I sent my man, Thomas Bowyer, to No 13 room, Millers Court, Dorset Street, owned by me, for the rent. Bowyer came back and called me, telling me what he had seen. I went with him back and looked through the broken window, where I saw the mutilated remains of deceased whom I knew as Mary Jane Kelly. I then despatched Bowyer to the Police Station, Commercial Street (following myself) to acquaint the police. The Inspector on duty returned with us to the scene at Miller's Court. I let the room about ten months ago to the deceased and a man named Joe, who I believed to be her husband. It was a furnished room at 4/6 per week. I sent for the rent because for some time past they had not kept their payments regularly. I have since heard the man Joe was not her husband and that he recently left her.

Living on immoral earnings, even indirectly, was by that date a criminal offence, and the landlord's assertion that he believed Joe to be his tenant's husband was probably intended to assure the police his was a respectable house.

Inspector Walter Beck arrived, bringing Constables, and looked through the window. At 11.15 Dr. Phillips arrived. At 11.30 Abberline arrived.

It had by this time been established that they could not get in, as the door did not open. This means either that McCarthy did not tell them that the bolt on the inside could be slid back by putting an arm through the hole in the window, or that the murderer had locked the door behind him with the key Mary Kelly had lost.

In that case, he must have stolen it, on a previous visit. That introduces an element of premeditation into the crime. Even if he had, after leaving, put his arm through the hole in the window to bolt the door on the inside, that betrays a familiarity with the premises and with Mary's custom.

In the end, McCarthy fetched a pick-axe, and the door was broken in.

Dr. Phillips now suggested that, as bloodhounds had been promised them, they should not go in, so as not to confuse the scents for the dogs. Abberline agreed. They waited for the bloodhounds. The bloodhounds did not arrive.

This may have had something to do with the fact that Sir Charles Warren, who had been under considerable pressure since his removal of the writing from the wall in Goulston Street, had resigned in the night, and his successor, the Assistant Commissioner, Sir Robert Anderson, had not yet taken over as Commissioner of the Metropolitan Police.

At 1.30 Superintendent Thomas Arnold arrived, to say the bloodhounds would not be coming. Abberline, therefore decided they should enter.

The room was sparsely furnished. There was only one chair, a bedside table, another small table and the bed. On the bed, Mary Kelly was lying, soaked in blood. Her breasts had been removed, and laid, in slices, on the bedside table. Her nose had been cut off and laid with the breasts, on the bedside table. Her throat had been cut across, from left to right, ear to ear, to the backbone. Her left arm had been so nearly severed as only to be connected with the body by skin, but had been arranged so that her left hand was in the abdominal cavity. She had been disembowelled. Her liver had been dragged from the body and placed between her legs. Her left thigh had been defleshed so as to expose a portion of the bone, and the slices of flesh removed from the thigh placed with her breasts and nose on her bedside table. Her right leg had been flayed, from the knee to the ankle, and the roll of skin turned back. Her forehead had been skinned.

Dr. Phillips formally pronounced life extinct.

A photograph was taken, which includes a corner of the bedside table, with what it bore. A close up was also taken of her eyes, in case there should be anything to the popular belief that the face of the murderer was imprinted on the eyes of his victim. The plate did not show this.

The bed was against the partition wall, but although there was a lot of blood on this, as well as on the bed, there was so much blood on the floor that Dr. Phillips thought death must have been caused by the initial cutting of a carotid artery, and that it must have been after this that the murderer placed her on the bed. He thought the perpetration of the mutilations would have required at least two hours. (That would mean that the murderer could not have left before about 6.00).

In the grate, there had been an enormous fire. Some of the cinders were still warm. So intense had been the heat that the spout and handle of the kettle had melted. The remnants of woman's clothing were found in the ashes, including a bit of the brim of a hat. The clothes were not Mary's. Mary's clothes were neatly folded over the chair at the foot of her bed. Probably they were Maria Harvey's, since, of all that she had left, the evening before, only the overcoat remained.

Mary's poor mutilated body was naked.

Many people have wondered why the murderer built up such an enormous fire. It was suggested he needed a light, to see what he was doing. But then he could have lit the candle. Maria Harvey testified that when she left earlier in the evening, not much of it was consumed. We are not told where this stood - probably not on the bedside table, used by the murderer for the parts of her body, or we should have been told of it. Perhaps it stood on the other small table, in the window. It has been suggested the murderer burned his bloodsoaked clothes. But clothes heavily blood-soaked would retard the blaze, and burn with a peculiar smell. He would have to have brought a change of clothing with him, in which to leave, and that again would imply premeditation. It has been suggested he took off all his clothes, to avoid getting them bloodstained, and during the two hours that he was naked at his task needed the fire to keep him warm. Perhaps, but this would have been to take a terrible risk. All lit up by firelight, he would have been dramatically visible from the dark court.

I ask myself what these things can mean; the fire, the burnt clothes, the clothes folded over the chair.

I think it possible the murderer managed to avoid getting his clothes so heavily soaked in blood that to put them on the fire would extinguish it, yet thought it best to burn one or two garments which did bear splashes of blood. Why did he not just taken them off and leave them? Perhaps he felt they were distinctive and could be traced to him. In that case, he would have needed to build the fire up big enough to consume them. Probably Mary had not much coal, and Mrs Harvey's clothes were to hand as fuel. Also, their remains would become mixed with, and so disguise, the remains of his own clothes.

He would have wanted to wash, but the room had no washstand or basin. How had Mary and Joe washed? How had they cooked? Cooking of a simple kind can be done on the hob of an open fire. There were public baths in the London of that time, but for a quick wash they probably went to that small fountain set back from Dorset Street. That was probably where the murderer counted on being able to wash when he left, as he had washed there after murdering Catherine Eddowes.

Ripperologists have concentrated on the fire, asking themselves the man's motive in making it. They have not interested themselves in Mary's clothes, neatly folded over her chair. Perhaps because I am a woman, it is these I think about, and the circumstances in which she took them off and folded them.

Women's clothing in those days was voluminous and complicated. There were whaleboned bodices. The laces had to be drawn tight from behind. Unless one had a maid or member of the family to do one up, it was a difficult matter. There is a contemporary picture in the *Penny Illustrated News* which shows Mary entering the room in the court with her murderer. The artist has made several mistakes. He has positioned the window and its hole wrongly and shown Mary using a key to open the door, unaware she had lost it. He is less likely to have been mistaken as to her dress. He shows her with a bustle, and with the wasp-waist that betrays tight-lacing above. If prostitutes were not excempt from the restrictions of fashion, I doubt if they undressed very far for their clients.

Yet Mary had undressed leisurely, folding each garment as she removed it and hanging it over the chair.

The question is, whether the murderer was the man seen by Hutchinson to go in with her. If he was, then entering about 10, he stayed until between 3.30 and 4.00, when the murder screams were heard. That is, an hour and a half. What were they doing all that time? I would have suggested, having a meal, but that the pathologist found the deceased had not eaten for some hours before death. Having a kettle on the hob, she could have made him a cup of tea. We are not told if there was an opened packet of tea in the room. We are not told of used teacups. In any case, to drink tea does not take that length of time. So, were they in the bed or out of it? I would think that in sexual murders, the stabbing is either a substitute for intercourse or a complement to it. Therefore, if it followed intercourse it would follow quickly. It is difficult to imagine that a sexually driven murderer would have had intercourse with her, then sat about for an hour and a half before producing his knife. His blood would no longer have been hot. So, if the hour and a half elapsed before the intercourse, how was it occupied?

It is also possible that the man watched by Hutchinson left, soon after Hutchinson gave up his vigil. I do not think she would have gone out again. It was a long time since she had eaten. She was cold and tired, and, having undressed, folded her clothes and gone to bed, she would have stayed there. Another man could have let herself in by pulling his arm through the window to slide the bolt.

At 2.00 a Dr. Thomas Bond arrived at Miller's Court. He was consultant surgeon to A division, and had been called in as a second opinion.

Friday 9 November was the day of the Lord Mayor's Show, but since word of the murder had got about, Miller's Court had been providing a rival attraction. Abberline had it cordoned off, letting nobody in or out, but when, at 3.45, a cart arrived to convey the body to the mortuary, there were many who had deserted the civic pageantry to watch it go. The window of Room 13 was now boarded up and the door - what remained of it - padlocked, and a policeman posted to keep the idle away.

The body was taken not to the mortuary in Whitechapel but to the one in Shoreditch, and thus the inquest came to be held in Shoreditch Town Hall, before Coroner Roderick MacDonald. When it opened, on 12 November, there was a dispute about this. Some people said it ought to be in Whitechapel, before Mr Baxter, but MacDonald replied, 'I may tell the juryman that jurisdiction lies where the body lies, not where it was found.' Before evidence was taken, the jurymen were conducted to the mortuary. They were only required to see the head of the deceased, the rest being mercifully covered.

Back in the Town Hall, the first witness called was Joseph Barnett. His evidence is so important that I will give it in full, as reported in *The Daily Telegraph* of 13 November.

Barnett: I was a fish-porter, and work as a labourer and fruit-porter. Until Saturday last I lived at 24 New-Street, Bishopsgate and have since stayed at my sisters's 21 Portpool Lane, Gray's inn Road. I have lived with the deceased one year and eight months. Her name was Marie Jeanette Kelly, with the French spelling as described to me. Kelly was her maiden name. I have seen the body, and identify it by the ear and eyes, which are all that I can recognize but I am positive it is the same woman I knew. I lived with her in No 13 room at Miller's Court for eight months. I separated from her on Oct 30.
Coroner: Why did you leave her?
Barnett: Because she had a woman of bad character there, whom she took in out of compassion, and I objected to it. That was the only reason. I left her on the Tuesday between five and six p.m. I last saw her alive between half-past seven and a quarter to eight on Thursday night last, when I called upon her. I stayed there for a quarter of an hour.
Were you on good terms? - yes, on friendly terms; but when we parted I told her I had no work, and had nothing to give her, for which I was very sorry.
Did you drink together? - No, sir. She was quite sober.
Was she, generally speaking, of sober habits? - When she was with me I found her of

sober habits, but she has been drunk several times in my presence.

Was there anyone else there on the Thursday evening? - Yes, a woman who lives in the court. She left first, And I followed shortly afterwards.

Have you had conversation with deceased about her parents? Yes, frequently. She said she was born in Limerick, and went when very young to Wales. She did not say how long she lived there, but she came to London about four years ago. Her father's name was John Kelly, a 'gaffer' or foreman in an iron-works in Carnarvenshire, or Carmarthen. She said she had one sister, who was respectable, who travelled from market place to market place. This sister was very fond of her. There were six brothers living in London and one was in the army. One of them was named Henry. I never saw the brothers to my knowledge. She said she was married when very young in Wales to a collier. I think the name was Davis or Davies. She said she had lived with him until he was killed in an explosion, but I cannot say how many years since that was. Her age was, I believe, 16, when she married. After her husband's death deceased went to Cardiff to a cousin.

Did she live there long? Yes - she was in an infirmary there for eight or nine months. She was following a bad life with her cousin, who, as I reckon, and as I often told her, was the cause of her downfall.

After she left Cardiff did she come direct to London? - Yes. She was in a gay house in the West-end, but in what part she did not say. A gentleman came there to her and asked her if she would like to go to France.

Did she go to France? -Yes; but she did not remain long. She said she did not like the part, but whether it was the part or purpose I cannot say. She was not there more than a fortnight, and she returned to England and went to Ratcliffe-highway. She must have lived there for some time. Afterwards she lived with a man opposite the Commercial Gas Works, Stepney. The man's name was Morganstone.

Have you seen that man? - Never. I don't know how long she lived with him.

Was Morganstone the last man she lived with? - I cannot answer that question, but she described a man named Joseph Fleming; who came to Pennington Street, a bad house, where she stayed. I don't know when this was. She was very fond of him. He was a mason's plasterer, and lodged in Bethnal Green Road.

Was that all you knew of her history when you lived with her? -Yes! After she lived with Morganstone or Fleming - I don't know which one was the last - she lived with me.

Where did you pick up with her first? In Commercial Street. We then had a drink together, and I made arrangements to see her on the following day, - a Saturday. On that day we both of us agreed that we should remain together. I took lodgings in George Street, Commercial Street, where I was known. I lived with her, until I left her, on very friendly terms.

Have you heard her speak of being afraid of anyone? - Yes; several times. I bought newspapers, and read to her everything about the murders, which she asked me about.

Did she express fear of any particular individual? No Sir. Our own quarrels were very soon over.

The Coroner: You have given your evidence very well.

Yes, Joseph Barnett had given his evidence well; he comes over to us as a responsible and honest man, who genuinely cared about her. What is odd is the complete suppression of the period during which she was employed as nursery governess by Sickert. Barnett says she first entered into prostitution, lured into it by her cousin, in Cardiff. She told Florence she had been in employment in Cardiff that was respectable, though dull and ill paid. Perhaps she lied to Florence. Yet the job she had had as sales assistant in the tobacconists's in Cleveland Street was respectable, if likewise dull and ill paid. To Barnett she represented herself as having gone straight from prostitution in Cardiff to a brothel in London. This is not so. Unlike Morganstone and Fleming, Sickert is not named, though she was with him for a long time, and he is represented as a client to the brothel, from which he took her on the holiday to France which she did not enjoy, whereas their association was much more respectable than that. He introduced her to Florence, and so probably to other friends who called at the studio in Cleveland Street. She was on the fringe of an artists' circle.

One would understand that a woman would suppress a period in her life during which she had been in prostitution, if she had since escaped from it. What is difficult to understand is that a woman, thought of as fallen, should suppress that there had been a period in her life during which she had been respectable. Why? Why did she tell Barnett, or let him think, that it was as a client to the brothel she had known Sickert? Why did she suppress that it was from a shop, not from a brothel, he had taken her - to become a nursery governess?

I can only think of one reason, that Sickert had told her not to talk about that child. He must have been saying, even before the murder of Mary Kelly, that to talk about the paternity of that child was dangerous. He did not only tell that to Florence to prevent her from talking about the murder of Mary Kelly - as having been organized by the Government to keep the secret of the child's paternity from being divulged by Mary Kelly - he told it to Mary Kelly, and he must have told it to her back in 1886, during the time she was helping him to look after the child. This is very odd, yet I feel must be so. Perhaps he was really, on the subject of that child, not quite sane. Had royalty gone to his head?

Yet, if he had even while she was with him as nursemaid told her she must never tell whose child she knew this to be, and so embued her with the danger of the knowledge she kept everything to do with it from Joseph Barnett, that makes it unlikely she was gossiping about it to the other women who were murdered. But yet again, if he had been representing the child's paternity as such a tremendous secret, that could have given her the idea of levying money on it, for her silence. Sickert told Florence he had received a blackmailing letter or letters from Mary Kelly. Joseph Barnett certainly did not know she had been trying to blackmail anybody. She was living a secret from him.

In that case, Florence was absolutely right in telling Mother the paternity of that child lay at the root of the murders. I believe it did. To go on with the inquest -

Mary Ann Cox, questioned as to what if anything she had head after she returned to her room for the last time, at 3.00, said she heard a man who lived 'in the court leave for work in Spitalfield market.' After that, 'I heard a man go down the court at 6.15. That would be too late for the market.' Questioned, she said she did not hear a door bang behind him, as though he had gone into a house, and agreed with the coroner he could have walked up the court and back again, and could have been a policeman on his beat.

Mrs Prater, called, explained that her room was directly above no 13. She had been out on the streets all Thursday night, and after her return to Miller's Court at 1.00 stood for 20 minutes on the corner, hoping to pick up a customer. No one passed and there was no light in Room 13. On returning to her own room, Mrs Prater barricaded her door with two tables and went to bed. (So she, at least, thought of the neighbourhood as dangerous, though her room, being in the main part of the house, was less dangerously situated than Mary's). She thought it was about 3.30 or 3.45 that the kitten disturbed her and she heard the screams. She heard no sounds as of beds or tables being pulled about. When she woke again it was 5.0 By 5.45 she was in the Ten Bells. She saw no strangers there.

Mrs Lewis, called, was now able to give a description of the man she had seen on the corner. 'He was stout, not very tall, and he wore a black, wide-awake hat.' (If only note had been made of the appearance of Hutchinson when he turned up, apparently later in the day, at the police station, this would enable us either to confirm or deny that it was he whom she saw).

Mrs Lewis continued, saying that she had dozed in a chair at Mrs Keyler's until she heard the clock of Christ Church, Spitalfields, strike the half hour. 'I sat awake until nearly four, when I heard a female voice shouting 'Murder' loudly. It seemed like the voice of a young woman. It sounded at our door. There was only one scream.'

So, now we have the time of the murder more narrowly boxed down.

When Mrs Lewis left Mrs Keyler's it was 5.30 and she saw no one.

The murderer would still have been at his work, though nearing the end of it. It would still have been dark and it is a pity the Coroner did not ask her whether she saw a light, firelight or anything through the window of Room 13, which she specified as opposite to Mrs Keyler's in the court, so must have been seen by her on leaving. Since she did not mention it, I can only think the fire had, by then, died down. The candle not being lit (or most likely she would have mentioned that) he did not catch her eye as moving around, if indeed the mutilation occupied as long as was thought and he was still there.

The evidence of Caroline Maxwell should also be considered, though this has always been a nuisance to Ripperologists, as it seems to be against all sense.

She was the wife of the deputy of 14, Dorset Street, lodging house, which was opposite to the entrance to Miller's Court. She had earlier made a

Mary Kelly

statement taken down by Abberline:

I have known the deceased woman during the past 14 months, she was known as Mary Jane and that since Joe Barnett left her she had obtained her living as an unfortunate. I was on speaking terms with her though I had not seen her for 3 weeks until Friday Morning 9th instant about half past 8 o'clock. She was then standing at the corner of Miller's Court in Dorset street. I said to her, what brings you up so early. She said, I have the horrors of drink upon me as I have been drinking for some days past. I said why don't you go to Mrs Ringers (meaning the public house at the corner of Dorset Street called the Britannia) and have half pint of beer. She said, I have been there and had it, but have brought it all up again. At the same time she pointed to some vomit in the roadway. I then passed on and went to Bishopsgate on an errand and returned to Dorset Street about 9am. I then noticed deceased standing outside Ringers public house. She was talking to a man, age I think about 30, height about 5ft 5in, stout, dressed as a Market Porter. I was some distance away and am doubtful whether I could identify him. The deceased work a dark dress, black velvet body, and coloured wrapper around her neck.

It is the date, 'Friday 9th instant,' that troubles. One could have taken this as an aberration, either of hers or of Abberline's, but in the Coroner's Court she stuck to it. She had seen her at eight on Friday morning. 'It was unusual to see her up at that hour, I spoke across the street. 'What, Mary brings you up so early?' She said, "Oh Carrie, I do feel so bad."'

The Coroner reminded Mrs Maxwell that she was on oath. W. Waddell of Scotland Yard wrote to me that her evidence can be totally disregarded. Indeed, unless it was with Mary's ghost she had this conversation, I would suggest that it took place not on the morning after but on the morning before her murder. The shock could have confused her as to the time elapsed.

Mrs Prater breakfasted on rum. Was it the measure of their drinking problem? In Mary's case, having to go out and round the corner to enter the common kitchen of 26 Dorset Street may have assisted her to the idea it was easier to go out and round the corner to enter the common kitchen of 26 Dorset Street to breakfast at Ringer's. (Incidentally, she would have had to go out and round the corner to a lavatory).

Dr. Phillips began to give his evidence and said he believed the cause of death to have been the cutting of a carotid artery. The Coroner said more detailed evidence could be given later. Then he turned to the jury and told them that if they were satisfied death had been caused in this way, they could return a verdict of wilful murder by person or persons unknown, and the inquest closed after less than a day. The others had gone on for much longer.

Of course, Coroner MacDonald may have had in mind the reluctance Dr. Phillips had expressed at the Chapman inquest to give full details in open court, but we are denied the benefit of hearing him asked to estimate the time of death; and Dr. Bond was not called. That he would have had a good deal to say is evident from his memorandum to the Home Office, which happily has survived and is now in the Public Record Office. He was consultant surgeon to Metropolitan Police A Division, and also the Great Western Railway, a lecturer on Forensic Medicine and author of several medical publications. In addition to making, jointly with Dr. Phillips, the post mortem on Mary Kelly, he had been shown the papers regarding the previous murders and asked for his comments. He wrote:

7 The Sanctuary,
Westminster Abbey
November 10th '88
Dear Sir
Whitechapel Murders
I beg to report that I have read the notes of the four Whitechapel Murders viz:-
1   Buck's Row
2   Hanbury Street
3   Berner's Street
4   Mitre Square.
I have also made a Post Mortem Examination of the mutilated remains of a woman found yesterday in a small room in Dorset Street.
1   All five murders were no doubt committed by the same hand. In the first four the throats appear to have been cut from left to right in the last case owing to the extreme mutilation it is impossible to say in what direction the fatal cut was made, but arterial blood was found on the wall in splashes close to where the woman's head must have been lying.
2   All the circumstances surrounding the murders lead me to form the opinion that the women must have been lying down when murdered and in every case the throat was cut first.
3   In the four murders of which I have seen the notes only, I cannot form a very definite opinion as to the time that had elapsed between the murder and the discovery of the body. In one case, that of Berner's Street the discovery appears to have been immediately after the deed. In Buck's Row, Hanbury Street, and Mitre Square three or four hours only could have elapsed. In the Dorset Street case the body was lying on the bed at the time of my visit two o'clock quite naked and mutilated as in the annexed report.
Rigor Mortis had set in but increased during the progress of the examination. From this it is difficult to say with any degree of certainty the exact time that had elapsed since death as the period varies from six to twelve hours before rigidity sets in. The body was comparatively cold at two o'clock and the remains of a recently taken meal were found in the stomach and scattered about over the intestines. It is therefore, pretty certain that the woman must have been dead about twelve hours and the partly digested food would indicate that death took place about three or four hours after food was taken, so one or two o'clock in the morning would be the probable time of the murder.
4   In all the cases there appears to be no evidence of struggling and that attacks were probably so sudden and made in such a position that the women could neither resist nor cry out. In the Dorset Street case the corner of the sheet on the right of the woman's head was much cut and saturated with blood, indicating that the face may have been covered with the sheet at the time of the attack.
5   In the four first cases the murderer must have attacked from the right side of the victim. In the Dorset Street case, he must have attacked from front or from the left, as there would be no room for him between the wall and the part of the bed on which the woman was lying. Again the blood had flowed down on the right side of the woman and spurted on to the wall.
6   The murderer would not necessarily be splashed or deluged with blood, but his hands and arms must have been covered and part of his clothing must certainly have been smeared with blood.

7   The mutilations in each case excepting the Berners Street one were all of the same character and showed clearly that in all the murders the object was mutilation.

8   In each case the mutilation was inflicted by a person who had no scientific nor anatomical knowledge. In my opinion he does not even possess the technical knowledge of a butcher or horse slaughterman or any person accustomed to cut up dead animals.

9   The instrument must have ben a strong knife at least six inches long, very sharp pointed at the top and about an inch in width. It may have been a clasp knife, a butchers knife or a surgeons knife, I think it was no doubt a straight knife.

10   The murderer must have been a man of physical strength and of great coolness and daring. There is no evidence that he had an accomplice. He must in my opinion be a man subject to periodical attacks of homicidal and erotic mania. The character of the mutilations indicate that the man may be in a condition sexually, that may be called Satyriasis. It is of course possible that the Homicidal impulse may have developed from a revengeful or brooding condition of the mind, or that religious mania may have been the original disease but I do not think either hypothesis is likely. The murderer in external appearance is quite likely to be a quiet inoffensive looking man probably middle aged and neatly and respectably dressed. I think he must be in the habit of wearing a cloak or overcoat or he could hardly have escaped notice in the streets if the blood on his hands or clothes were visible.

11   Assuming the murderer to be such a person as I have just described, he would probably be solitary and eccentric in his habits, also he is most likely to be a man without regular occupation, but with some small income or pension. He is possibly living among respectable persons who have some knowledge of his character and habits and who may have grounds for suspicion that he isn't quite right in his mind at times. Such persons would probably be unwilling to communicate suspicions to the Police for fear of trouble or notoriety, whereas if there were prospect of reward it might overcome their scruples.

There are a number of points to note. From the evidence of other witnesses, we know that Mrs Nichols, Mrs Chapman and Mrs Eddowes can only have been dead a few minutes when found, and that the time of Mary Kelly's death must have been nearer to 4.0, but Dr. Bond does say that estimating the time backward from the onset of rigor mortis cannot be exact as the time at which it sets in varies.

Dr. Phillips felt sure in the case of Annie Chapman, that the placing of the rings and other articles taken from her person, at her feet and around her, was by some design. Dr. Brown felt that the placing of Mrs Eddowes, intestines over her right shoulder, save for the piece detached and placed between the trunk and left arm was deliberate. Both doctors felt they were in the presence of deliberate arrangements by the killer. If he had to pick up from the floor the parts of Mary which he had thrown behind him as he worked, then was his placing them on the corner of the table beside her left shoulder, likewise with deliberate thought?

Of notable importance to our enquiry is that whereas Dr. Brown and Dr. Phillips thought that the cutting up of Mrs Eddowes and Mrs Chapman showed considerable anatomical knowledge, Dr. Bond's opinion was that the murderer had none whatever. In fairness, it should be remembered Dr. Brown had been looking at the body of Catherine Eddowes, Dr. Bond at that of Mary Kelly.

According to the *East London Advertiser*, Mary was given a proper funeral, paid for by Henry Wilton, who had been clerk of St Leonard's Church, Shoreditch. The service was held at St. Leonard's at noon on Sunday the 18th, and her coffin was inscribed: Marie Jeanette Kelly, died 9th November 1888, aged twenty-five. It bore a floral cross, paid for by boys at Leytonstone school, and two wreathes, from the Britannia (Ringer's) and Ten Bells, inscribed 'from friends of the deceased woman using certain public houses in common with the deceased woman.' Joseph Barnett followed the hearse in the first carriage. In the one that followed were women, among whom were distinguished Maria Harvey and Mary Ann Cox. The procession made its way to St Patrick's Cemetery, Leytonstone. It was a Catholic one.

The burial service was performed by Father Colomban. May it have eased her soul.

Chapter 16
The Exclusion of Eddowes

Joseph Sickert had been told by his father that 'Kelly was involved with three prostitutes, into whose class she had descended in order to fight off starvation, and at their instigation had resorted to blackmail.' (1) Knight, explaining this a couple of pages further on in his book, says, 'One poor woman [meaning Annie Crook] shrieking for her truths to be heard...could easily have been dismissed as mad. But four apparent lunatics crying out the same tale, even though they were East End whores, would have produced a pattern many would have been eager to interpret.'(2) Blackmailers do not usually shriek their truths, they hoard them so as to be able to demand money for not shrieking them, but no matter. The claim made by Sickert is that Mary Kelly had told what she knew of the parentage of Annie Crook's child to three other prostitutes. The three were Mary Nichols, Annie Chapman and Elizabeth Stride. As I found it impossible to believe Lord Salisbury had known and advised Gull that Mary Kelly had told the child's parentage to Mary Nichols, Annie Chapman and Elizabeth Stride, and that therefore these three, as well as herself, were to be got rid of, I first inclined to pass over Knight's chapter entitled 'All Roads Lead to Dorset Street.' Yet it is a fact that these three and Mary Kelly lived very close together, much closer than one would suppose from the places at which they were murdered.

Dorset Street (the name will not be found on the map for it has been changed to Duval Street) is a very short street, running from Commercial Street to Crispin Street, parallel to and between Brushfield Street and White Street. Mary Kelly, though her door opened into the passage to Miller's Court, at the back, lodged in 26 Dorset Street. Annie Chapman lodged at 35 Dorset Street, and they used the same pub. This we learn when we put together statements made by witnesses at their two inquests. At the inquest on Chapman, a prostitute, Amelia Farmer, said she had been a witness to a fight between the deceased and another woman, Liza Cooper. It was over a bar of soap which the deceased had borrowed and not returned, and began in Ringer's though continued outside. For the inquest, the point of importance was that the bruises on the face and breast of the deceased had been inflicted by Liza Cooper, not by the murderer. For us, what interests is the mention of Ringer's.

What this was emerges only when we look at Caroline Maxwell's statement that she had advised Mary Kelly to have half a pint of beer at Ringer's meaning the public house named the Britannia, kept by a Mrs Ringer, and that

Mary said she had already done so but brought it up. So, this public house, on the corner of Dorset Street and Crispin Street, was patronized both by Mary Kelly and Annie Chapman.

Elizabeth Stride's address was given at the inquest as 32 Flower and Dean Street, but as it emerged in the evidence which followed, she had only spent a couple of nights there and really lived with Michael Kidney, whose address was 35 Dorset Street, the same as Annie Chapman's. So that was where Elizabeth Stride had lived, in the same house as Annie Chapman, and, as she drank, she too was probably a patron of Ringer's.

Only a very close scrutiny of the evidence given at the inquests would have brought these interconnections out. They were not picked out by newspapers as significant.

Mary Nichols lived a little further away, on the other side of Commercial Street, in Thrawl Street, as did Catherine Eddowes, in Flower and Dean Street, but Walter Sickert told his son that Mary Nichols was one in whom Mary Kelly had confided, and Catherine Eddowes was not. Her murder was a mistake.

Now this is extraordinary. Everyone has heard of Jack the Ripper, but his victims are usually just referred to as prostitutes. People do not know their names, unless they have specially studied the crimes. Sickert not only knew their names, he certainly talked to his son as though he knew a lot about them, as individual persons. To the public they are hardly individualised. But Sickert presumed to know that Mary Kelly was associated with Mary Nichols, Annie Chapman and Elizabeth Stride in a way that she was not with Catherine Eddowes. That is presuming to know a lot.

Their names appeared, of course, in the newspapers of 1888, but even then never in large print. If he was right about there being connections between Kelly, Chapman and Stride from which Eddowes was excluded, it is extraordinary that a close examination of evidence should reveal a likely basis for such an assertion in as much as Kelly, Chapman and Stride, at any rate, all lived in the same street, at only a few doors from each other, with Ringer's to bring them together. These little streets are so small and insignificant as never to have been heard of by most people, excepting of course those who live in them.

Walter Sickert was claiming to know a lot about the women, as individuals. Did he know them?

Amongst the statements taken for neighbours of Mary Kelly there is only one that speaks of a man in her life other than Barnett. That is the one taken from Julia Venturney:

I occupy No 1 Room at Miller's Court. I am a widow but now living with a man named Harry Owen. I was awake all night and could not sleep. I have known the person occupying No 13 room opposite mine for about 4 months. I knew the man who I saw down stairs (Joe Barnett) he is called Joe, he lived with her until quite recently. I have heard him say that he did not like her going out on the streets. He frequently gave her money. He was very kind to her. He said he would not live with her while she led that course of life. She used to get tipsy occasionally. She broke the window a few weeks ago when she was drunk. She told me she was very fond of another man named Joe, and he had often ill used her because she cohabited with Joe (Barnett). I saw her last yesterday, Thursday, at 10.am.

I could have asked myself if this other man was Sickert, except that Mrs Venturney said his name, too, was Joe. He could have been Fleming.

Walter Sickert had apparently given his son no explanation of the 'mistake' by which Catherine Eddowes was murdered, but Knight thought he had found one when he noticed she had been living with a man named Kelly. Gull and the others must have thought, when they got her, that they had got Mary Kelly. Mary Kelly had been eventually tracked down, Joseph Sickert told him, with the aid of the portrait - he did not say by his father, but I have never heard of any other artist to whom she might have sat. I do not, however, believe that, even with a Sickert portrait in hand, it would have been possible for a stranger to pick her out from amongst the twelve hundred prostitutes said to be soliciting in Whitechapel at that time, unless at least the area was known. Sickert, of course, must have known the street, for he had received the blackmailing letter or letters, which must have born an address for the hoped for money to be paid to.

The plan - Gull's plan - Walter Sickert told his son, was to kill Nichols, Chapman, Stride and Kelly within one month, by Masonic ritual, but, something having gone wrong, the killing of Mary Kelly had to be postponed, until 9 November, when it was judged the police would be occupied with the preparations for the Lord Mayor's Show. Notice that Sickert is claiming to know what was in the murderer's mind.

In telling a story, some things may be added for drama, but the mistake over Catherine Eddowes does not add to this. It is odd to have made up, as it is odd that the missing part of Eddowes' apron as found on the way to Kelly's. The discovery of the apron in Goulston Street was published at the time but not Major Smith's discovery of the blood in the basin beneath the fountain in Dorset Street. Even Knight missed it, though it had appeared in Rumbelow (whom perhaps Knight thought not worth reading very thoroughly), Rumbelow's obvious source being a work listed in his (but not Knight's) bibliography, *From Constable to Commissioner* by Sir Henry Smith, 1910. Smith is not a particularly striking name and, there being nothing about the Ripper in the title, Knight thought probably that it was because Rumbelow was a policeman he had included in his background reading this memoir of a police officer, and did not consult it to see if it held anything for Ripperologists. Would Sickert have thought to obtain and read it? The name of Smith had never been publicized with regard to the murders. Sickert seems to have known the names of the very high ranking officers of the period. I would be surprised if Smith was his source for his assertion the Ripper intended to get Kelly that night. Smith did not know that. Nobody had told him of Mary Kelly's special personal interest to the

Ripper, the ultimate, intended victim. All he saw in his discovery of the blood in the fountain was that the murderer must have been sufficiently familair with the district to know there was in Dorset Street a small fountain at which he could wash his hands.

Now I am going to stick my neck out and offer a suggestion. When the first of Mary Kelly's letters arrived, insisting that he still owed her money and must pay it because she was hard up. He went to see her, to try to talk things out in a friendly manner. They went into Ringer's. Mary brightened up. Mary Nichols, Annie Chapman and Elizabeth Stride came in and she introduced him to them. Making the most of him, she told them this gentleman had once taken her to France with him, and she had once looked after a child for him, in Cleveland Street, and there was quite a tale to be told about the parentage of that child...Later on, when the tone of the relationship had darkened and he conceived the idea of killing her, he realized he would have to eliminate those three as well, or they would remember and be likely to tell the police. So that he should not be suspected, he would make it look like a madman's work. On the night of 30 September, he killed Elizabeth Stride and meant to go on to Mary Kelly's. What route would he have taken? From Berner Street he would have gone along Commercial Road to that circus of roads, one of the radii of which is Commercial Street. He thought to go up that to Dorset Street, but seeing Catherine Eddowes standing about was side-tracked by her to Mitre Square. He had just killed, his blood warm, and he killed again, pointlessly, and, angry with himself, made a real mess of the body, and then resumed his way - up Goulston Street this time. He discarded the piece of apron he was carrying and went to the fountain in Dorset Street to wash his hands and so appear respectable when he knocked on the door. Why did he not go in?

He would have found Joe Barnett there.

1   Knight p 35
2   Knight p 37

Chapter 17
Hogarth's Murders

It is very many years now since the afternoon when my mother and I strolled into the Soane Museum, Lincoln's Inn. We had thought to see the Canalettos (not hung in a very good light,) but there was a guide, who insisted on showing us everything. The pride of the place was Hogarth's original paintings of *The Rake's Progress*, from which the famous engravings had been made, and other series. We found ourselves in a corner concerned with torment. There was a man with torturers gathered around him. Mother and I shied away from it, refusing to look. The guide, trying to get us back, said, 'It's a satire on the medical profession.' Mother exclaimed, 'Was that his opinion of doctors!' People who took your insides out instead of making you well? He must have had bad experience. We said we did not want to look at horrors, and walked resolutely on.

Now I find in Knight's book a reproduction of that picture, entitled *The Reward of Cruelty*. Knight said it showed three Freemasons performing a Masonic murder. The rope knotted round the victim's neck was a cable-tow and stood for the cutting of his throat...I was not partial to Knight's idea of three Masonic murderers setting out to get the women who knew the royal secret, and for a long while avoided looking too closely into the drawing. Ultimately, I steeled myself to look into the drawing. The heart and entrails were on the floor, about to be eaten by a dog. Ropes from the ceiling suspended what looked like a screw through the victim's forehead. Knight declared this was a lewis.(1)

I took down from the shelf Leadbeater's *The Hidden Life in Freemasonry*, and found a drawing of the thing. The accompanying text read:(2)

The smooth ashlar is generally suspended from a pulley, and held by the lewis, an implement consisting of wedge-shaped pieces of steel which are fitted into a dovetailed mortise in the stone to be hoisted.

Leadbeater's exposition related to a form of Masonry adapted to suit Theosophists, so need not therefore necessarily correspond with the orthodox Craft. I thought I had better check on it. I therefore telephoned a friend whom I knew was a Mason, the same one whom I consulted on the theme of Juwes and asked him if the Hogarth print reproduced in Knight's book was Masonic.

This time, he was positive. 'Yes,' he said. 'that is Masonic, at least in part.' There was a pause, whilst he searched for his copy. Then he said, 'you see, there is a dog about to eat something. Also the shape of the room suggests a lodge. In the upper right and left hand corners you can see there are words. They are too blurred to be legible, at any rate in this reproduction, but I know what they should be.' Nevertheless, the mutilation of the leg was not masonic.

It was obvious I had misjudged the picture. The candidate for initiation, for such I now took the recumbent figure to be, took an oath, calling down all manner of horrors upon himself should he break it. Was this a nasty idea of the artist to show these as though they were being perpetrated? Or did the picture relate to the symbolical death undergone by the candidate for the highest degree? It was probably the same in the Eleusinian mysteries, and before that in the mysteries of Egypt, outwardly the drama of the seed, falling to the ground in the autumn, lying buried beneath the earth as though it were dead through the winter, and sprouting in the spring: symbolically a way of telling the candidate he must die to the things of the world to be reborn of the spirit. Osiris was dismembered before he was resurrected.

I telephoned my Masonic friend again, and said 'I don't want you to tell me more than you feel you should, but that picture represents either one of two things. On first being made a Mason the candidate takes an oath, on pain of suffering all kinds of mutilations should he fail to keep it. But then, much further on in Masonry, at the initiation to a higher degree, the candidate is murdered...'

'Symbolically murdered!'

'Symbolically murdered, and perhaps things are symbolically done to him. It is one of those two things.'

'It's what would happen to him if he broke his oath.'

I sat back and thought again; and reached again for the Leadbeater. This time it opened itself as if by magic at a page referring to 'the p.. mentioned in the O.' The 'p...' must stand for penalty and the O for Oath. 'Among the Egyptians,' it went on, 'the same p...existed, and even before them among the Nilotic negroes in Egypt, and probably in other places as well. It mattered enormously to an ancient Egyptian that his body should be cast into the waves, and that he should not be decently buried with proper rites.' (3)

So that was it. It was the improper disposal of the remains that was the essence of the penalty. Obviously, to have one's heart and entrails eaten by a dog was improper disposal, without hallowed rites.

I felt it, now, imperative I should know the context in which this picture appeared. Knight said it was 'the final stage in Hogarth's *Four Stages of Cruelty* series - ostensibly a caricature of the medical profession. In fact a Masonic ritual killing in progress.' If this was stage IV what were stages I, II and III? Knight did not say. Perhaps he had not seen them - if Joseph Sickert had shown him just the one picture, as showing his father's idea that the murders were masonic. This final picture must relate to a story of which it was the culmination, in which its meaning could be found. I wrote to London Library and asked them to send me anything they had on the life and work of William Hogarth.

Prate V.
Behold the Villain's dire disgrace!
Not Death itself can end.
He finds no peaceful Burial Place,
His breathless Corse, no friend.

Torn from the Root, that wicked Tongue,
Which daily swore and curst!
Those Eyeballs from their Sockets wrung,
That glow'd with lawless Lust!

His Heart, expos'd to prying Eyes,
To Pity has no Claim:
But, dreadful! from his Bones shall rise,
His Monument of Shame.

Designd by W. Hogarth

Published according to Act of Parliament Feb 1 1751

IV. The Four Stages of Cruelty

They sent me *Hogarth's Progress*, by Peter Quennell, and *William Hogarth*, by Austin Dobson. In the Quennell I found a passage relating to the *Four Stages*. It followed on a discussion of certain of the other moralities:(4)

> The lesson taught in the *Four Stages of Cruelty* is no less deliberately rammed home. Tom Nero, an undeserving Charity Boy, begins by torturing a stray dog, as the driver of a hackney carriage unmercifully thrashes his broken-down horse, murders a servant-girl whom he has previously seduced and persuaded to sell her master's silver, and last appears as a disembowelled corpse, exposed to the cold scientific brutality of the anatomists of Surgeons' Hall.

So the sufferer was not an innocent. He was being punished for his cruelties to others. Why should the punishment meted out to him take the form special to the candidate who breaks his oath? Masonry is thought of as a system of moral training. The sponsors have probably given the candidate a preliminary talk about the nature of the conduct that will be expected of him, and this may include some idea of chivalry towards the weak and defenceless. In perpetrating cruelties such as this, he is, therefore, forsworn. Or perhaps it is just Hogarth's idea of making the punishment fit the crime, the sins of the wicked catching up on him...Nemesis.

Quennell had some excuse for taking the persons attending the corpse to be anatomists, for the skeletons in the alcoves might suggest anatomical research.

Certain of those gathered round wear mortar-boards, which would have suggested doctors of learning. Yet the dignified personage who sits in the chair with high back and triangular top, between pillars, looks like the Master of the Lodge, to me. One of the knives in use has a triangular form like that of the little trowels which builders use to place the mortar between bricks in a wall, the mortar, of course, being carried on a square board which might be called a mortar-board. The symbolism of Masonry is all to do with building and its tools and, even in those days, surely scientific men would not have had so little sense of hygiene as to let a dog be running round, eating up the parts as they fell from the body to the floor - which would defeat their purpose of obtaining them for scientific examination.

I came across another reproduction of the Hogarth in an unexpected place. I went to the Wright of Derby exhibition at the Tate (7 February-22 April 1990), and, opening the Catalogue, was surprised to find it in the Introduction by Judy Egerton; it was for comparison with two of Wright's scientific pictures. She wrote: that 'both the *Orrery* and *Air Pump* paintings appear to make specific borrowings from Hogarth's gruesome disembowelling scene from *The Four Stages of Cruelty*...' Beneath this reproduction, one saw a verse, presumably of the satirist's composition, engraved:

Behold the Villain's dire disgrace!
Not death itself can end.
He finds no peaceful burial place:

III: The Four Stages of Cruelty

His breathless Corpse no friend.
Torn from the Root, that wicked tongue,
* * *

That his tongue should be torn from the root is part of the penalty the candidate calls down on himself should he break his Oath.

Yet my masonic friend did not think the killings were by a Mason. The only point of a Masonic killing would be to 'teach somebody a lesson,' and would fail to do so unless unmistakably Masonic. The body ought to be 'within a cable-tow' of the sea, or at least of water. He would have thought that a Mason would have tried to leave the bodies close to the Thames.

Indeed, I do not think Sickert was a Mason. Masons have to believe in God. Sickert did not believe in God. Yet, without being a Mason; he could have had a source of Masonic symbols.

It is not uncommon for Masonic symbols to be hidden within pictures that are ostensibly of something else. During my research for some of my earlier books, particularly the *Bacon*, I had had occasion to look at many such drawings. A volume in which they are particularly evident is Gibson's catalogue of Bacon's works.(5) In the title-pages of a number of them that were printed just after his death, they can be discerned. The symbols are veiled just sufficiently not to catch the eye not trained to look for them. Hogarth's pictures, with their intricate wealth of detail, afford among the endless arches, columns, time-pieces, triangles and squares, infinite hiding places. Why is it that in the first scene of *The Rake's Progress*, there leans against the mantelpiece a gavel, the double-headed hammer which is the symbol of authority of the Master of the Lodge? Why is that form taken by the hinge to the pew in *The Sleeping Congregation*? It was not the wastrel or the sleeping member of the congregation who was the holder of the gavel. I think Hogarth was saying to those who recognized the symbol, 'This picture may seem to you but a slight thing, but know the status of the artist who made it.'

Knight thought Hogarth was out to 'expose' Masonry as a secret society dedicated to wickedness. I do not think that at all. I feel sure he thought of it as a school for virtue, and took his responsibilities seriously. Sickert refers often to Hogarth in his writings, but in one of his articles says: (6)

...we know that the brush is didactic at its peril. A surgeon must neither blush nor preach. Hogarth's moralities are no more true, on their side, than are the conjugations of Miss Maude Goodman on the other.

I am not sure what he means, there. Does he mean that it is not true that those who do a bad deed suffer bad fates, as Hogarth says they do, or that Hogarth was in some way insincere, like those newspapers that headline vice on the pretext of condemning it? Hogarth freely admitted that his series on *The Harlot's Progress* started from two studies of harlots, done spontaneously, and that the idea for embodying them in a series with a moral to it came later, but that does not make him insincere.

Hogarth's Murders

Hogarth, like Pope, was genuinely shocked by the cruelty to animals prevalent in that day. His self-portrait shows him with his palette and his dog, Trump, a large pug or boxer, to whom he was devoted, and he wrote an epitaph to his bullfinch, which died aged eleven years. I do not think one need doubt the sincerity of his own statement of his purpose in making these four cruelty pictures. Their 'leading points', he said, he had:(7)

made as obvious as possible, in the hope that their tendency might be seen by men of the lowest rank. Neither minute accuracy of design, nor fine engraving, were deemed necessary, as the latter would render them too expensive for the persons to whom they were intended to be useful...To expressing them as I felt them, I have paid the utmost attention; and as they were addressed to hard hearts, have rather preferred leaving them *hard*...The prints were engraved with the hope of in some degree correcting that barbarous treatment of animals, the very sight of which renders the streets of the metropolis so distressing to every feeling mind. If they have had this effect, and checked the progress of cruelty, I am more proud of being their author, than I should be of having painted Raphael's Cartoons.

So his intention was to stop people from being cruel, by threatening them with a picture of what might happen to them if they were - Hell fire, cast in Masonic terms, or a Westerner's version of the oriental idea of karma.

There is no doubt as to the power of the pictures, only they can be misunderstood. I do not know if they could give some hard person pause before proceeding to cruel behaviour. To perverted natures, they could act as incitement.

It was in the book by Austin Dobson I found reproduced the scene which preceded the last one in the series. I do not think Knight can have seen it, or he must have said something about it.

I could not believe my eyes. I was looking at a picture of the murder of Annie Chapman. There she lay, against the wooden palings, on a step in the yard at the back of a building, her throat deeply cut through, from ear to ear, her right hand almost severed from the arm, her two rings at her feet and her trinkets about her. I would have thought the drawing had been commissioned to illustrate what Inspector Chandler and Dr. Phillips found, save that it had been made more than a century earlier. For a moment, I had the sensation of a time-slip. The engraving had been issued in 1751. And they are not two rings at her feet. They are two watches. When one takes a magnifying glass one sees the figures on the dials. Each has a chain, to which is attacked the key to wind it up, but, from the angle at which they are seen, the gold rims framing the dials give the impression of rings. and they are at her feet, as they were at Annie Chapman's feet. The trinkets include a small treasure-box from which are falling a bijou hymn-book and a Bible, or perhaps volume of the sacred law, open at the words 'God's Revenge Against Murder.' A paper-case was amongst the 'trumpery articles' ranged round Annie Chapman. Here these included a bag, from which are falling a candle-stick and a tea-pot or kettle - but wait, there is something odd about the handle, something across it, not quite at right angles. It is a double-headed hammer, a gavel. Tom Nero, a real Ripper's knife in his hand, is being seized by outraged townspeople. They have also found the letter she wrote him, signed, 'yours till death, Ann Gill.'

No, I am not suggesting Sickert went looking for wooden palings against which to pose and murder Annie Chapman, but the thought comes to me that when he saw her lying there, struck down against the palings, she looked so like the Hogarth engraving that the fantasy possessed him to pull off her rings and set them at her feet, and open the little pocket he found sewn to the inside of her petticoat and strew its treasures round her, to complete the likeness.

It was not the Rossetti poem but the Hogarth picture which had inspired the arrangement. Did this train of thought continue?

Curiously enough, I found reproduced both in the Quennell and in the Dobson,(9) a drawing which provided a link with one of the other murders, the one he told his son had been by mistake - Catherine Eddowes. It was a comical invitation sent by Hogarth in the form of a drawing, to a friend, a Mr King, inviting him to dine with him at the Mitre Tavern. Hogarth has drawn a knife and a fork, and between them a plate. In the middle of the plate is a pie, and in the middle of the pie is a mitre. Around the pie are arranged the words 'Mr Hogarth [sends his] Compts to Mr King and desires the Honour of his Company at dinner on Thursday next to Eta Bita PY.'

Mitre Tavern stood at the entrance to Mitre Square. Knight writes that Mitre Tavern was the meeting place of three Masonic Lodges, the Hiram Lodge, the Union Lodge and the Joppa Lodge. No, I am not going to go down Knight's road and agree with him that Catherine Eddowes had been murdered elsewhere and her body conveyed to Mitre Square in order Masonically to sign the murder. I am not even going to suggest she was lured to it because of its name. Sir Henry Smith, observing that her beat was small and well known to the police, said that at Bishopsgate Police Station they should have known she was making for Mitre Square and followed her. Though too dark and secluded a place in which to solicit, it was probably a place to which she took clients whom she had met while standing on the main road. All the same, I do have the feeling it was unlucky for Catherine Eddowes that it was to Mitre Square she took a man the night she was murdered - and lost a kidney, one half of which was said in the letter that accompanied the other half to have been fried and eaten. There is the link with the Mitre and the pie. I do not want to be horrid. It may not really have been eaten.

Forget the pie, if you will. But can a man be driven mad by pictures?

Scrutinizing again the last in *The Four Stages of Cruelty* series, I notice something I did not before. Whilst the eye is first caught by the long rope of the intestine being pulled out from the abdomen by the man with the bucket, from which it is falling, like the heart, to the dog, there is a smaller piece of intestine, between the left arm and the body. At the inquest on Mrs Eddowes, Dr. Brown, answering the City Police solicitor, had said a small detached piece of intestine, had been placed between the left arm and the body, and that the placing had been deliberate. Retailing his evidence, I said earlier that I could not interpret it but felt it should be noted. Now I am glad that I noted it. I had wondered how Dr. Brown could have been so sure the placing by the murderer had been deliberate. If a piece had just been lying along the depression between limb and trunk, it could have fallen there. But if it was placed as shown here, passing over the body and under the arm, to reappear the other side, since she was dead before she was disembowelled, the murderer must have lifted her left arm in order to arrange the piece of intestine passing beneath it, as in this picture. Yet Brown said the piece of intestine so arranged was detached. In the picture, it is detached on one side only. It has been cut off or peters out below the arm, but above the arm, comes, like the longer intestine, from the abdomen - but here the artist is in error. Though it is common to speak of the intestines, in fact there is only one intestine. It has many convolutions and changes of shape, but it is all one tube. Hogarth shows two tubes. To do with the insides of a real woman what is shown here would, therefore, be impossible. There was not a second tube. The only way in which Hogarth's arrangement could be imitated would have been by detaching a piece to place between the left arm and the body.

Knight - carried away by his argument - says that Mary Kelly's heart was removed. It was not. It was her liver that was taken out. But that puts me in mind of something else. Shelley was cremated on a beach, and one of the mourners rescued from the flames what he took to be his heart, and later gave it to his widow. In my biography, *Shelley*, I felt obliged to take note of a scientific person's observation that the part that resists consumption longest is not the heart but the liver, that none of those present at the funeral had sufficient anatomical knowledge to tell the difference, and that a mistake upon this point could account for the legend that Shelley's heart was unusually large.(10) It has now been lost, so the question cannot be resolved. The point is, a mistake could be made. Perhaps Mary Kelly's killer was trying to get her heart, got hold of something, and only when he had dragged it to visibility in the light of the fire, realized it was not her heart but something other, and abandoned it between her legs. Being under the ribs, the heart may be difficult to get hold of. Perhaps the breasts were a substitute.

It has been noticed before that the parts which the Ripper most mutilated were not the private ones, which are in most sex murders the focus of the attention. He worked to get insides out, and to mutilate extremities. There is nothing particularly sexually inviting about a shin, yet Mary's left shin is flayed, from knee to ankle, in exactly the way the left shin is drawn by Hogarth being flayed from knee to ankle.

There is a smaller point. The forehead is even less sexual than the shin. Yet the murderer had skinned Mary Kelly's forehead. He would not have possessed a lewis, and even the point of his knife would not penetrate the bone, but by removing the skin from the part he could pay his homage to the illustration.

It is a small detail and others may not agree, but to me it feels conclusive. Sickert was not a Mason, but the mutilations and arrangement seem to imitate not lodge ritual but the Hogarth drawings.

I have hesitated for a long time before accusing Sickert, but none of the other candidates had his acquaintance with Hogarth.

1 Knight, p 169
2 *The Hidden Life of Freemasonry*, C W Leadbeater, (Theosophical Publishing House, Adyar) second ed., 1928 pp 113-4
3 Leadbeater, p 226
4 *Hogarth's Progress*, Peter Quennell (Collins, 1955)   p 210
5 *Francis Bacon, a Bibliography of his work and of Baconiana to the Year 1750* R. V. Gibson, (OUP, 1960)
6 Sitwell, p 195
7 Quennell, p 208
8 *William Hogarth*, Austin Dobson (Sampson Lowe, 1890) pp 134 and 274
9 Quennell, p 138 and Dobson, p 85
10 *Shelley, a Biography*, Jean Overton Fuller (Cape, 1960) p 314 A.S. Bicknell, *The Athenaeum*, 1885; *Flight of the Skylark, The Development of Shelley's Reputation*, Sylvia Norman (Reinhardt, 1954), p 265

Bibliography

Unpublished Typescript

Letters to Florence, from Sickert, Conder and Moore, edited by Violet Overton Fuller, with a commentary based on Mrs Humphrey Holland's reminiscence and other sources

Other Sources

Sickert

(in order of publication)

The Life and Opinions of Walter Richard Sickert, Robert Emmons (Faber, 1941)

A Free House, or The Artist as Craftsman, being the Writings of Walter Richard Sickert, ed. Osbert Sitwell (Macmillan, 1947)

Sickert, Lillian Browse (Hart-Davis, 1960)

Sickert, The Painter and His Circle, Marjorie Lilly (Noyes, 1973)

Sickert, Wendy Baron (Phaidon, 1973)

Walter Sickert, a Biography, Denys Sutton (Michael Joseph, 1976)

Walter Sickert, Richard Shone (Phaidon 1988)

The Set of Sickert and Florence: Conder, Moore, Beerbohm and Blanche

Conder

Charles Conder, His Life and Work, Frank Gibson, with a catalogue of the Lithographs and Etchings by Campbell Dodgson MA Keeper of the Prints and Drawings, British Museum, with one hundred and twenty-one illustrations (Lane 1914)

The Life and Death of Conder, John Rothenstein (Dent, 1938)

Moore

Portrait of George Moore in a Study of His Work, John Freeman (Werner

Laurie, 1922)
Irish Literary Portraits, John Eglington (Macmillan, 1935)
GM, Memories of George Moore, Nancy Cunard (Hart-Davis, 1936)

Beerbohm

Max, A Biography, David Cecil (Constable, 1964)
The Lie of Art, Max Beerbohm's Parody and Caricature, John Flestiner (Gollancz, 1973)

Blanche

Portraits of a Lifetime, The Late Victorian Era, the Edwardian Pageant, 1870-1914, Jacques-Emile Blanche, translated and edited by Walter Clement, with an introduction by Harley Granville-Barker (Dent, 1937)

Impressionist Background

The French Impressionists, Clive Bell (Phaidon, 1951)
The Impressionists, William Gaunt (Thames & Hudson, 1970)
Impressionism, Phoebe Pool (Thames & Hudson, 1967)
The Impressionists, Pierre Courthion (Galley, 1982)

Degas, François Fosca (World Publishing, USA 1954)
Monet, Vasile Nicolescu (Bucharest, 1972)
Monet, Alfredo Martini (New York, 1982)
Monet, John House (Phaidon, 1981)
Sisley, Richard Shone (Phaidon, 1979)
Van Gogh, the Life and Work of, Carl Nordenfalk (Elek, 1953)
Whistler, Francis Spalding (Phaidon, 1979)
The Pre-Raphaelite Dream, William Gaunt (Reprint Society and Cape, 1943)
Christina Rossetti, Lona Mosk Packer (Cambridge, 1963)
A Victorian Romantic, Dante Gabriel Rossetti, Oswald Doughty, (Oxford, 1960)

Hogarth

Hogarth's Progress, Peter Quennell (Collins, 1955)
William Hogarth, Austin Dobson (Sampson Low, 1890)
Painting of the British Social Scene from Hogarth to Sickert, E D K Johnson (Weidenfeld, 1986)

Ellen Cobden

Wistons, Miles Amber [pseud Ellen Cobden] (Fisher Unwin, 2 imp, 1902)
Sylvia Saxon, Ellen Millicent Cobden, (Miles Amber) Author of *Wistons* (T. Fisher Unwin, 1914)

The Ripper

Police Officers' Memoirs

Anderson, Sir Robert *The Lighter Side of My Official Life* (Hodder and Stoughton, 1910)
Suspect: Pizer

Smith Sir Henry K.C.B., *From Constable to Commissioner, the Story of Sixty Years, Most of them Misspent* (Chatto, 1910)
No Candidate

Later Studies

Cullen, Tom, *Autumn of Terror, Jack the Ripper, His Crimes and Times,* (Bodley Head, 1965)
Suspect: Druitt

Daniel, Mark, *Jack The Ripper* (Penguin, 1988)
Choice of four suspects: Gull, Lusk, Spratling or Clarence. The accompanying ITV programme opted for Gull

Farson, Daniel *Jack The Ripper* (Michael Joseph, 1972)
Suspect: Druitt

Harris, Melvin *Jack the Ripper, the Bloody Truth,* (Columbia, 1987)
Suspect: D' Onston Stephenson

Harrison, Michael *Clarence* (W.H. Allen, 1972)
Suspect: J K Stephen

Howells, Martin and Keith Skinner *The Ripper Legacy* (Sidgwick and Jackson, 1987)
Suspect: Druitt

Knight, Stephen *Jack the Ripper, the Final Solution* (Panther, 1977) My references are to the latter edition
Suspect: William Gull

McCormick, Donald *The Identity of Jack the Ripper* (Jarrolds, 1973)
Suspect: Pedachenko

Rumbelow, Donald *The Complete Jack the Ripper* (W.H. Allen, 1975)
No Candidate

Spicer, Robert 'I caught Jack the Ripper,' in the *Daily Express,* 16 March 1931
Stowell, T E A 'Jack the Ripper ' a solution?' *Criminologist,* 1 November 1970
Suspect: Clarence

Wilson, Colin *Jack the Ripper, Summing Up and Verdict* (Bantam, 1987)
No Candidate

Background and Miscellaneous

Chester, Lewis, David Leitch and Colin Simpson, *The Cleveland Street Affair* (Weidenfeld, 1977)
d'Arch Smith, Timothy *Love In Earnest, Some notes on the lives and writings of English 'Uranian' Poets from 1889-1930* (Routledge, 1970)
Fuller, Jean Overton *The Magical Dilemma of Victor Neuburg* (Mandrake 1990)
Hidden, Christopher, ed *Queen Victoria in Her Letters and Journals* (Murray, 1984)
Hyde, Montgomery, *The Cleveland Street Scandal* (W H Allen, 1976)
Napley, Sir John *The Camden Town Murder* (Weidenfeld, 1987)
Quennell. Peter, *Mayhew's London, being Selections from 'London Labour and London Poor' by Henry Mayhew* which was first published in 1851 (Pilot, 1949)

Index

Bibliography and Index